Feedback

"In my MBA courses on strategic management, I encourage my students to apply the tools of strategy analysis to their own careers. Well, here's a book that explicitly (and engagingly) advocates precisely that approach. Viewing one's career as a business to be nurtured offers a new and insightful perspective on career development. Our careers are by far the biggest investments we make in our lives. Vaughan Evans encourages us to deploy the same tools of rigorous business analysis to evaluate career decisions as a venture capitalist would to evaluate an investment in a start-up business."

– **Professor Robert M. Grant**, Professor of Strategic Management at Georgetown University, Washington D.C. and author of *Contemporary Strategy Analysis.*

"This is a thorough work on achieving career success, full of innovative tools and charts, which I love! Readers will appreciate how they clarify the issues that are key to career development."

– **Daniel Porot**, lecturer on career design at London Business School, IMD, INSEAD, et al., author of *The PIE Method for Career Success* and summer workshop co-leader with Richard N. Bolles, author of *What Color Is Your Parachute?*

"This book not only points out common challenges for career changers and entrepreneurs, but shows scenarios for overcoming them. Most definitely a win-win book, the kind I like best."

– **Carol Christen**, career strategist, California, and co-author with Richard N. Bolles of *What Color Is Your Parachute?: For Teens.*

"Vaughan Evans's book will re-ignite your passion. Rich, detailed examples bring his innovative ideas to life. As you apply his time-tested business tools to your career, you'll gain insight, clarity, and the motivation to succeed!"

– **Carol L. McClelland, Ph.D.**, career coach, California, and author of *Green Careers for Dummies* and *Your Dream Career For Dummies.*

BACKING YOU, MBA!

How Thinking of Yourself as a Business Can Advance or Transform Your Career

VAUGHAN EVANS

Published by Business & Careers Press
PO Box 59814
2 Mortlake High Street
London SW14 8UR
www.businessandcareerspress.com

Printed and bound in the United States of America

First printing 2011

ISBN 978-0-9561391-2-2

**ATTENTION CORPORATIONS, UNIVERSITIES, COLLEGES, AND
PROFESSIONAL ORGANIZATIONS:** Quantity discounts are available on bulk
purchases of this book for educational, professional, or gift purposes, or as premiums
for increasing magazine subscriptions or renewals. Special books or book excerpts can
also be created to fit specific needs. For information, please contact the publisher.

To Wuk

Table of Contents

Part I: Would You Back You?

Competing by segment
Competing in the future
Getting past first base
Risks to your position

Laying out your plan in a market context
Is it achievable?
The bottom-up approach
Implications for employees
Assessing revenue or profit plans
Risks in your plan

The Suns & Clouds chart
What the chart says about:
    »   Extraordinary risk
    »   The balance of risk and opportunity
Making your chart sunnier
    »   Would you have backed the Beatles? Oprah?
The risks of backing you

Developing a storyline
    »   Sharon Stone's storyline
My storyline: why I wrote this book
Writing your own storyline

Part II: Becoming More Backable

Foreword

People choose to do an MBA for a host of reasons. They relish the intellectual stimulation. They plan to tap into an extended alumni network. They want to have fun again in a collegiate environment through a continuation or nostalgic recreation of their carefree university days.

Some see an MBA as a straight investment: U.S. $100k down for what will hopefully be a $20–30k/year bump in salary.

But most choose to invest in an MBA for solid career development purposes. They seek to acquire the broader knowledge and skills needed to fully develop their managerial or professional careers.

Some part-time MBA students have every intention of carrying on with their current employer upon completion of their MBA. They and others, particularly those in Executive MBA programs, may be part-financed by their employers, limiting their career options when they graduate.

Most MBA students, however, are self-financed and come with minds wide open over career choice. They may well choose to return to their pre-MBA employer, but want to see what the alternatives are.

Many come direct from completing their bachelor's degree or after just a couple of years in the workplace. For them, future career choice is often an exciting blank canvas.

For most MBA students, therefore, one of the main benefits of the program is the chance to learn more about and evaluate alternative career paths.

Does this sound like you? If so, this book is for you.

Backing You, MBA! is tailor-made for the MBA student.

It asks you to think of yourself as a business. It suggests you look at the business strategy tools you are learning at business school in a new way...*by using them on yourself!* Not on some real or imaginary company in a case study, but on you.

The book deploys three sets of tools:

- ▷ Strategic Due Diligence (Part I)
- ▷ Business Strategy (Part II)
- ▷ Strategic Mergers & Acquisitions (Part III)

Part I of this book starts by asking whether you are backable in your current job or business, if you're doing a part-time MBA, or pre-MBA job, if you're a full-timer. In other words, would an investor put money on you? To address this question, we deploy the tools of Strategic Due Diligence— the very tools a strategy consulting firm would use on behalf of a private equity client looking to invest in a target company. These tools have been especially modified here for the individual: for you.

If you're one of the many who have not had a serious job prior to business school, but who have come direct from a bachelor's degree, no problem. Skim through Parts I and II to get a feel for where they're heading and start reading in depth at Part III. In Chapter 17 you'll be asked to return to Part I to undertake Strategic Due Diligence on your *target* job post-MBA.

If you find in Part I that you are indeed backable in your current or pre-MBA job, the question becomes: How can you make yourself *more* backable? This is Part II and these are the tools of Business Strategy, the very same ones you have been using in your case studies on transforming the competitiveness of a firm. Here again, they have been modified for use on the individual.

If, however, you find that you are *not* backable in your current or pre-MBA job, if only for the reason that your heart is no longer in it, how do you then shift to a new job? And not just to any old job, but one that you feel deeply passionate about—*and* where you will be backable. These are the tools of Strategic Mergers & Acquisitions ("M&A"), adapted for you and set out in Part III.

You will be using the tools learnt at business school to plan your own career. This book will help you to see these tools in a new light, perhaps showing through in your final MBA exams!

I have developed the tools in this book over the years through my work on business strategy, strategic due diligence, and strategic M&A for businesses large and small. I have found them remarkably apposite when adapted and applied to the needs of the individual. Tools like the Suns & Clouds, Going for the Goal, Strategic Bubble Bath, and *Hwyl* Star charts help clarify the thinking of the individual as much as of the corporate manager or financier. They work whether you plan to be a manager or an engineer, an investment banker or a journalist, a consultant or a property developer. They help you decide if you would back you in the post-MBA job of your dreams.

These tools work for employees as well as the self-employed—as long as you can think of yourself as a business. Employee or self-employed, you will have your own distinctive set of customers, competitors, and capabilities. You will work with your own set of market demand prospects, competitive forces, and personal strengths and weaknesses. You will face your own set of challenges and risks—along with all the opportunities out there waiting to be grabbed. The only difference is that while the self-employed person genuinely runs a business, the employee needs to *think* of him or herself as a business.

Backing You, MBA! is divided into three parts:

1. *Would You Back You?*—Are you backable in your current or pre-MBA job or business?

2. *Becoming More Backable*—If you are backable, how can you become more so and improve your chances of success?

3. *Backing Your Passion*—If you are not backable, or if you came straight from a bachelor's degree, how can you find a career that inspires you *and* where you'll be backable?

Part I assesses how sound your prospects will be in your current or pre-MBA job once armed with an MBA. If you're self-employed, what are the chances that your business will be hit by a market downturn or tougher competition? Will your MBA make your business more competitive?

If you're an employee, what are the chances that your company—or your job within your company—will be affected by a market downturn? Are there too many people with your skills? In which ways will an MBA make you more competitive? Will your attitude work for you? As the management pyramid narrows, will it be you who moves up or will you be one of the many cast aside?

In short, *would you back you* in your current or pre-MBA job?

If the answer to Part I is in the affirmative, Part II shows you how to do better and how you can improve your chances of success, be promoted, or shift to a more attractive role within your organization. It shows you how to set your sights, build on your strengths, and work on your weaknesses. Perhaps you will decide to voluntarily outsource yourself and set up your own company. In short, it shows you how to *become more backable*.

Part I may conclude, however, that you are *not* backable in your current or pre-MBA job—that it's time to look elsewhere. If this is the case, Part III is for you. It is also for you if you have come to business school direct from university.

Where would you love to be? Which jobs or businesses will inspire you, fulfill you, consume you with passion? Part III shows you how to work out whether these jobs are as attractive as they seem and how well placed you would be, once you're an MBA, if you aimed for them. Some of your dream jobs or businesses may lose their shine; others will prove unattainable. But some will be promising and worthy of pursuit.

Part III shows you how to find a job which you feel passionate about *and* in which you will be backable. It will encourage you to *back your passion*.

Before we launch into the meat of Part I, let's pause to meet our main cast of characters. All four MBA students are fictional, but aspects of their situations may have been influenced by people I have known over the years. We'll dip into their lives and work challenges throughout this book whenever we need to translate theoretical advice into everyday reality.

Three of these exemplars were employees before arriving at business school; one was self-employed. All are seeking to embark on a career post-MBA where their passion lies *and* where they'll be backable:

1. Gary, a middle manager in a utilities company doing a part-time MBA at Kellogg, will use his MBA to broaden his responsibilities in the company.

2. Valerie, a self-employed economic consultant now studying at London Business School, will use her MBA to break into new product/market segments.

3. Jennifer, formerly an accountant specializing in financial due diligence and now at Harvard, will shift to strategy consulting or private equity.

4. Formerly a fast-track management trainee with a multinational, Hari is studying at Stanford and will launch his own startup business venture.

These four exemplars won't cover every situation pertinent to every reader, but you will likely find aspects of their career planning process relevant and illuminating.

We'll meet Valerie regularly throughout this book. Gary will surface late in Part I and again in Part II as he endeavors to make himself more backable in his job. Hari will feature in Chapter 13 on Backing YouCo, as he dreams up his own venture, while Jennifer's deliberations on her future career will form the main case study in Part III.

Valerie the Economist

Valerie is a self-employed economic consultant in her early 30s. Compared to many of her fellow students at London Business School, her work and lifestyle thus far have been exotic in the extreme. Graduating from Cambridge University with a first-class degree in economics, her first job was a two-year posting with the Ministry of Economic Development in Swaziland. After six months of touring much of sub-Saharan Africa on a motorbike, on her own (!), she returned to England to work with a leading economic consulting group, EconCo.

Valerie was with EconCo for five years, largely on long-term assignments in Uganda, Nepal, and Bangladesh, before she set out on her own at the age of 28 to give herself greater freedom of choice. She didn't find business hard to get, and worked in yet more wonderful locations from the Caribbean to the Pacific, but she wondered for how much longer she could lead such a carefree, nomadic lifestyle. If she ever wanted to settle down and start a family, she would need a more stable base. So she enrolled in the Alfred P. Sloan Program, a one-year Executive MBA program (also held in the U.S. at MIT and Stanford), with the aim of shifting from economic consulting overseas to management consulting nearer to home....

Gary the Manager

Gary's background prior to arriving at Kellogg Graduate School of Management business school could hardly have been more different from Valerie's. He was born and brought up in one of the North Shore communities adjoining Lake Michigan, went to his local university, Northwestern, and left with a good degree in electrical engineering. He joined a large Illinois-based electric utility company, UtiliCo, as a trainee manager straight from college. There he remained for ten good years, joined for much of that time by a wife, two children, and a large mortgage. Foreign travel to Gary meant popping over to the country on the other side of the Great Lakes. Gary has enrolled for the part-time, three-year MBA program down the road in Evanston to develop his managerial career, conceivably with another local employer, but he and his family have no desire whatsoever to move away from the North Chicago area....

Hari the Would-be Entrepreneur

Hari is in his late 20s, a graduate in electrical engineering and for the last few years a manager at a multinational electronic goods company based in Sacramento, California. An undisputed high-flier, his prospects were rosy at his company. But his real passion lies elsewhere. What excites him are tales of entrepreneurs who conceptually create, launch and develop their own businesses—especially those with Asian backgrounds, like him. They are his role models. Therefore, Hari has enrolled at Stanford Graduate School of Business to broaden his perspective. There, within six months, he has fallen in love with and married a Latina fellow student, Concha, whose background is in IT consulting. Together, when not working flat out to complete their assignments, they ponder new business ideas....

Jennifer the Aspiring Consultant or Financier

Jennifer is 28 years old, a graduate in modern languages from Dartmouth College and an employee of one of the Big Four accounting groups in Boston, Massachusetts. She started off in auditing, but moved to the transaction services group once qualified, where she worked mainly on financial due diligence assignments for private equity clients. She put in long hours, and learned a lot, but felt that other advisers not only did more interesting and intellectually challenging work, but earned more, too! She sees her MBA at Harvard Business School as her entry ticket to strategy consulting, and conceivably to private equity itself—where people her age appear to earn far more with far less effort....

Part I

Would You Back You?

What is your "business"?
Where is market demand headed?
What about the competition?
What do customers need?
What must you do to succeed?
How do you measure up?
Will you make your plan?
How risky is backing you?
What's the story?

Introduction

Think of yourself as a business. How sound are your prospects? Would an investor back you? Would *you* back you?

That's what Part I aims to find out.

What should you look for when considering whether to back a business? What would a serious pro-investor, someone who does this day in and day out, look for?

Investors are highly selective where they invest their money. Backing entrepreneurs because they like the idea, the sector, the location, or the product, because they like the people, or, worst of all in this business, because they sympathize with them, may make them great guys, but won't keep them in business for long.

If before investing, however, they undertake a rigorous, systematic series of checks, the odds of their losing money become much smaller. And the prospect of getting a good return on the investment becomes much higher.

This systematic checking process is called "due diligence." It has many components—strategic, financial, operational, IT, environmental, managerial, legal, and others—each of which tends to be carried out by a specialist provider.

Of these components, strategic due diligence is arguably the most vital. It tells the investor whether the target business has a sustainable competitive advantage in an attractive market.

If it has, it is worth the investor probing deeper into the details, the other components of due diligence—the finances, the operations, the legal issues.

If the target is not competitively strong, or if its markets are unattractive, the investor will walk away. Period.

Having specialized in strategic due diligence for over 25 years, I have found it to be as relevant for the individual as for a company.

If you are in a job or business with an attractive market and where you have a sustainable competitive advantage, you are backable—subject to completion of due diligence. If you are not, you are probably not backable.

> In Part I, we'll take it that your "current" job or business is the one you're continuing to do now, if you're on a part-time MBA program, or the one you were doing beforehand, if you're a full-timer. This makes explanation of the Strategic Due Diligence tools much easier.

To do Strategic Due Diligence on you, you need to find answers to one basic and one supplementary question.

The basic question is: *Are you likely to achieve your plans over the next few years?*

The supplementary is: *Do the opportunities to beat your plan outweigh the risks of your not achieving it?*

You'll look for risks and opportunities in your job or business in four main areas:

1. *Demand risk*—how risky is future market demand?
2. *Competition risk*—how risky is future competition?
3. *Your position risk*—how risky is your competitive position?
4. *Your plan risk*—how risky are your plans?

Each of these areas of risk and opportunity goes toward making up a *Risk Jigsaw*, as shown in the diagram. Your challenge will be to piece together the four pieces of the jigsaw, assess the overall balance of risks and opportunities, and conclude whether or not you should back you.

The nine chapters of Part I are therefore arranged around how to piece together your Risk Jigsaw:

1. What is your "business"?—preparation for the risk analysis to follow
2. Where is market demand headed?—Demand Risk
3. What about the competition?—Competition Risk
4. What do customers need?—preparation for Chapter 6
5. What must you do to succeed?—more preparation for Chapter 6
6. How do you measure up?—Your Position Risk
7. Will you make your plan?—Your Plan Risk
8. How risky is backing you?—the Risk Jigsaw completed
9. What's the story?—assembling the storyline on whether to back you

First, you need to understand the nature of your job or business....

1

What Is Your "Business"?

What Are Your Services and for Whom?
The Employee's "Business" and "Customers"
Your Plans

What services do you offer, to whom? And which count the most? Which services to which customer groups really matter in your business?

You need to know this because you don't want to waste your time. You should focus your efforts on researching and analyzing those bits of your business that are most important. There is little point in spending hours analyzing a service you offer to a customer group that only contributes to 1% of sales. You should put in the work on the 80%.

This first step is relatively straightforward for the self-employed. But if you're an employee, you need a little more imagination. We'll start with the self-employed, but employees need to read this section too.

What Are Your Services and for Whom?

A self-employed person is a businessperson. You have customers. Revenues from those customers need to more than cover your costs. You live off the profit. You're a business.

As a business, what services, or less frequently in today's world, products do you offer? To what groups of customers?

Most self-employed people tend to offer a number of services to a number of customer groups. The services are typically related, but each is distinct. The line-up of the competition tends to differ. Some competitors may offer all of your services; others may specialize in just one or two of them. Others still may offer only one of them as a sideline to another business.

Likewise, most self-employed people also tend to serve more than one customer group. Customer groups we can define as sets of customers with distinct characteristics and typically reachable through distinct marketing routes.

Each service to each customer group is called a "product/market segment," or a "business segment."

If you offer two services to one customer group, you have two business segments. If you stick with the same two services but develop a new customer group, you'll have four segments. If you now introduce a new service, offered to both groups, you'll have six segments.

How many services do you offer? To how many customer groups? Multiply the two numbers together and that's how many business segments you operate in.

But these segments are not of equal importance to the success of your business. And your backer needs to know which are the most important.

Which segments count most toward your overall profit today? Ideally your management information system will give you contribution to overheads in each segment. If not, you'll have to make do with gross profit by segment.

Simplest of all is when all your segments have a similar cost profile. Then you can just take sales by segment.

Which two, three, four or more segments contribute to over 80% of your business? These are your most important segments.

But what if you were not self-employed pre-MBA, but, as is more typical, an employee in a company or other organization, large or small?

The Employee's "Business" and "Customers"

Just a reminder: This step-by-step guide and toolkit works just as well for an employee as it does for a self-employed businessperson. But first you have to *think of yourself as self-employed*—as a business.

Think of your whole earnings package, including salary, vacation, sickness benefits, medical insurance, pension contribution, and so forth, as *revenues* for your business. What services are you providing to your organization to merit those revenues? Which people or groups of people in your organization find your services so useful that they are prepared to pay, in effect, those revenues for them?

And *voilà*. You're a "business"! You provide services and you have "customers." All you have to do is carve up the main tasks you undertake in your job into distinct services. Then, if appropriate, allocate the people who use your services into customer groups. These are your business segments.

How much time, how many hours a week on average, do you spend on each segment? Which are the most important? Which are the two, three, four or more which account for over 80% of your working week?

If you find it difficult to visualize your job as a business, it may help if you try to imagine what would happen if your job were "outsourced."

You would no longer be an employee, but you would still be doing the same job. You wouldn't be on the payroll, so you would have no salary. Nor would you have any vacation, pension, or other benefits paid by the company. You would have revenues. Your services would be the same as you're providing today. Your "customers" would be those same colleagues who today use your services as an employee. Each customer would pay you directly for the services you provide. Scary, perhaps, but that's your "business."

If you were a manager pre-MBA, it may be more difficult to consider yourself as outsourced. Management is often defined as the core competence of any organization. It can be what distinguishes one group of people—one "company" of people—from another. But some tasks in a manager's job may be outsourced, such as project work or advisory work for the CEO, so imagining the job being outsourced might help managers assess which segments contribute most in their "business."

Your Plans

You have already worked out which segments currently contribute most in your business, whether you're an employee or self-employed. But what of the future?

Things change. Your most important business segments of today may not be those of tomorrow. Will market forces favor some at the expense of others? Do you have any plans to invest in one segment or launch into a new segment?

Which are the three, four, or more segments which together will account for 80% plus of the profits of your business (or "business") over the next three to five years?

These will be the business segments to focus the research and analysis of Part I on.

Do you have a "business plan" as such? If you're self-employed, you may well have. This book will help you assess how realistic this plan is, whether or not it's backable.

Most readers, especially employees, will have no such plan. If that's you, let's assume for now that *things stay more or less as they were before* on your return to your former job or business. Sure, as an employee, you may hope to receive some additional responsibility, a promotion, a pay rise (hopefully above inflation). Sure, as a self-employed person, you may hope to win some new customers and grow the business somewhat. But if you have no specific plans, let's for the time being assume that your "plan" for a return to your former job in five years' time is a steady, unspectacular improvement on what it was pre-MBA.

The advantage of this assumption is its clarity. Because after you've worked through the tools in Part I of this book, you'll have a much firmer idea of whether carrying on with your current job or returning to your pre-MBA job is a practical scenario. Is it realistic to believe that you would thrive in that same job in three or five years' time?

If you were a frustrated, dissatisfied employee pre-MBA, will you lose out on your return to colleagues—present or yet to be hired—who are less frustrated and more satisfied? How will you compete with colleagues who actually love their work? Would you back you in those circumstances?

Part I's analysis may produce some stark results.

Valerie's Economic Consulting Business

Valerie has created a good business since going independent four years ago. The grounding she received working initially for an African government and subsequently at a top economic consulting group has given her the credibility needed to pitch for and win a stream of projects, each lasting anywhere from three to 18 months. She has turned over an average of U.S. $100,000 a year—less than she would have earned had she stayed full time at EconCo, but this has been more than offset by her perceived benefits of independence—the ability to be more selective in where to work and on what, and the opportunity for lengthy post-project travels around the globe.

Economic competitiveness advice is Valerie's specialty: helping developing countries create a framework whereby internationally competitive industries can be nurtured and developed. She loves this work and has built up much experience in it, but it isn't possible to do this type of work all the time. It all depends on what project comes up when she is available. So she has also done a couple of projects on regulation, one in utilities, and one in transport.

Valerie has two routes to market. Her favored route is direct to the end-user, the contracting government department or aid agency— but this route is wholly reliant on her contacts. She did manage to win a one-year economic competitiveness project in Uganda, building on her relationships both with the Ministry of Economic Development and with UN managers on the ground in Kampala. This was a happy conjunction of influences, but difficult to replicate in other countries.

To maintain workflow Valerie has also had to subcontract. She keeps in close touch with her old friends at EconCo and has acquired new contacts at former competitive groups, as well as at those in other areas, such as management, engineering, and planning consulting. But the kinds of jobs offered through the subcontracting route tend to be the least attractive—and Valerie felt compelled to take on a ten-month project to reorganize a customs department in Bangladesh, work that did not inspire her. Having said that, it still enabled her to embark on a fantastic three-month tour around South-East Asia once it came to an end.

Overall, Valerie offers three services (competitiveness, regulation and administration) to two customer groups:

- Direct clients, whether government departments or aid agencies
- Prime contractor clients, for whom she is a subcontractor

Therefore Valerie has six business segments, of which two are most prominent. Competitiveness to direct clients is happily the largest in terms of revenues (see Figure 1.1), but, less happily, administration to prime contractor clients emerges next. These two segments together account for 65% of her revenues.

Figure 1.1. Valerie's Revenues from Economic Consulting

Product	Revenues by Customer Group ($000)		
	Direct Clients	Sub-Contracting	Total
Competitiveness	**45**	15	60
Regulation	15	-	15
Administration	-	**25**	25
Total	**60**	**40**	**100**

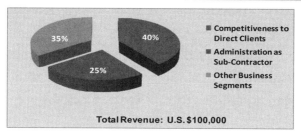

Total Revenue: U.S. $100,000

Clearly these two segments need to be examined in depth...or do they? Valerie has plans. If she decides to stay in economic consulting after getting her MBA, she would like to use her new knowledge and qualification to break into the market of business strategy consulting to private sector enterprises in developing countries. In three years' time she hopes that the segment of strategy advice to direct clients will be up there with economic competitiveness, ahead of regulation, in terms of importance to her business (Figure 1.2). She plans to move right away from subcontracting, especially on administration projects.

Valerie would therefore need to examine her prospects not just in economic competitiveness to direct clients, but also in business strategy and regulation. Should she bother with her subcontracting segments? Yes, because if things don't work out as planned in selling to direct clients, she will find some comfort in knowing that she can fall back upon subcontracting, even on administration projects.

Figure 1.2. Valerie's Forecast Revenues after Three Years

Product	Revenues by Customer Group ($000)		
	Direct Clients	Sub-Contracting	Total
Competitiveness	60	10	70
Regulation	30	-	30
Administration	-	0	0
Business strategy	**50**	-	50
Total	**140**	**10**	**150**

Valerie must therefore check out her prospects in four business segments: competitiveness, business strategy and regulation to direct clients, and administration to prime contractor clients.

2

Where Is Market Demand Headed?

Weaving Your Web of Information
The Four-stage Process for Gauging Future Demand
For Employees: Gauging Demand at Two Levels
Market Demand Risk

This chapter is about demand for the type of services you provide. You are not alone. There are others out there who do what you do. This chapter asks you to think about how market demand for *all* these people, including you, has changed in the last few years and how it is likely to change in the future. Will demand for *you all* grow? We need to know this before we address the crucial question in the next chapter: Is there any chance there may be too many of you competing for the same jobs or business in the future?

Again, if you're an employee, it will help if you think of yourself as a business. You need to think about what will happen to demand for your kind of service over the next few years. That's demand for your services not just within your current company but *overall demand for your type of service across all companies and organizations.*

Any market is made up of demand and supply. Whether the market is for things or people—apples or actors, MP3 players or musicians, trucks or truckers—the fundamentals of economics apply. When demand and supply are in balance, that's good news for all concerned. When demand outstrips supply, that's good for the suppliers—though usually only for a while, until more supplies and/or suppliers arrive.

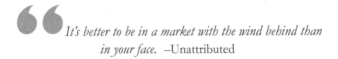

It's better to be in a market with the wind behind than in your face. –Unattributed

When demand falls and supply exceeds demand, that's bad news for suppliers. In the labor market, these suppliers include you. You're a supplier of labor.

We're going to apply those fundamentals to the market for *your* services. We'll look at market supply in the next chapter, but first at market demand. We'll forecast what's going to happen to market demand over the next few years. Your backer will also want to know what the risks are of things turning out worse than that. And, on the other hand, what the opportunities are of things turning out better.

Is market demand going to grow? This is the big question. Is demand for providers of your kind of services, in each of your main business segments, going to grow over the next few years? Is it going to be bigger in a few years' time, or smaller? Or more or less the same?

It's not the only question, of course. Equally important, as we'll see in the next few chapters, is the nature of the competition you're going to face and how you are placed to compete.

But it's a question of odds. You have a better chance of prospering in a market that's growing than one that's shrinking.

Weaving Your Web of Information

I've been advising clients on market trends for over 35 years. In the old days, you used to have to call up trade associations, write to companies active in the market asking for their annual reports, visit reference libraries to wade through reams of trade magazines, journals, and so forth. Or you might have to purchase an expensive market research report, often only of tangential relevance to the market you were researching.

Now it's a breeze. All you have to do is switch on your laptop, click onto your Internet connection, pop into Google, Yahoo, or Bing and type in the name of your market alongside such words as "market," "growth," "forecasts," "trends."

You'll find that Google comes up with hundreds—maybe thousands—of websites to visit. Most of them will be irrelevant. Two, three, or more will be spot on. You'll begrudge having to waste time trawling through dozens of useless sites, but hang on! Think of the hours and hours of effort you're saving compared to the old days. You just need a bit of patience and perseverance and systematically wade through the referred sites. Open up a Word file, and whenever you come across an article on a website that seems useful, copy it and drop it into your document.

You're weaving your own web of information on your market.

You may find that your search directs you to reports produced by specialist market research companies. These should be used as a last resort. Some can be quite good, reflecting the direct access they have had to market participants and observers, but too many turn out bland. And expensive. Better to do your own digging around on the web.

There are some good news websites where you can search directly without having to subscribe. The National Public Radio website, www.npr.org, offers fully searchable archived broadcasts, as does www.pbs.org. Also try the major newspaper websites. Both *The New York Times* (www.nytimes.com) and the *Washington Post* (www.washingtonpost.com) offer free searchable archives for a limited period (one and two weeks, respectively). That should be time enough for you to research what you need for your own market, although while you're there you may choose to do a couple more searches on new markets you're interested in (see Part III of this book) before your allotted time runs out. *The LA Times* (www.latimes.com) offers free abstracts on searches through its archives, but you pay for the full article. For more detailed company and financial information, *The Wall Street Journal* website (www.online.wsj.com) will cost you U.S. $1.99 per week.

In Britain, the BBC's website (www.bbc.co.uk) is a hugely informative, internationally focused resource and doesn't cost a penny. Similarly international in outlook, the website of *The Economist* (www.economist. com) offers free search on articles less than a year old, but subscription is needed for older articles. The websites of the main broadsheet national and regional newspapers are also good sources, such as *The Guardian* (www. guardian.co.uk), which is free and requires no registration. There are also *The Times* (www.timesonline.co.uk), *The Daily Telegraph* (www.telegraph. co.uk), *The Independent* (www.independent.co.uk), *The Western Mail* (www. icwales.icnetwork.co.uk), *The Scotsman* (www.scotsman.com), and *The Irish Times* (www.ireland.com), some of which require registration. *The Financial Times* website (www.ft.com,) offers a wealth of financial, company, and market information, but to search through back copy requires you to subscribe at £171 (roughly U.S. $250) per year.

You can find similarly useful websites from the main national television, radio, newspaper, and magazine companies in most countries.

You can also find out much about the companies working in your market. Many will have their own websites you can tap into. Smaller companies tend to use their websites just as product or service showcases, but some may provide snippets of information on where the market is heading, such as a press release summarizing a recent speech by the CEO at a trade conference. Publicly quoted companies will attach their annual reports and Form 10-Ks, in which you'll be able to find the company's views on market trends.

Another good source of market info on the web is online trade magazines. Typically they will have at least some sections open to the public without subscription, which can often be expensive. If you work in the automotive industry, for example, you could look up www.automotive-news.com. If you're in the wine business—lucky you—how about www.

wine-spirit.com? Whatever sector you work in, there will likely be an online trade magazine.

The Four-Stage Process for Gauging Future Demand

There is a four-step process you should follow in any assessment of market demand trends. Get this process right and all falls logically into place. Get it out of step and you may end up with a misleading answer. You should apply these steps for each of your main business segments. The four steps are:

1. *Assess past growth:* Check how market demand has grown in the past
2. *Assess past drivers of growth:* Identify what has been driving that growth in the past
3. *Assess changes in drivers:* Assess whether there will be any change in influence of these and other drivers in the future
4. *Forecast future growth:* Forecast market demand growth, based on the influence of future drivers

Let's look at each of these briefly, then at some examples.

1. Assess past growth

This is where it would be good to get some facts and figures. It's surprising how the most straightforward of searches can reveal recent growth rates in the markets you're looking for.

Be careful not to fall into the trap of relying on one recent number. Just because demand for a service jumped by, say, 8% last year doesn't mean that trend growth in that market has been 8% per year. The latest year may have been an aberration. The previous year might have seen a dip in the market, possibly by 5%, followed by the 8% recovery. That would give average growth over two years of just over 1%, not 8%!

You should try to get an average annual growth rate over a number of recent years, preferably the last three or four. As long as there haven't been serious annual ups and downs (if so, see box), you can usually get a usable approximation of average annual growth by calculating the overall percentage change in, say, the last four years and then annualizing it. The annualizing should strictly speaking be on a compound basis (see box again), but you're not going to get a rap on the knuckles from your backer (that's you!) if you just divide the overall percentage change by the number of years to get a simple average. Then you can use that number as the top of a narrow range, as in, say, 5 to 7%/year.

Many markets served by the self-employed professional, however, may be so small, so "nichey," that there is little or no data to be found on them. No matter. Useful information can still be uncovered. All you need to find out is whether the market has been growing fast, growing slowly, holding flat, declining slowly, or declining fast. We can define growing slowly as moving along at the same pace as the economy as a whole (Gross Domestic Product), which tends to average out at 2 to 2.5%/year in the United States, Britain, and other large Western economies. That's in "real" terms—in other words, in terms of tangible, wealth-creating growth. On top of that sits inflation, typically around the same 2 to 2.5%/year, although it has been much higher in the past. Slow growth in terms of "money of the day," or in "nominal" terms, can therefore be defined as roughly 5%/year.

A Moving Average Approach to Deriving Trend Growth Rates

There is one major complication in deriving trend growth rates, and that is when annual changes have been irregular, showing no consistent trend. The best way to deal with this is to plot a graph and draw a line (or curve) of best fit through the points. Another way is to translate your data into three-year moving averages. This smooths out annual fluctuations, making it easier to derive trend growth rates.

An example may help.

Here's a set of market data (in U.S. $ millions, say) for the 2000s:

Year	2000	2001	2002	2003	2004	2005	2006	2007
Market Demand	1476	1223	1150	1201	1387	1452	1582	1555
Change	n/a	-17%	-6%	4%	15%	5%	9%	-2%

If we were to ignore all that happened in the middle years, and just consider growth between the start point of 2000 and the end point of 2007, that would give us an overall increase of 5.4%, or growth (compound) of 0.75%/year.

But 2000 was the peak of a boom, so using that as the base year has underestimated growth in the 2000s. Likewise, if we'd used the trough year 2002 as the base, that would have over-estimated growth in the 2000s. We therefore translate the above data into three-year moving averages—namely the sum of this year's number plus the previous year's number plus the following year's number, divided by 3—as follows:

Year	2000	2001	2002	2003	2004	2005	2006	2007
Market Demand	n/a	1283	1191	1246	1347	1474	1530	n/a
Change	n/a	n/a	-7%	5%	8%	9%	4%	n/a

This has the effect of smoothing the annual fluctuations and we begin to see a clearer pattern. Taking 2001 as the start point and 2006 as the end point now gives an overall increase of 19%, or an average of 3.6%/year. The 0.6 figure suggests spurious accuracy, but a conclusion of 3.5%/year, plus or minus 0.5%/year (in other words, a conclusion of 3 to 4%/year), seems more reflective of trend growth in the 2000s in this market.

---

2. Assess past drivers of growth

Once you have uncovered some information on recent market demand growth, you now need to find out what has been influencing that trend. Typical factors that influence demand in many markets are:

- Per capita income growth
- Population growth in general
- Population growth specific to a market (for example, of pensioners or baby boomers, or general population growth in a particular area, possibly influenced by net migration)
- Some aspect of government policy
- Changing awareness, perhaps from high levels of promotion by competing providers
- Business structural shifts (such as toward outsourcing)
- Price change
- Fashion, even a craze
- Weather—seasonal variations, but maybe even the longer-term effects of climate change

Not all of these drivers will be relevant for your business segments. You need to pick those that are the most important. There may also be factors that are purely specific to your market. Fashion, fads in particular, can have a huge effect on some markets.

3. Assess changes in drivers

Now you need to assess how each of these drivers is going to develop over the next few years. Are things going to carry on more or less as before for a particular driver? Or may things change?

Will, for instance, immigration continue to drive local population growth? Is the government likely to hike up a particular tax? Could this market become less fashionable?

The most important driver is, of course, the economic cycle. If it seems the economy is poised for a nosedive, that could have a serious impact on demand in a business segment over the next year or two. You need to think carefully about the timing of the economic cycle when approaching your backer.

4. Forecast future growth

This is the fun bit. You've assembled the information on past trends and drivers. Now you can weave it all together, sprinkle it with a large dose of judgment, and you have a forecast of market demand—not without risk, not without uncertainty, but a systematically derived forecast nevertheless.

Let's take a simple example. You're offering a relatively new service to the elderly. Step 1: You find that the market has been growing at 5 to 10%/year over the last few years. Step 2: You identify the main drivers as (a) per capita income growth, (b) growth in the elderly population, and (c) growing awareness of the service by elderly people. Step 3: You believe income growth will continue as before, the elderly population will grow even faster in the future, and that awareness can only get more widespread. Step 4: You conclude that growth in your market will accelerate and could reach over 10%/year over the next few years.

A simple chart can help in coming to the final judgment, especially when things are not as straightforward as in this example (see Figure 2.1). The chart shows clearly whether demand is set to grow faster, or slower, and what drivers are causing that. It concludes that this service seems to have the wind behind. I wonder what it is....!

Figure 2.1. Market Demand Prospects for a New Service to the Elderly

| Demand Drivers for a New Service to the Elderly | Impact on Demand Growth | | | Comments |
	Recent Past	Now	Next Few Years	
Growth in incomes	-	o	+	• U.S. to resume economic growth in 2011-12, assuming no double-dip?
Growth in elderly population	+	+	++	• Proportion of U.S. population aged 65+ forecast to grow from 13% to 18.5% by 2025 (U.S. Census Bureau)
Increased awareness of service	++	++	+++	• Newspaper coverage, national and local, greater all the time
Overall Impact	+	+	++	
Market Growth Rate	*5 to 10%/yr*	*5 to 10%*	*Over 10%/yr*	

Key to Impact		O	None
+++	Very strong positive	-	Some negative
++	Strong positive	- -	Strong negative
+	Some positive	- - -	Very strong negative

For Employees: Gauging Demand at Two Levels

So far we've looked only at market demand prospects for self-employed people. If you're an employee, the approach is similar but a little more complicated. You need to look at market demand prospects at two levels:

▷ At the level of the economy (local, regional, or national, as for the self-employed, depending on your willingness—or ability—to relocate): Where's overall market demand for your type of service heading?

▷ At the level of your company: Where's demand for your type of service heading *within your company*?

You should look at both these levels because your backer needs to know how employable you would be if things go wrong in your current company or organization and you need to leave. This could be for a whole variety of reasons. It could involve personality conflict. Your boss may move on and you don't get on with the new one. Maybe an ingratiating colleague is promoted undeservingly above you. It might be that you can't tolerate working in the same room as a colleague.

Companies are no more than gatherings of people. People fall out. You may be forced to leave your company even though you do your job extremely well and everyone knows it.

But there's another reason. If there's a chance that your company gets into trouble—performing badly relative to the competition—then that could have a major impact on the *demand by your company for your type of services*. If your company is forced to restructure, then you and your colleagues may face a redundancy program. If the worst happens, and your company closes down, you and your fellow service providers will find yourselves on the labor market all at the same time. Not a good place to be.

Suppose you were a production line foreman at the grand old British motorcycle manufacturer, BSA, in the early 1960s. Originally a gunsmith, the Birmingham Small Arms Company ventured into bicycles in the late nineteenth century and motorcycles in the 1900s. After its acquisition of Triumph in the 1950s, it was the largest motorcycle company in the world. By the time that the Japanese motorcycle company, Honda, opened a plant in Britain in the 1960s, BSA virtually owned the British motorcycle market and was highly profitable. This wasn't surprising, since it had been spending precious little on research and development for years. Within a year or two, BSA was hemorrhaging cash. It never recovered.

Japanese motorbikes were technologically streets ahead of BSA, not in performance perhaps, but in reliability, fuel efficiency, and style. They were also much cheaper. Competition had for years been so fierce between the half-dozen Japanese motorcycle producers on their home turf that taking on foreign producers in their domestic markets was a cakewalk. Within 10 years or so, the British motorcycle industry virtually disappeared. Much the same happened in the United States, with producers like Harley-Davidson surviving only through refocusing their strategy to become a distinctive, cult, high-performance, high-price, niche producer.

If you, a foreman at BSA, were looking for backing in the early 1960s, you'd have thought it straightforward: yours was a prestigious blue-collar job in a venerable, respected, highly profitable company. But if your prospective backer had done her job properly and rigorously analyzed the prospects for your employer over the next three to five years, she may have unearthed some advance warnings (for example, capital expenditure less than depreciation) of the impending catastrophe for the British motor-cycle industry. She may have suggested that you started looking elsewhere before you were forced to do so—along with hundreds of fellow employees.

If, however, your company is performing well, and from what you can tell, better than most of the competition, then that's good news. Demand in your company for your type of service is likely to be higher than overall market demand (whether nationally, regionally or locally, however you choose to define your market).

To assess market demand prospects for employees, therefore, we need to use the same four-stage checking process we used for the self-employed, but at two levels—that of the broader economy and that of the company:

1. *Assess past growth:* Check how market demand for your type of service has grown in the past, both in general, in the economy as a whole, and specifically within your company; has demand for your type of service in your company been growing on a par with, above or below that found elsewhere?

2. *Assess past drivers of growth:* Identify what has been driving that growth in the past; what are the drivers specific to your company? —has your company been under/out-performing the market? —has it been adopting differentiating policies which affect demand for your type of service?

3. *Assess changes in drivers:* Assess whether there will be any change in influence of these and other drivers in the future; are there any changes likely to impact your company more than elsewhere?

4. *Forecast future growth:* Forecast market demand growth, based on the influence of future drivers, both in the economy and specifically in your company

We shall see how market demand forecasting for an employee works in practice with the example of Gary in Chapter 8. Until then, we shall continue with our main exemplar, Valerie, who is a self-employed businesswoman but needs to address market demand issues little different than if she were an employee in the same marketplace thinking of herself as a "business."

Market Demand Risk

Whether you're self-employed or an employee, you've now come to a reasonable forecast of what's likely to happen to market demand for your type of service over the next few years. But your backer needs to know a little more than that. You've assessed what's *most likely* to happen. But what are the risks of something happening to market demand that could make things worse than that? What could happen to make things *much* worse? How likely are these risks to happen?

On the other hand, what could make things better than you have forecast? What could make things *much* better? How likely are these opportunities to happen?

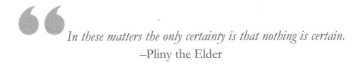

In these matters the only certainty is that nothing is certain.
–Pliny the Elder

Your backer's going to be very interested in these risks and opportunities. She's going to use your market demand forecasts to help her assess whether you're going to make your plan in Chapter 7. But then she's going to look at all the risks and opportunities around that plan in Chapter 8. And market demand issues will be the first set to be factored in.

It may help if you draw up a table, setting out each main risk or opportunity in the left-hand column and assessing in the next two columns first the likelihood of it happening and then the impact on your forecast if it should happen. This will help you to assess how important are each of the issues that you identify, as follows:

- ▷ If likelihood is medium (or high) and impact is high, that is a big issue
- ▷ If likelihood is high and impact is medium (or high), than that too is a big issue

Any other issues that you don't include in the table can be assumed to be either unlikely to happen or not to have much impact if they do happen. An example of such a table can be found in Appendix A, Figure A.2.

This table on market demand risks and opportunities, together with similar tables you'll draw up on those concerning competition (Chapter 3), your capabilities (Chapter 6) and your plan (Chapter 7), will form the inputs for completing your Risk Jigsaw in Chapter 8.

Valerie's Market Demand Prospects

Valerie knows full well that there is no way to get reliable data on market size and growth in economic consulting, certainly not in the segments that are pertinent to her. But she believes, rightly, that it is trends, not necessarily numbers, that are of most importance. She needs to use her familiarity with the market to come up with a robust assessment of these trends.

Valerie starts with her main segment, economic competitiveness, and judges that the five main demand drivers are aid levels, aid policy, awareness of the benefits of globalization, product life cycle, and civil conflict. She suspects that the main driver of growth in the past, product life cycle, could well be the main driver of deceleration in the future, since many, perhaps most, developing countries have now carried out competitiveness projects. Add-on projects are likely to be lower key and less likely to be aid-funded, hence involving expatriate economists (see Figure 2.2). This will apply to both her work for direct clients and as a subcontractor.

Figure 2.2. Market Demand Prospects for Economic Consulting

Demand Drivers for Competitiveness Product to Direct Clients	Impact on Demand Growth			Comments
	Recent Past	Now	Next Few Years	
Aid levels to LDCs	++	o	+	▪ Aid to resume growth as recession abates?
Aid policy	++	++	++	▪ Aid agencies keen to promote internationally competitive industries in LDCs
Awareness of benefits (and costs) of globalisation	++	++	++	▪ LDCs eager to follow S-E Asia, China, India
Product life cycle	++	+	+/o	▪ Many countries now have structures in place
Civil conflict	+/-	+/-	+/-	▪ Down during conflict, up with rehabilitation
Overall Impact	++	+	+	
Market Growth Rate	*Fast*	*Slower*	*Steady*	

Demand Drivers for Administration Product to Prime Contractor Clients	Impact on Demand Growth			Comments
	Recent Past	Now	Next Few Years	
Aid levels to LDCs	++	o	+	▪ Aid to resume growth as recession abates?
Aid policy	+	+	++	▪ Aid agencies keen to see greater efficiency
Product life cycle	+	++	++	▪ Still many LDC Govts/Depts run inefficiently
Prime contractor utilisation	++	- -	+	▪ Use of sub-contractors to resume with pick-up
Overall Impact	+	+/o	+/++	
Market Growth Rate	*Steady*	*Slower*	*Medium*	

Ironically, demand prospects in the segment with which Valerie is less enamored, public administration and governance, may well be set for faster growth. Aid organizations are now paying more attention to the efficient operations of the organizations to which funds have been disbursed, hoping that aid flows will be better channeled where they are most needed. Once prime contractor utilization has picked up, following the credit crunch-induced dip, demand for subcontractors in this segment could again be buoyant.

Valerie moves on to look at the market demand risks and opportunities in independent economic consulting, taking all her segments together. No serious risks stand out (Figure 2.3). Aid flows since the G8 Gleneagles summit in 2005 have been buoyant and have remained reasonably protected during the credit crunch. Civil conflict remains a serious risk, but it tends to balance out—as one country erupts, another abates.

Figure 2.3. **Market Demand Risks and Opportunities for Economic Consulting**

Market Demand Risks	Likelihood	Impact	Comments
Double-dip recession	Low/ Med	Low/ Med	• World economic growth set to resume in 2011-12, but sovereign and corporate indebtedness remain. Impact on aid levels limited, but severe in depression
Aid policy switches priority to e.g. poorest of poor	Low	High	• For long the top priority, but agencies recognise need for growth and trickle-down effect
More civil conflict	Low	High	• It's swings and roundabouts – e.g. Vietnam and Rwanda move forward, while e.g. Thailand and Kenya wobble
Market Demand Opportunities	Likelihood	Impact	Comments
New products to extend life cycle, such as cluster industries, firm-level competitiveness	Med	Med	• All leading economic consulting groups liaise with LDC governments and aid agencies to develop new ways of accelerating LDC competitiveness
More stellar success stories	Low/ Med	High	• For a generation and more the world has awaited the first "Asian tiger" on the African continent. Just one would lift the whole continent

On balance, market demand opportunities seem to outshine the risks, especially with the potential for product extensions—with economic consulting groups offering add-on products to extend life cycles, including in the competitiveness segment.

On balance, Valerie believes market demand prospects in independent economic consulting seem promising and will be of little concern to a backer. She suspects, however, that one identified trend, the demand shift from competitiveness to administration projects, may well resurface in Chapter 6, given her attitude to work in the latter segment....

You're Fired...Up!

Our first real-life exemplar is not in fact an MBA, but he did study economics at the Wharton School of the University of Pennsylvania and is too large a personality to omit from this book. He emerged from Wharton with his heart urging him to go to film school, but his head telling him to join his father in the real estate business. He went with his head. One reason was because of market demand. The main underlying demand drivers in real estate are population growth and economic development: supply limitations ensure that real estate prices rise in real terms over the long term, and as long as you get the timing right, and don't build or buy at the peak of the cycle, you can make good money. Donald Trump was born into the business, focused on it, and thrived in it—despite all but going under in the construction recession of the early 1990s. And, following his success fronting the TV show, The Apprentice, Trump even ended up with his own star on the Hollywood Walk of Fame. Who needed film school?!

3

What about the Competition?

This chapter is in some ways unfortunate. Life would be simpler if you were the only person who could provide your services, who could do your job. If your customers (or colleagues if you're an employee) had no choice but to come to you, you could shape your job to suit your own needs… and charge the customer what you wanted, within reason.

Life isn't like that. First, if a job's worth doing, there will be more than one of you wanting to do it. Second, none of us is irreplaceable. Don't kid yourself. There's always someone who can do your job just as well as you.

A screenwriter may have a certain actress in mind when he creates a screen role, but there's no guarantee she'll be available or willing to take the part. And when the second or fourth choice wins the Oscar for Best Actress, who then remembers the actress for whom the role was initially created?

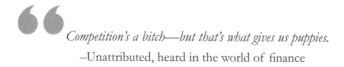

Competition's a bitch—but that's what gives us puppies.
–Unattributed, heard in the world of finance

There's always competition. There are others out there, often many others, who are either doing, or may be thinking of doing, what you are doing. This chapter asks you to think about what's happening, and what's likely to happen, to *all* these people doing your kind of job or business. And whether competition among all of you is getting tougher or slacker, or staying about the same. Above all, you need to know if there may be too many of you competing for the same jobs or business in the future.

Not only is there always competition but industry participants usually believe the competition to be tough. This is true even in near monopolies. Microsoft may have cornered the world market in personal computer operating systems, but it hasn't been an easy ride. Competition has been fierce and will only get tougher in the future.

What you must think about is whether competition will actually get *tougher*. Whatever your competitive situation today, it results in you making a profit or earning a salary of however many thousand dollars a year. But that's today. What your backer needs to know is what's going to happen *in the future*. Will the competitive environment enable you to continue to make that income, or grow it in line with your plans in three or five years' time?

Knowing the Competition
For the self-employed

First, you must be clear about who your competitors are. Think about when you provide a particular service to a particularly good customer of yours. Who else could she have gone to? Think about all your services to all your customers. What other names frequently crop up—who do they go to, or who could they have gone to? They're your competition.

Next, you should find out all you can about your competitors. If you're self-employed, this shouldn't be too difficult. How big are your competitors relative to you? How big were they a few years ago? How fast have they grown? Faster or slower than you? How long have they been around? How long have they offered this competing service?

What sort of service do they offer? What quality, price? Similar to yours? More upmarket, pricier? More downmarket, cheaper?

Do you know what financial resources your competitors have? If they need to expand, can they do it from their own (or spouse's) pocket, or will they need a backer? What are their plans? Do they intend to broaden their service offering, reach out to a new customer group? Or are they likely to be content carrying on doing what they do now?

For the employee

It's a little more tricky, but it can be quite revealing to think about who your competitors are if you're an employee. Your competition is not just your fellow employees who do the same job as you. It's also fellow employees who could and would like to do the same job as you.

It's also independent contractors who could be engaged by your boss to do the job you do temporarily. Or they could be engaged on a longer-term basis should your employer decide to outsource your job.

Finally, it's all those in your marketplace who are doing similar jobs at other companies, or who would like to do similar jobs at other companies, who would apply for your job if they knew there was a vacancy. Or who might apply on spec anyway even if there were no vacancy. These are all your competitors!

It's important that you as an employee consider all sets of competitors, direct and indirect, current and potential. Your backer has to understand the labor market in which you work, both within your company and—should you have to leave your employer—outside.

May the Five Forces Be With You!

There's no better tool to assess the competitiveness of a marketplace than Porter's five forces model. Indeed, it remains the most memorable and useful tool I learnt at business school in the early 1980s—and it may well be the same for you too!

The five forces model first appeared in Professor Michael Porter's *Competitive Strategy: Techniques for Analyzing Industries and Competitors* in 1980. It was designed for business markets rather than labor markets, but the principles work just as well here.

Porter identified five main sets of forces that shape the competitive intensity of a marketplace, as shown in Figure 3.1. Here's a quick word on each of them.

Figure 3.1. **Market Demand Risks and Opportunities for Economic Consulting Worldwide**

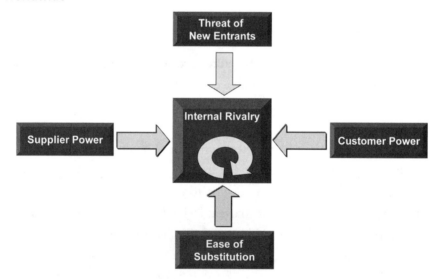

Internal rivalry

Internal rivalry for the self-employed (and remember that employees should think of themselves as self-employed here) is shaped by three main sub-forces: the number of players, market demand growth, and external pressures.

The number of players. The more numerous the players, the tougher typically the competition. Are there many players in your marketplace?

Market demand growth. The slower growing the market, the tougher typically the competition. How fast is your market growing?

Here's an example: fast-growing, labor-scarce markets, such as plumbing (in the United States), tend to have less internal rivalry than slow-growing, labor-abundant markets, such as bus driving.

External pressures. External bodies, in particular government and the trade unions, have the power to influence the nature of competition in many workplaces. Whether this is through introducing (or raising) a minimum wage, capping hours of work, toughening health and safety regulations, or imposing restrictive practices, competition can be greatly affected. In general, pressures from both government regulation and trade unions tend to reduce competition, though they are of course aimed at bringing about compensating benefits of other kinds. What external influences are there in your marketplace?

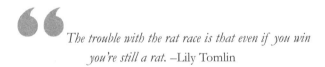

The trouble with the rat race is that even if you win you're still a rat. –Lily Tomlin

There are other factors influencing internal rivalry, which may be relevant in your workplace. One is high barriers to exit, where providers have little choice but to stay on competing when they should be withdrawing (for example, a restaurant with many employees, hence potentially high redundancy costs, or a shop with a long lease on the property which is difficult to offload). Another is seasonal or irregular overcapacity due to fluctuating levels of demand (for example, fruit picking).

How many providers are there in your marketplace? Too many? Enough? Too few (Great!)? How fast is the market for your services growing (Chapter 2)? What about the other factors? Put all these together and ask yourself how tough is the internal rivalry in your marketplace. High, low (Lucky you!), medium? And in a few years' time? Why?

Threat of new entrants

The lower the barriers to entry to a market, the tougher typically the competition. In a labor market where there are low barriers to new entrants, such as for unskilled labor, competition in times of low market demand, say during economic recession, can be very tough. In a labor market where barriers to entry are very high, for example in medicine, law or scientific research, competition is typically moderate—unless the regulating authorities have made a mess of long-term human resource planning.

Qualifications, training, and experience are the main entry barriers in most labor markets. But there can be others, such as:

> High investment costs to set up in business (for example, higher for dentists than for barbers, though higher for barbers than for cleaners)

> High costs of switching from one supplier to another (for example, higher for doctors than for restaurateurs)

> Reputation, or "brand equity" (for example, very high for non-executive directors, psychologists, actors)

How high are the entry barriers in your services? How serious is the threat of new entrants? High, low, medium? Is the threat going to get more serious over the next few years, less serious, or stay more or less the same? Why?

Ease of substitution

The easier it is for customers to use a substitute product or service, the tougher typically the competition. In labor markets, it is difficult for users to substitute for teachers or nurses, for example, but less difficult to substitute for cleaners (clever vacuum cleaners), TV or PC repair people (upgrade to a new model), or gardeners (drag Dad off the golf course).

How big is the threat of your type of service being substituted? High, low, medium? Is the threat going to get bigger over time? Why?

Customer power

The more bargaining power the customer has over the service provider, the tougher typically the competition. In labor markets, this is often a reflection of the number of providers in a particular marketplace, compared with the number of customers. The more choice of provider the customer has, the tougher the competition.

Customer power is also influenced by switching costs. If it's easy and relatively painless to switch suppliers, such as for your Realtor, competition is tougher. If switching costs are high, such as for your doctor, competition is less tough.

How much bargaining power do customers for your type of service have over providers like you? High, low, medium? And in the future? Why?

Supplier power

The more bargaining power suppliers have over the service providers, the tougher typically the competition. In labor markets, this force is not always so relevant. The main suppliers needed by most self-employed are their fellow self-employed, working as subcontractors. Thus the main supplier to a self-employed handyman could be his subcontracted apprentice, who should be readily replaceable if he were to move on.

In my own business of independent management consulting, I am often reliant on fellow independents to jointly provide the service needed by my clients. My associates can have strong bargaining power when they know they are ideally placed to do the work, whether because of their experience or because they just happen to be available at the right time.

How much bargaining power do your suppliers have over providers of your kind of service? High, low, medium? And in the future? Why?

Overall competitive intensity

These then are the five main forces shaping the degree of competition in a marketplace. Put them all together, perhaps as in the diagram above, and you'll have an idea of how competitive your marketplace is. How tough is it? High, low, medium? Is it set to get tougher? Why?

Your Job Market: Balance and Pricing

With your analysis of market demand (Chapter 2) and of industry competition (here), you will now have a good idea of whether market demand and supply are more or less in balance, now and over the next few years. This could have major implications for pricing prospects in your marketplace, hence on your earnings.

Suppose you're self-employed. If you conclude that you're in a balanced market and that market demand and supply are likely to remain balanced, then prices for your services may well carry on rising as they have done in the recent past—probably along with inflation, just above or just below.

If, however, your market is due to move from balance to oversupply—where supply exceeds demand—that will place a dampener on prices. You and your competitors will have to fight more fiercely for custom, and any planned price increases to meet rising costs may have to be put on hold.

If, conversely, the market is due to move from balance to undersupply (or excess demand), when more people want your type of service than there are services available, that's good news for you. You may be able to nudge up pricing above inflation.

Likewise, if you're an employee, it's unlikely that you and your colleagues are going to be awarded a significant salary increase when your company is facing a situation of oversupply in the market and not enough market demand. Conversely, in times of excess demand and overflowing order books, that's when you stand a good chance of pushing through a hike in salary or bonus.

What's likely to happen to market pricing is very important to your backer. This is because any extra dollar on the selling price of your service drops straight down to the bottom line. Conversely, every dollar off the selling price hits the bottom line.

There's a similar effect for employees. Let's take a simple example.

Ricardo, a bus driver in Calgary, Alberta, has wages equivalent to U.S. $40,000 a year. He puts a regular $200 per month in a save-as-you-earn scheme and spends what's left after tax living a reasonable, sensible, non-extravagant life style. Suppose his company is facing recruitment difficulties, due to Calgary's booming oil-driven economic growth, and awards all bus drivers a pay hike of 7.5%. That's $3,000 per year extra pay gross, say $2,400 per year after taxes. Assuming Ricardo doesn't want or need to spend the extra cash on anything else, his monthly savings may now be $400 per month. They've doubled! He hasn't had to work harder, put in more hours, look for extra work outside bus driving time, yet he's doubled his potential savings.

The possibility of a significant pay raise is important information for your backer.

Competition Risks

Doubt is not a pleasant condition, but certainty is absurd. –Voltaire

Now it's time to pull out all the main competition and pricing risks facing you and other providers of your services over the next few years. As you did in Chapter 2, it may be helpful to draw up a small table and highlight the most important risks and opportunities. You can find an example of such a table in Appendix A, Figure A.2.

These competition and pricing risks and opportunities are the second component of your Risk Jigsaw. Along with those on market demand (Chapter 2), your position (Chapter 6) and your plan (Chapter 7), you'll be taking them into account when considering whether to back you in Chapter 8.

Valerie's Competition

Valerie does two separate five forces diagrams, for each of her two distinct customer groups in independent economic consulting—direct clients and subcontracting. There is much overlap so, for the sake of brevity, we show just the combined version in Figure 3.2.

Figure 3.2. Competition in Economic Consulting

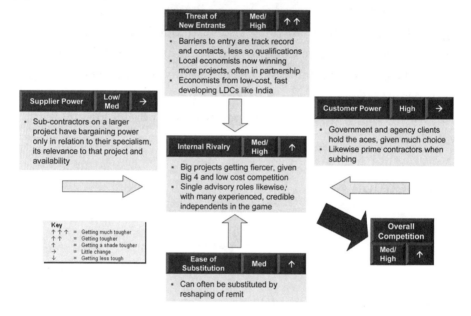

Internal rivalry in Valerie's business is medium to high, she figures. Amongst the larger groups, the Big Four accounting firms, her old firm EconCo, a couple of U.S. groups, and two or three European groups, are the major players, all supported, to varying extents, by their own government's aid agencies. Each major contract undergoes an open bidding process, but there are ways in which the result can be skewed in favor of the domestic group.

Independent players like Valerie can take on these groups only on much smaller projects and where they have excellent contacts. More often, they subcontract to the larger groups. Competition between these independents is conducted in a sporting manner, but is nevertheless more intense than a decade ago, due to their greater numbers. Many now possess the credibility gained from genuine experience in the field.

The biggest threat to both the economic consulting groups and the independents comes from new entrants. On the one hand, independents and now sizeable groups have sprung up in many developing countries, starting off as counterparts to expatriate parties and now increasingly competing for and winning contracts on their own. And on the other hand, Western consulting groups are facing competition from low-cost but highly educated third party countries like India. The independents likewise face growing competition both from local and low-cost rival individuals.

Overall, Valerie adjudges industry competition in independent economic consulting as medium to high, but getting tougher.

She compares this with her findings on market demand in Chapter 2, and concludes that the market for economic consulting has a slight imbalance. It has some excess supply, and given her forecasts of steady growth in her favored segment of competitiveness, though faster in administration, she suspects that there will be little opportunity for players to nudge up pricing over the next few years.

Finally, Valerie considers the threat of new entrants or, more pertinently, the growing establishment of recent entrants as being the only risk she would consider "big"—in other words, of medium to high likelihood and of medium to high impact. This will need to be factored into her decision on whether she would back herself in Chapters 8 and 9.

A Star Competitor

This student at Harvard Business School actually left three months before graduation to take up an offer at Westinghouse. He went on to lead the management services unit at Arthur D. Little before setting up his own business in 1963 under the sponsorship of a local bank, the Boston Safe Deposit and Trust Company. Competition in consulting has always been ferocious—barriers to entry are low and the client often has the luxury of choosing between three, four, or more highly credible proposals. At the time, competition between leaders like Arthur D. Little, McKinsey, and Booz was toughest in areas of overlap like operations management. Bruce Henderson was interested in the new area of strategy consulting and believed he could create a viable business within that niche alone. He was right. The Boston Consulting Group turned out to be no dog, not even a question mark, but a star—and has remained so since, despite having spawned numerous competing offspring over the years.

4

What Do Customers Need?

What Customers Need
The E2-R2-P2 of Customer Needs
How Needs May Change

We dealt with market demand risk in Chapter 2 and market supply risk in Chapter 3. In Chapter 6 we move on from the overall marketplace and look at you, at how you rate in your job or business in comparison with your competitors or colleagues. That's your competitive position risk.

But before we get there, we need to do some careful preparation and take another look at the marketplace as a whole. We work out what's common to all players in your business in the pursuit of success. What do you *all* need to do if you are to become successful?

To answer this, we have to address it in two parts. First, *what do customers need* from providers of your type of service? Or if you're an employee, what do your "customers"—your managers, or those to whom you report—need? That's this chapter. Then in Chapter 5 we'll ask: *What do you need to do to meet customers' needs* and succeed in your job or business?

First, let's be clear about what Part I of this book is trying to do and what it's not. Here we're defining "success" as being able to bring home, with a reasonable balance of risk and opportunity, the kind of earnings you've envisioned in your business plan. It's a narrow definition, but it's the only one that's of interest or use to your backer.

Of course, this begs questions regarding job satisfaction and job fulfillment. These we'll return to in Parts II and III. For the time being, your backer is not particularly interested in how spiritually meaningful your work is—*unless any dissatisfaction is going to impair your performance*. If this is so, as we'll examine in Chapter 6, then a major risk will be slotted into your risk jigsaw.

We should keep in mind yet again the most important segments in your "business." Customer needs often differ by segment. Customers in one may be sensitive to price and will look around for the cheapest service on offer. In another, customers may place quality of service as paramount and are prepared to pay a premium to achieve that. In a third segment, customers may be sensitive to time and will pay more for a service that is delivered promptly.

You should assess customer needs in each of your most important business segments.

What Customers Need

What do customers need from providers of your type of service? If you're an employee, what do your managers need from you and your peers?

If you're self-employed

What are customers looking for when they buy your type of service in one of your business segments? Are they looking for the lowest possible price for a given level of service? Are they looking for the highest quality service irrespective of price? Or, more likely, something in between?

Do customers have the same needs in your other business segments? Do some customer groups place greater importance on certain needs?

What exactly do they want in terms of service? The most luxurious? Delivery on time? The most jovial camaraderie?

We're all customers of service providers. Depending on what we're buying, our expectations differ. Think of what you look for when you engage a gardener, a PC repairer, or a subcontractor for your business.

Different customer groups have different needs for different types of service. You, as a self-employed businessperson, need to know what each of your customer groups expects of you and your competitors. And how they rank each need in order of importance.

> *Quality in a product or service is not what the supplier puts in. It is what the customer gets out and is willing to pay for.* –Peter Drucker

If you're an employee

The same holds true if you're an employee. You need to know what exactly the people to whom you report—your "customers"—expect from you in each of your business segments. You need to know how important each need is in relation to the others.

The E2-R2-P2 of Customer Needs

In the business world, customer needs from their suppliers are referred to as customer purchasing criteria (CPCs). For companies that provide services to (or produce goods for) other companies, namely business-to-business (or B2B) companies, CPCs typically include product quality, product range, delivery capabilities, pre-sale service, post-sale service, relationship, reputation, financial stability, and so forth. And of course, price.

For companies that provide services to the consumer directly, namely business-to-consumer (or B2C) companies, CPCs tend to be similar, although typically with less emphasis on product range and financial stability. Depending on the service being offered, the consumer will place varying importance on quality, service, and price.

For self-employed people, CPCs, or more simply, customer needs, are again little different in nature. Except that customer needs can often pertain to the provision of services by *one individual*, not the collection of individuals that is a company. They can be grouped into six categories. They are needs relating to the:

> ▹ *Effectiveness* of the service.
> ▹ *Efficiency* of the service.
> ▹ *Relationship* with the individual service provider.
> ▹ *Range* of services provided.
> ▹ *Premises* (only applicable if the customer needs to visit the service provider's premises).
> ▹ *Price* of the service.

They can be conveniently remembered, with perhaps a faint redolence of a cult science fiction movie, as the *E2-R2-P2* of customer needs.

Likewise "customer" needs of employees fall more or less into the same categories. Your managers expect from you the appropriate balance of service and price, that is, salary and benefits. But they provide the premises.

Let's look at each in turn.

E1: Effectiveness

The first need of any customer from any service is that the job gets done. Not half-done, not over-done, just done. You want a crew cut. You go to the barber. He gives you a crew cut. You pay and go home. Job done.

You may have other requirements, like how long the haircut took, the interaction with the barber, whether he also offers a wet shave, how clean the barbershop is, or how reasonable his price. But the most basic requirement is that he is effective at giving you a crew cut. At getting the job done.

Suppose, however, that it's not a crew cut you want, but the cool cut sported by some movie star? Now you start to get a bit more demanding. You'll want your barber, or hair stylist, to be competent technically at delivering such a haircut, to know about the pros and cons of living with such a haircut and to have done a few of these before—you don't want to be a guinea-pig, not with your hair!

In other words, you as the customer will have certain expectations as to what constitutes job effectiveness. You'll have expectations in three areas: *skills, knowledge and experience*. We'll take one at a time.

Skills

A skill is defined in dictionary.com as a "proficiency, facility, or dexterity that is acquired or developed through training or experience." It's not what you learned at school, it's what you were trained for in the world of work.

Customers need different skills from different services. The dramatic skills of an actor are of little use if you need advice on financial planning. Rather you want your advisor to have the skill of wrapping financial planning tools around your particular financial circumstances.

What skills does a customer expect from the service you offer? How important are these needs to your customers, relative to other needs? Are they of high, low or medium importance?

Knowledge

"Knowledge" has six definitions in dictionary.com, as follows:

- ▷ The state or fact of knowing
- ▷ Familiarity, awareness, or understanding gained through experience or study
- ▷ The sum or range of what has been perceived, discovered, or learned
- ▷ Learning, erudition
- ▷ Specific information about something
- ▷ Carnal knowledge

Each of these definitions, leaving aside the last one, may add some understanding of what the customer may need from your service. Customers will expect you not just to have certain skills but to possess knowledge associated with those skills.

In many services, customers will expect you to have knowledge of the benefits to them from the provision of your services. Thus the customers of an economic consultant like our exemplar, Valerie, will expect her to know what the benefits to the country will be from embracing her suggested reforms in economic competitiveness.

What knowledge, general or specific, do your customers expect you to have in the provision of your service? How important are these needs relative to others? High, low, or medium?

Experience

"Experience" is defined in dictionary.com as "active participation in events or activities, leading to the accumulation of knowledge or skill." So it's an integral part of the concepts of both skill and knowledge. It appears in their definitions. They appear in its definition.

Yet it's wise to pull out experience as a specific customer need, because it can sometimes be crucial. It may be important, but not as important as skill or relationship, for example, in selecting your physiotherapist. But what about your cardiac surgeon? No matter how well qualified she is, how adept she is with the scalpel, or how well you know her, if she hasn't had much experience in the precise surgical procedure that you need, would you opt for her?

It's not just in life-and-death situations where experience is important. It's important in virtually all services. Would you want your new boiler to be installed by a lad in his teens?

The trouble with working in a career where experience is a major customer need is how to get started. The answer is in building it however you can. Sometimes we need to swallow our pride and work for free, or at a big discount, just to build the experience.

Do your customers require much experience from the providers of your service? How important a need is it, relative to others? High, low, medium?

E2: Efficiency

We've looked at effectiveness, the most basic of customer needs for any type of service, and its three main components—skills, knowledge, and experience. The second distinct area of customer need is the second "E," efficiency. *How long will it take to deliver this service effectively?* How capable is this service provider in delivering one level of service in one space of time, another level in another space of time, and so on? In other words, how efficient is this service provider?

All customers place *some* level of importance on efficiency for all types of service. You may not care if your crew cut takes 10, 15, even 30 minutes, but you would care if it took all Saturday afternoon and you missed the big football game.

Different customer groups may place different levels of importance on efficiency for the same service. The direct clients of our independent economic consultant, Valerie, do not place as much emphasis on efficiency as her prime contractor clients—who sometimes want the answer by yesterday!

How much emphasis do your customers place on the efficiency of your service? How important is it relative to other needs? High, low, medium?

R1: Relationship

Your barber gives a good crew cut and he does it quickly. But do you like the guy? Is he the sort of guy you feel comfortable with having his hands on your head? Do you want your barber to chat or stay quiet? How do you want to interrelate? Does it matter to you if he seems bored and disinterested? Or would you prefer him to be interested and enthusiastic?

Never underestimate the relationship component in providing a service. A successful builder knows how to keep the homeowner as content as possible during the extension works. He'll try to ensure minimum disruption to everyday living—no wheelbarrows across the living room carpet—and be of good cheer at all times. He knows that his business depends on personal referrals. If the stay-at-home spouse tells a neighbor that he's not only a good builder but an okay guy to have around under trying circumstances, his chances of converting the next sale are improved.

It's the same in the workplace. When the redundancy program comes along, it's not the boss's favorite who's first shown the door.

Dictionary.com defines relationship as "a particular type of connection existing between people related to or having dealings with each other." But it's useful to divide customer expectations of relationships in two: *rapport* and *attitude*. Rapport, defined as "mutual trust or emotional affinity," is the set of one-on-one relationships built up between your customers (or managers, if you're an employee) and you.

It is not your aptitude, but your attitude, that determines your altitude.
–Zig Ziglar

Attitude is best singled out. It can be a major issue in career planning. And it can often be a paramount factor in the provision of services. A positive attitude, conveying enthusiasm, cheer, conviviality, optimism, humor, energy, and other uplifting attributes, can leave the customer feeling she has received exceptional value from the service.

A negative attitude, conveying grumpiness, gloom, pessimism, misery, lethargy, and other down-spiriting attributes, can leave the customer feeling glad to be rid of the service provider.

A negative attitude may be the result of dissatisfaction with the job. If this is so for you, it may impinge on your competitive position (Chapter 6) and you may need to consider changing career—hopefully following your passion (Part III).

How much emphasis do customers place on personal relationships in your service? On rapport? On attitude? High, low, medium?

R2: Range

The second "R" and fourth area of customer need is the range of services provided. This is an area customers can find important for some services, even most important, and for other services of no importance at all.

Let's return to the example of a hair salon. No self-respecting hair stylist would offer any less than haircuts, perms, and colorings. But is that enough? Would customers prefer a salon that can also offer techniques such as relaxing, straightening, plaiting, and braiding? How important to the salon's target customer group is the range of services provided?

At the other extreme lies the functional barbershop. If most customers only want a crew cut, they're going to look for a barber shop that is effective and efficient, and where the barber is a good guy. If the barber were also to offer head massage, big deal! Yet to some customers, the head massage may the unique offering that draws them through the door.

How important a need is range to your customers compared with others? High, low, medium?

P1: Premises

This only applies to a small portion of the self-employed and not to employees. Many of the self-employed, such as management consultants, web designers, and professional speakers, don't need a storefront. Accountants, insurance brokers, health practitioners do. Premises can be important, depending on how you are pitching your services.

Think on hair salons again. If you're aiming for the rich and famous, then you'll need a storefront on 5th Avenue, New York, or in Mayfair, London. And it had better be spectacular. If you're going for the middle-class, suburban housewife, you'll need a storefront on the local main street, and it should be clean and tasteful. Premises should be appropriate for the pocket of the customer.

How Can You Find Out?

All this is very well in theory, you may ask, but how do you know what customers want? Simple. Ask them! Or if that's impractical, since you're now immersed in your MBA studies, ask a former colleague to ask them for you.

It doesn't take long. You'd be surprised how after just a few discussions with any one customer group a predictable pattern begins to emerge. Some may consider one need "very important," others just "important." But it's unlikely that another will say that it's "unimportant"—unless perhaps for one out of a range of services provided. Customers tend to have the same needs.

The comprehensive way to find out customer needs is through "structured interviewing," where you ask a selected sample of customers a carefully prepared list of questions. (More on this in Chapter 6 and Appendix B.)

This is one of the steps in the *Backing You, MBA!* process that is typically easier for the employee. Most employees have regular reviews with their managers, at least once a year when it's time to decide pay raises. Your boss tells you what she needs from you and your colleagues. Dig out your notes from your last such review before you left for the MBA—what did she need?

Do you need a storefront for your type of service? What do customers expect of your premises? How important a need is it relative to others? High, low, medium?

P2: Price

This is the big one. Set your prices sky high and you won't have many customers.

Think about the buying decisions you make regularly and the influence of price. For nonessential services, we tend to be more price sensitive.

When your eight-year-old son's hair is flopping over his eyes, you look for a barber. He has little interest in his appearance (for the time being!), so you may look around for the cheapest. But how cheap are you prepared to go? Would you take him to a barber's that is (literally) dirt cheap, where the combs are greasy, the floor is covered with hair, and the barber is a miserable so-and-so? Probably not. You set minimum standards of service and then go for a reasonable price.

For essential services, we tend to be less fixated with price. When your central heating system breaks down in the middle of winter, will you go for the cheapest service engineer? Or will you call around your friends and acquaintances to find someone who is reliable, arrives when he says he will, fixes it with no fuss, and charges a price that is not exactly cheap but at least is no rip-off?

What are customers' pricing needs from providers of your type of service? How important is it relative to other needs? High, low, medium? Very high?

Your most unhappy customers are your greatest source of learning.
–Bill Gates

How Needs May Change

While you're talking to your customers, or to your managers, you also need to find out how their needs may change in the future. If they believe one need is highly important to them now, will it be as important in a few years' time? You need to know.

One factor that often tends to change over time is the emphasis a customer will place on price. Think of your laptop computer. Just a few years ago laptops were rather expensive, but when choosing between one of a half-dozen manufacturers to buy from, you might have paid a premium for a solid, well-known brand name. You may have been reluctant to buy a cheaper laptop and take the risk of it breaking down a year later (just as it came off warranty!). Now that laptops have become more commoditized, you may take a punt on the cheaper machine—especially for the kids!

It's the same with services. When a service is new and innovative, customers may be happy to give it a go despite the seemingly high price. A few years later, when there are many other providers, customers will expect more reasonable pricing. Consider a spa vacation in the tropics. A few years ago you would have had to pay an arm and a leg to have them pampered in a five-star spa resort in the tropics. Now dozens of three-star hotels in Thailand offer excellent spa services. In a few years' time, some new angle on the spa theme will come out. It'll cost a bomb for a while, but if it's popular the price will soon come down.

It's similar for employees. Price may not be the most important consideration of prospective employers when there is a national or local shortage of people with your skills. They'll be prepared to pay top salaries and benefits to recruit employees who can do the job. But that won't last. Over time there will be new entrants and labor supply will come more into balance with demand. Employers will then pay more attention to price. Think of the pay packages offered to Internet-savvy software developers in the late 1990s dot-com boom. It couldn't last, and it didn't.

How are customer needs from providers of your type of service likely to change over time?

You've assessed customer needs for your type of service, by major segment, now and over the next few years. In Chapter 5, we'll look at what capabilities are needed from providers like you to meet those customer needs and perform your service successfully.

Customer Needs in Valerie's Business

Valerie figures she has a pretty good idea of what her customers' needs are in independent economic consulting, but she's been at business school for eight months now and feels she could do with a refresher. So she arranges to meet up at a pub with a former fellow independent, David, and do some brainstorming.

After a smooth pint of Greene King, a trusty shepherds pie, and some catch-up chat, they turn to customer needs. Qualifications are essential, they agree, and the basic skills of analysis, reporting, and presenting important, but it is experience and relationship that direct clients place in highest priority (see Figure 4.1). They want the comfort of knowing that their supplier has done it all before and will bring that experience to bear when dealing with unfolding events. And they greatly value a personal relationship with the supplier.

Figure 4.1. Customer Needs from Economic Consulting

Customer Needs of Direct Clients		Importance	Change
Effectiveness **- Skills**	▪ Rigor of analysis ▪ Clarity of reporting ▪ Clarity of communication	Med/High	→
- Knowledge	▪ Qualifications	Essential	→
- Experience	▪ Understanding of approach and process	High	→
Efficiency	▪ Guarantee of supply ▪ Effort ▪ Timeliness	*Med** Med/High *Med**	→ → →
Relationship	▪ Rapport ▪ Enthusiasm	*High** High	↑ ↑
Range		Low	→
Premises		N/a	
Price		*Med**	↑

*Customer needs of Prime Contractor Clients are found to be the same as for Direct Clients, other than in guarantee of supply *(High)*, timeliness *(High)*, rapport *(Med)*, and price *(Med/High)*

Prime contractor clients have a different emphasis. Guarantee of supply is critical, because they need the supplier to join the project team exactly when required. And they place a greater emphasis on price and the timeliness of reporting (some direct clients are relatively laid back, happy to say "sometime next month" for the next report!). Prime contractors place correspondingly less emphasis on relationship.

Valerie and David then move on to what they as suppliers need to do to meet those needs, but that's for the next chapter....

5

What Must Providers Do to Succeed?

Key Kapabilities (K2s)
Converting Customer Needs into K2s
  » Service-related
  » Cost-related
Two More K2s
  » Management
  » Market Share
Applying Weights
Beware Must-have K2s!

In Chapter 4 you found out what customers need from your type of service. Or if you're an employee, what those to whom you report need from your type of service. You rated each of these customer needs by degree of importance.

In this chapter, you'll set out what you and all other providers of your services must do to meet those customer needs. You'll also determine what else providers have to do in terms of managing themselves as a business, whether employed or self-employed, to provide a competitive service. Then you'll be in a position to rate your own performance against all these factors in relation to your peers—that's for the next chapter.

Key Kapabilities (K2s)

We define Key Kapabilities as what providers like you need to do to succeed in your type of business or job. They are what you need to get right to be able to meet customer needs *and* run a sound business (if self-employed).

In the world of business, they are called Key Success Factors (KSFs). They are what a company needs to get right to succeed in that marketplace. Typical KSFs are product (or service) quality, consistency, availability, range, and product development (R&D). Companies also need to get their service right, with such KSFs as distribution capability, sales and marketing effectiveness, or post-sale technical support. Other KSFs relate to the cost side of things, such as location of premises, scale of operations, state-of-the-art equipment, and operational efficiency.

But this book is about you as an individual, and many of these KSFs will relate to the skills and attributes, or *capabilities,* required of *an individual person* providing your type of service. But not all. If you're self-employed, factors such as the range and skills of your subcontractors, or location and standard of premises, relate to your business, not to you as a person.

We'll call them Key Kapabilities, or K2s for short. Not to be confused with the second highest mountain in the world, Mount K2 of the Karakoram range in the Himalayas, but the term may serve as a reminder of the peaks we need to climb in order to succeed.

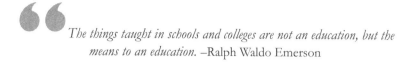

The things taught in schools and colleges are not an education, but the means to an education. –Ralph Waldo Emerson

Converting Customer Needs into K2s

First, we convert the customer needs we researched in the last chapter into K2s. In other words, we need to work out *what providers such as you must do in order to meet those customer needs.*

There are two types of K2s relating to customer needs: service-related and cost-related.

Service-related

Conversion is fairly straightforward for most customer needs. An associated K2 can often seem similar to, even the same as, a customer need. Suppose, for example, that you as a customer want your hair stylist to be good at coloring. That's one of your needs. So she or he needs to be skilled at coloring. That's a K2.

But K2s generally tend to take a different perspective from customer needs. Here's an example. When you call up your Internet service provider technical help desk, you want the technician to fix the problem. You as a customer need someone who can understand and fix your problem. The associated K2s for the technician are an appropriate technical qualification, subsequent completion of relevant training and experience of handling this and similar problems.

Here's another. When you jump on the city tour bus in Acapulco, Rome, or Kyoto, you expect to be able to understand clearly what the tour guide is saying. The customer need is clarity of communication. The associated K2s are proficiency in the language of delivery and clear communication skills.

What do providers of your type of services need to do to meet customer needs? What are the associated K2s for each customer need in your business or job?

When converting a customer need, you may find that the associated K2 can sometimes be the same as you've already associated with another customer need. In other words, one K2 can sometimes be sufficient to meet two or more customer needs. Returning to the tour guide, for example, another customer need may well be rapport with the guide. Rapport will be greatly eased through fluency in the language of delivery. In this example one K2, language proficiency, serves two customer needs, namely (1) clarity of communication, and (2) rapport.

Cost-related

There's one customer need that needs special attention, and that's price. Customers of most services expect a keen *price*. The service providers need to keep their *costs* down. Price is a customer need, cost competitiveness a K2.

In a competitive service business like car repair, middle-income customers tend to be sensitive to price, among other needs such as quality of work and integrity. The self-employed car mechanic will therefore try to keep his rental costs of premises down by locating his garage well off the Main Street, maybe off the side streets too and on to some commercially zoned land alongside the railway line.

What importance rating did you give to price as one of your customers' needs in the last chapter? If you gave it a "low," you're in luck.

For most of us, price is typically rated by customers as of high importance, or medium-high at best. In which case, we need to figure out how to keep costs down, or at least reasonable.

If you're an employee, this is all about your pay package. If you've rated price as highly important to your "customers," you and your peers need to be careful not to push too hard with your requests for a pay raise. Or you should think about offering your employer more flexibility within the overall package—lower basic, potentially higher bonus relating to performance, for example.

If you're self-employed, and price is highly important, you typically have four main cost levers to play with: cost of materials, use of subcontractors, overhead control, and profit flexibility:

> ‣ There may be little you can do about the cost of materials or equipment. If you're a sole trader, you'll have precious little bargaining power over your suppliers. What you can do, though, is keep as much control on material wastage as you can, for example on paper and printer ink.

> ‣ Careful use of subcontractors may be a K2 in your line of business. A self-employed businessperson should only use subcontractors when she doesn't have the capability or time available to do the work herself. But it's not always as easy as that. You may choose to keep your subcontractor happy and toss him some extra work, just to help him get by and stay in business, thereby being available to you when you really need him. It's a trade-off.

> ‣ Control of overhead is usually an important K2 for the self-employed. If you need premises, then they should be appropriate to the market positioning of your business. If you need to advertise, it should be carefully targeted. And you might reconsider whether your business really needs its customers to be taken to so many lunches or trips to the opera/baseball/Hawaii to succeed!

> ‣ Flexibility in profit level may be a K2. What's left of revenues after subcontractor and any other direct costs, and after overhead, is profit (pretax), the pay of the self-employed person. The ability to accommodate fluctuating profit levels, especially during market downturns, may be a K2. If you've leveraged up your lifestyle to an extent where a sharp fall in profits one year would put you and your family in financial distress, you are at a disadvantage to a competitor with greater personal flexibility. Acceptance of a long-term lower level of profit may also be a K2. If similarly competent competitors have come into your market

prepared to work at lower levels of pay—for example recent migrants—are you prepared to do the same?

There's one more set of cost-related K2s that is important. There's not a lot you can do about it if you are an individual, self-employed person. But you should know about it because this is a source of competitive advantage that lies with your larger competitors. Size may matter. Other things being equal, the larger the provider the lower their costs should be *for each unit* of business sold. This can be true for many overhead cost items, even for engaging subcontractors (the more work they're given, the lower the negotiated rate per day). These are "economies of scale."

Two areas of overhead where these economies tend to be most relevant in the service sectors are in rental space costs and marketing expenses. Think of two hair salons competing against each other on the Main Street. One has double the amount of space of the other and serves on average 80 customers a day, compared to the smaller salon's 40. They are thus similarly efficient and they charge similar prices. But the larger one has lower rental costs *per customer* because of a discount negotiated with the landlord on the second commercial unit rented. The larger salon also pays lower marketing costs *per customer*, since advertising space in the Yellow Pages or in local glossy magazines costs the same per column inch for both salons, irrespective of how many customers the advertiser serves.

What are the main cost-related K2s in your business? Cost of materials? Use of subcontractors? Overhead control? Profit flexibility? Economies of scale?

Two More K2s

So far, we've derived two sets of K2s from the customer needs laid out in Chapter 4: service-related and cost-related K2s. There are two more sets that should not be forgotten, especially for the self-employed: management and market share.

Management

Management-related K2s may be very important in your business. As a one-man-band, a freelancer, a self-employed individual, you have to do every job, play every role in your business. You're chairman of the board, chief executive officer, chief finance officer, chief operating officer, sales director, marketing director, IT director, even company secretary, all rolled into one. You may even have to act as HR director when you contemplate what training course you should go on and then discuss with the CEO (you again!) whether the business can afford your absence.

All of this might sound glamorous. Not so fast! You also have to do the un-glam jobs. You're the gofer. You go to the post office to mail your packages, you lug the PC to the repair shop, you answer the phone, you make the coffee. You do the bookkeeping. This requires discipline and time management, attributes that everyone struggles with and none more so than the self-employed. Trust me, I know. Especially when running your business coincides with the soccer World Cup (as I write!) or the Wimbledon tennis championships (next week!) on TV.

How important a K2 is management to your business? Scheduling customers? Bookkeeping? Cash collecting? Keeping lines of communication open through land line, cell phone, and email?

Above all, how important is sales and marketing to your business? Most self-employed or small businesses fail not because the individuals aren't competent at the service they offer. Quite the contrary. Very often they're the best and that's what gave them the confidence to break out on their own in the first place.

They fail because no one knows they're there.

Selling and marketing are the lifeblood of the self-employed person. If prospective customers don't know you're a player, or if they don't know how good you are, you have no business.

And if you don't like selling and marketing, or if you're no good at it, you'd better find a partner who can.

How important is management to your business? High, low, medium?

Market share

There's one final K2—an important one—that we need to take into account that isn't directly derived from a customer need. This is the size of your presence in a particular business segment—in other words, your share of that particular market. The larger the relative market share, the stronger should be the provider.

A high market share can manifest itself in a number of different competitive advantages. One such area is in lower unit costs, but we've already covered this under economies of scale in cost-related K2s, so we must be careful not to double count.

Market share is an indicator of the breadth and depth of your customer relationships and your business reputation. Since it is more difficult to gain a new customer than to do repeat business with an existing customer, the provider with the larger market share typically has a competitive advantage—*the power of the incumbent.*

For example, if your hair stylist fulfills all your customer needs—excellent hair styling, relaxing premises, rapport (aka gossip!), and a reasonable price, the fact that one or two of your friends are chatting about the excellent new stylist who has just set up further down the street will not necessarily tempt you away from your usual provider. Why switch? Your stylist would be most upset, especially when she has done nothing to deserve such disloyalty. This is the power of the incumbent. Customers don't like switching, unless they are sorely tempted (the pull factor) or forced to move through deficient service (the push factor). Keep the service levels high and your customers will tend to stick with the service they know.

It can even be costly to switch, for example, if your service provider offers you loyalty discounts. Sometimes it's costly in terms of time to switch, for example, if you change Internet service provider, you face the hassle of having to notify all your contacts of your new email address. Sometimes it's costly in emotional terms to switch, as we saw with the hair stylist. The higher the switching costs, the greater the power of the incumbent.

It's similar with employees. If your boss has found someone who looks like he could do your job a helluva lot better than you can, then you might find yourself being shifted sideways or even out the door. But if your boss finds someone who could do your job better, but not that much better, than you, then she's going to think twice about taking on the hassle of dealing with your disappointment, let alone risk falling foul of employment law, by edging you out.

Incumbency tends to rise in importance as a K2 where customers rely on their service provider for historical continuity. It's less of a wrench to change your shoe repairer, even your hair stylist, than to change your psychiatrist, or your accountant. The latter two have built up useful knowledge about you, whether it's your mind or your double-entry books. Switching to another provider may mean him taking a long time to build up the relevant understanding of you as an individual or business.

How great is the power of the incumbent in your job or business? How important is market share as a K2? High, low, medium?

Applying Weights

You've now worked out which are the most important factors for success, the K2s, in your business or job. Each one has been ranked as being of high, medium, or low importance, presently and in the next few years. Now you need to weight them.

A simple quantitative approach works best. Don't worry, you won't have to compute a weighting of, say, 14.526%. That would be horribly spurious accuracy. But it's helpful to derive a percentage for the weighting, whether to the nearest 5 or even 10%, so that in Chapter 6 you can easily tot up and rate your *overall* competitiveness relative to your peers.

So that 14.526% would become simply 15%. No more accuracy than that is needed. How to do it? There are two ways: methodically or eyeballing.

If you want a systematic approach, take a look at the text box. If you want to eyeball it, to get a rough and ready answer, start from the weightings taken for our main exemplar, the independent economic consultant, Valerie (see Figure 5.2). These can be taken to be fairly typical of a professional or managerial individual, but feel free to adjust them to what you

consider key to success in your job or business. And make sure that however you jiggle them they still add up to 100%.

One area where your K2 weightings may differ from Valerie's in the
importance of relative market share. In economic consulting, this is relatively low, due to the contractual nature of the business, the geographically
diverse client base, and the paucity of switching costs.

Once you've eyeballed the weightings in general, you need to assess to
what extent these weightings differ for each of your business segments. In
particular, different customer groups can often place a different emphasis
on price, so cost competitiveness may be more of an issue in one segment
than in others. Other customers in other business segments may be more
concerned about the effectiveness or the efficiency of the service.

A Systematic Approach for Deriving K2 Weightings

Here's a step by step systematic approach to weighting K2s:

- Use judgment on the relative power of the incumbent
  to derive a weighting for *relative market share* of i percent,
  typically in the range of 15 to 25% for professional and
  managerial workers.

- Revisit the importance of price to the customer. If you
  judged the customer need of medium importance, give
  cost competitiveness a weighting of 20%. If low, 10%. If
  high, 30%. Pro rata for in-between. Settle on c percent.

- Think on the importance of *management* factors to the
  success of your business, especially marketing. Settle on
  m percent, typically within a 0 to 10% range.

- You've now used up a total of $(i + c + m)$ percent of
  your available weighting.

- The balance, namely $100 - (i + c + m)$ percent, will
  be the total weighting for *service* factors, typically in the
  range of 50 to 65% for professional and managerial
  workers.

- Revisit the list of K2s relating to *service issues*, excluding
  price, which has already been covered. Where you've

> judged a factor to be of low importance, give it a K2 score of 1. Where high, 5. Rate pro rata for in between (for example, medium/high would be a 4).

- ▸ Add up the total score for these service-related K2s (excluding price) = S.
- ▸ Assign weightings to each service K2 as follows: weighting (percent) = K2 Score * (1—[i + c + m])/S.
- ▸ Round each of them up or down to the nearest 5%.
- ▸ Adjust further if necessary so that the sum of all K2 weights is 100%.
- ▸ Eyeball them for sense, make final adjustments.
- ▸ Check that the sum is still 100%.

Beware Must-have K2s!

There is one final wrinkle. But it may be crucial.

Is any one of your K2s so important that if you don't rank highly against it you shouldn't even be in the business or job? You simply won't begin to compete, let alone succeed? You won't win any business, or you won't be able to deliver on the business you win? In other words, it is a *must-have* K2, rather than a mere *should-have* K2.

Let's take an extreme example. Suppose you are thinking of backing Mr. Fayque, a locally respected psychotherapist working out of his smartly converted front room in a fashionable suburb of Tulsa, Oklahoma. You find that the most important K2s are psychotherapy techniques, communication skills, and experience. Qualifications are not regarded by most customers as important in their buying decision since "they all have the same diplomas."

Mr. Fayque rates highly against all the major K2s. His customers feel comfortable in his grasp of techniques, he's immensely personable, and he has years of experience. There's just the one problem: He's not qualified. You stumble upon this entirely by chance when talking to a friend of a friend who went to the same school at roughly the same time as Mr. Fayque. She knew him all right, but she also knew that he'd dropped out of school in a haze of drug-fuelled hedonism. She wasn't aware he had ever returned. A couple more calls, and you discover that the framed certificate in pride of place in Mr. Fayque's front room is a fake. He has been practicing under false pretences.

In this case, qualification is a must-have K2. Mr. Fayque doesn't have it. He shouldn't have been practicing, no matter how well he met all other K2s. You won't back him.

Are any of the K2s in your business or job must-haves? Keep a note of them before we assess your rating against all K2s in the next chapter.

One final thought. *Is Attitude a Must-Have K2?* How important is attitude in your current or pre-MBA job? Is it one of the many should-have K2s or could it be a must-have?

We've all seen it before: the best restaurant in town, exquisite cuisine, fine wines, conducive décor, pleasing ambience—yet surly, miserable, down-spiriting servers. Why, oh why, we wonder, does the manager put up with these guys? The answer is that he doesn't need to do anything about them. His tables are full, the cash rolls in daily. Courteous service is a customer need, and one of a number of K2s for every restaurant owner. In most restaurants, it's a must-have K2. Without it, people wouldn't come back. Regrettably it doesn't seem to be regarded as a must-have K2 in some of the best restaurants.

Think of other places where you have come across those same grim faces, or heard those same miserable voices—insurance claims personnel, immigration officers, local government officials, medical receptionists, product return desk staff, and so on. Attitude is no must-have K2 there.

Then think of summer camp. Imagine dropping off your 12-year-old daughter at a summer camp in the Rockies and meeting a couple of camp staff wearing those same miserable faces. You'd stuff your daughter back in the car, do a u-turn, and head for home. An enthusiastic, cheerful attitude is a must-have in the summer camp business. Likewise in most leisure, travel, and entertainment businesses—think how many people would carry on watching *American Idol* on TV if Simon Cowell never cracked a toothy smile after one of his gratingly pompous but telling putdowns!

How important is attitude in your job or business? Is attitude a must-have K2?

Key Kapabilities in Valerie's Business

Valerie has little difficulty in assessing the K2s needed to meet the customer needs she and former colleague David have already identified in independent economic consulting. Most important are track record, basic consulting skills of analysis, report writing and presenting, and inter-personal skills (see Figure 5.1).

Figure 5.1. Key Kapabilities for Economic Consulting

Customer Needs of Direct Clients		Importance	Change	Associated Key Kapabilities
Effectiveness - Skills	• Rigor of analysis • Clarity of reporting • Clarity of communication	Med/High	→	• Analytical skills • Report writing skills • People skills (presentation)
- Knowledge	• Qualifications	Essential	→	• Post-graduate economics degree
- Experience	• Understanding of approach and process	High	→	• Track record • Brand
Efficiency	• Guarantee of supply • Effort • Timeliness	High Med/High Med/High	→ → →	• Availability • Work ethic • Delivery
Relationship	• Rapport • Enthusiasm	High High	↑ ↑	• People skills (communication) • Positive, upbeat attitude
Range		Low	→	• Range of services
Premises		N/a		• Premises
Price		Med	↑	• Cost competitiveness

Trickier is the weighting. Valerie tries the eyeballing approach at first, but that seems a bit haphazard, so she switches to the systematic method. If she as an economist can't derive weightings methodically, who can?!

For direct clients, she considers that relative market share is not a huge advantage in winning each new contract, not in comparison with businesses such as health, financial, or legal services. Cost and management factors are important, but not as important as service factors, for which she has a total of 55% remaining to be allocated (Figure 5.2). Most important among these are effectiveness factors like track record/brand and basic consulting skills. She knows that when pitching directly to aid agencies or governments, her Achilles heel is often the absence of brand.

Figure 5.2. Weighting of Key Kapabilities in Economic Consulting

Key Kapabilities in Independent Economic Consulting	Weighting	
	Direct Clients	Sub-Contracting
Relative Market Share	15%	**5%**
Cost Factors: Overhead control, Scale economies	20%	**25%**
Management Factors: Marketing	10%	**5%**
Service Factors: Effectiveness—Analyse, Report, Present	10%	10%
Effectiveness—Qualifications	10%	10%
Effectiveness—Track record, Brand	15%	**20%**
Efficiency—Availability, Work ethic, Delivery	5%	**15%**
Relationship—Communication, Attitude	10%	**5%**
Range	5%	5%
Premises	0%	0%
Total	100%	100%

Note: Where different, K2 weightings in sub-contracting are highlighted in bold

For subcontracting, the weights change somewhat. Relative market share becomes insignificant and marketing and communication less important, but cost competitiveness and efficiency—being available when needed, delivering output on time—more so.

Now she's ready to assess how well she as an independent stacks up to the competition—but that's for Chapter 6....

6

How Do You Measure Up?

Your Competitive Position
Implications for Future Market Share
Competing by Segment
Competing in the Future
Getting Past First Base
Risks to Your Position

This is the easy part. You've done all the hard graft in the last couple of chapters, paving the way for the show-down of this chapter.

It may also be the rewarding part. You may be pleasantly surprised at how well you rate against your peers in your current or pre-MBA job or business.

But it may also be the shocking part. You may find that you're poorly placed to compete or even survive in the competitive arena in which you play. Your backer may back *off*, rather than back *you!*—in which case, you may need to move swiftly on to Part III of this book!

In this chapter you'll assess how you perform against each of the Key Kapabilities (K2s) you identified in Chapter 5. Taking into account each K2's weighting, you'll then tot up the ratings and see how your overall competitive position compares against your competitors (or colleagues, if you're an employee).

You should do this for each of your main business segments, since your position in one may be very different from in others. Then you should consider how your position is likely to change in each segment over the next few years and what you can do to improve it over time.

Finally, you need to do a reality check. Do you by any chance rate poorly against one of the *must-have* K2s we highlighted in Chapter 5? If so, that may mean you don't get past First Base. You shouldn't be in your former job or business. Period. Could it be your attitude?

The first thing to decide is who to compare yourself with. Sometimes that seems a no-brainer. Often it requires a little more thought.

Take a simple example. For the owner of one of three hair salons on a suburban Main Street, the comparison may seem obvious. She judges herself against the other two. But some of her potential customers may have their hair done in the city during lunch breaks or after work. Others may get it done when they do their weekly grocery shopping at the out-of-town supermarket. They are competitors too.

Don't be stingy. If you think another provider is serving clients who could potentially be yours, rate him too. Remember, this chapter is the easy bit. It takes just a few minutes to have a first shot at rating each competitor.

If you're an employee, you should first compare yourself with those who do the same job, who serve the same "customers." But think too about those who *could* do your job by moving sideways or upwards, even downwards, in your firm.

And don't forget to include the external supplier, which is what you could be if your job were outsourced. Consider how competitive she would be if your boss asked her to take over your job or aspects of your job while you were away, say, on maternity leave.

Your Competitive Position

How do you compare with your peers? Are you more or less competitive than them? What's your competitive position? And theirs?

To derive your competitive position, all you need to do is rate yourself against each of the K2s drawn up in the last chapter. If you use a numerical rating system, alongside the percentage weighting system you've already drawn up in Chapter 5, your competitive position will emerge clearly.

If you perform about the same as your peers against a K2, give yourself a score in the middle of a range of 1-5, a 3 (*good, favorable*). If you perform very strongly, a 5 (*very strong*). Poorly, a 1 (*weak*). If you perform not quite as well as most others, give yourself a 2 (*okay-ish, but below par*). If better than most, a 4 (*strong*).

Now do the same for each of your competitors against that K2. Who's the best performer? Does she merit a 5, or is she better but not *that* much better than everyone else, for a 4?

And so on against each K2.

Real knowledge is to know the extent of one's ignorance. –Confucius

If you've used Excel, your competitive position literally falls out at the bottom of the spreadsheet. For the first 25 years of my career, I had to do it by hand—either by totting up in my head or using a calculator if I was feeling lazy. For youngsters today, that must be difficult to imagine.

Excel makes things so much easier. But beware. The old manual approach encouraged you to think very carefully about each rating, because you really didn't want the hassle of having to do the calculation all over again. With Excel you do no calculating, so sloppy thinking incurs no time penalty. It's a trap, well known in financial planning these days. Think carefully.

Algebraically, your overall rating is the sum of each rating (r) against each K2 multiplied by the percentage weighting (w) of the K2. If there are n K2s, your overall rating will be (r1 * w1) + (r2 * w2) + (r3 * w3) + …. + (rn + wn). As long as the percentage weightings add up to 100%, you should get the right answer.

Implications for Future Market Share

The main use of competitive position for your backer is to give him some idea of how your business is likely to fare over the next few years *in relation to the market as a whole.*

If your competitive position turns out to be around 3, or good/favorable, he'll expect you, other things being equal, to be able to grow your business in line with the market over the next few years. In other words, to hold market share.

If your competitive position is around 4 or above, he'll expect you to be able to beat the market, to gain market share, again, other things being equal. Suppose he's already worked out from Chapter 2 that the market should grow at 10% a year. With a competitive position of 4, he'll feel more comfortable if your plan is to grow business at, say, 12% a year.

If your competitive position is around 2, however, your backer is going to be less confident about your business prospects. It's more likely you'll underperform the market and he'll be especially worried if your plans show you outperforming the market! He will wonder if he's backing the right horse.

If you're an employee, the main purpose of competitive position is to give your backer comfort on whether you should hold on to your job, thereby enabling you to achieve the earnings levels in your plan.

If your competitive position is around 3, then your backer will think there's no reason why you should fare any worse, or better, than other employees in your firm over the next few years. If she's deduced from Chapters 2 and 3 that your firm's prospects are sound, that your firm is doing well in a growing, not-too-competitive market, then your favorable competitive position may well give her sufficient comfort to back you.

If your competitive position is around 4, or above, then even if your backer has found out from Chapters 2 and 3 that the firm may be facing some troubled times, she may still be interested in you. Other things being equal, if the firm has to cut back on staff over the next few years, you're less likely to be among the first batch to leave than those who are less well placed.

If your competitive position is around 2, however, your backer's going to be concerned. Even if she finds that the firm's prospects are promising, she'll wonder if you're in the right job. She'll want to know what plans you have for strengthening your position. And if she's not convinced by those plans, she may recommend that you start looking elsewhere, before you're forced to.

How Can You Find Out?

Finding out your competitive position is easy for employees. Ask your boss! Or wait until your next review comes along and ask her then. Ask her how you rate against each of the service-related K2s. You could even try asking her which of your peers she thinks rates most highly against each K2, although she might be a bit hesitant revealing this. Ask her how you should go about improving your performance against one or two of the K2s.

For the self-employed, the first step is to do it yourself. Over the years, or months if you've only just started, you'll already have had occasional feedback from your customers: "Great piece of work" generally means you've done something right. "No way am I gonna pay you for that!" suggests the opposite.

Have a go at rating yourself. Then stick a question mark against those ratings where you're a little unsure on how you perform. Investigate those ratings one or two at a time. Next time you're with a customer, throw in the line: "By the way, you know that job I did for you a couple of months ago—were you happy with the turnaround time?

Did you expect it to be quicker?" Gradually you'll be able to start removing the question marks and firm up your rating.

While rating your own performance, you should also be rating your competitors. All performance is relative, so if you give yourself a 3 against one K2, it will be relative to a competitor whom you rate as a 4, or another a 2. Do a first draft of rating your competitors at the same time as your own. Again stick in question marks against the numbers where you're unsure. Then start throwing in the odd question with your customers, like: "What about Joe? Does he turn things round as fast as I do?" Gradually the question marks on your competitors' ratings should also disappear.

The methodical way for the self-employed to find out their ratings is through *structured interviewing*. This is what management consultants do on behalf of their clients to derive primary information on business strategy, marketing, or due diligence assignments.

A structured interviewing program differs from the more casual approach in two respects: You select a representative sample of interviewees, and you draw on a prepared questionnaire.

The advantage of a structured interviewing process is that it will in time give you all you need to know. There are two disadvantages. First, it takes up the time of your customers. There's a risk that you'll leave your customer thinking that you've just wasted a quarter or half hour of her precious time. Second, you may be a bit sensitive about your customers knowing that you're doing a strategy review. You don't want them to think that you may be moving on to bigger and better things, leaving them in your wake. You also may not want your customer to think too hard about your service compared to others, in case he suddenly realizes he'd be better off with a competitor!

These risks should, however, be containable as long as you prepare your story well in advance and try to make the experience as beneficial for the customer as for you.

For a detailed description on how to conduct a structured interview program with your customers, please turn to Appendix B.

Competing by Segment

We've talked this far as if there were only one business segment. But most people work in quite a few business segments. How does your competitive position compare in each segment?

You'll find that some ratings are the same, some are different. Take skills, for example. If the skills required for two segments are the same, then your rating against that K2 will be the same in each segment. But the weighting of that K2 may well differ by segment, thereby impacting your overall competitive position in each.

Other ratings may be different by segment. For instance, you may have years of experience in one segment, but you've only just started in another - rating a 5 in the first, but only a 1 or 2 in the other. Or awareness. You may have loads of contacts developed over the years in one segment, but you're finding it hard to get your name known in another.

Just as you've assessed market demand prospects and competitive intensity for each of your main business segments in earlier chapters, so too you need to evaluate your competitive position in each segment. Then in Chapter 7 you'll be able to assess your business prospects in each segment.

Competing in the Future

So far your analysis of competitive position has been static. You've rated your current competitiveness and that of others. But that's only the first part of the story. What your backer also wants to know is how your competitive position is likely to change over the next few years. He'll want to understand the dynamics. Is it set to improve or worsen?

The simplest way to do this is to add an extra column to your chart, representing you in, say, three years' time. Then you can build in any improvements in your ratings against each K2. These prospective improvements need, for the time being, to be both in the pipeline *and* likely for your backer to be convinced. We're going to look in more detail in Part II at how you can *proactively and systematically* improve your competitive position. How you can stretch your sights, identify the capability gap, and select a strategy to bridge the gap. But for now we'll just look at how your competitive position seems set to change naturally over the next few years.

One obvious area where you may well improve your rating is in experience, since you will by then be three years' more experienced. If you already have 20 years' experience in a business segment, then an extra three years won't make a difference. But if you've only had 20 months in the business, an extra 36 will make a big difference.

Remember, though, that the experience K2 can work the other way. If you've been in the game for 20 years and your main challenger just three years, you should have an edge—maybe a rating of 5 to his 2.5. Three years' hence, however, you've been there 23 years and he six years. You're still a 5, but he's become a 3, possibly a 3.5. The gap has narrowed. Much will depend on the extent to which experience is judged by customers to be relevant to their buying decision.

Other areas where you may be able to improve your competitive position over time may be in skills or qualifications. If you're set to undergo any further training, then that should be factored in. Your training may well be in an aspect of your job that will directly meet customer needs, such as in further skills or knowledge development. Or it may be in an area that improves your management-related K2s, such as a course in selling skills or public speaking.

Remember again, however, that improved competitive position is a two-edged sword. Your competitors too will have plans. This is where analysis of K2 dynamics gets challenging. It's easy enough to know what you're planning but what are your competitors up to?

Try adding a couple of further columns representing your two most fearsome competitors as they may be in three years' time. Do you have any idea what they're planning to do to improve their competitiveness in the near future? What are they likely to do? What could they do? *What are you afraid they'll do?*

By now you've added three columns and the table may start looking a bit unwieldy. Perhaps you should draw up a new table altogether, representing the competitive situation in three years' time? You'll need to do this anyway if there are any significant changes likely in the required K2s, or their weightings. In that case, you can't use the current weightings to apply to future competitive position. You'll need a new table.

How is your competitive position likely to change over time? And for your competitors?

Getting Past First Base

In the last chapter, we introduced the concept of the must-have K2—without a good rating in which you cannot even begin to compete.

Did you find a must-have K2 in any of your business segments? If so, how do you rate against it? Favorable, strong? Fine. Okay-ish? Questionable. Weak? Troublesome. A straight zero, not even a 1? You're out. You don't get past first base.

And what about in a few years' time? Could any K2 develop into a must-have? How will you rate then? Will you get past first base?

And even though you rate okay-ish against a must-have K2 today, might it slip over time? Could it slide below 2, into tricky territory?

This may be a case of being cruel to be kind. It's better to know. The sooner you realize that you're in the wrong business or job, the sooner you can move on. Part III can help you with that.

The ironic thing about must-have K2s is that you can rate superbly against all the other K2s, but if you don't rate at least a 2 (okay-ish) against a must-have, you may be nowhere. You're in the wrong business or job.

We saw the example of Mr. Fayque in the last chapter. He was accomplished in each of the K2s, bar the one must-have. He wasn't qualified.

Finally, is attitude is a must-have Key Kapability in your business?

If you return to your former job or business post-MBA, will your attitude be right?

Is it on the wane? Is there any chance it will slip so far that your rating against this must-have K2 will fall below threshold level, below favorable?

Might this adversely affect your performance on the job? If so, you may be among the first to go during the next shakeout.

Better to realize it now and take some affirmative action—see Part III of this book—than plod on until you're shaken out.

If you can't change your fate, change your attitude. –Amy Tan

Risks to Your Position

In Chapters 2 and 3, you pulled out the main market demand and competition risks and opportunities facing all providers of your type of service. Now you can add those that relate to your competitive position over the next few years. Again it might be helpful to draw up a small table, using the example shown in Appendix A, Figure A.2.

You've now completed the third component of the Risk Jigsaw. There's just one more to go, in the next chapter on meeting your plan. Then all the main risks and opportunities will be pieced together in Chapter 8.

Valerie's Competitive Position

Valerie uses the approach set out above to see how her competitive position in independent economic consulting will improve with her MBA. She's a trifle dismayed, though not wholly surprised, that her position in her main business segment, economic competitiveness to direct clients, whether governments or aid agencies, will improve only slightly.

But this doesn't concern her for long. She didn't set out on her MBA to strengthen her standing in a segment where she was already strong. She did so to venture into business strategy work for her same or related clients in economic consulting or, ideally, to move into mainstream strategy consulting to European corporate clients with a top-tier management consultancy.

In this segment, Valerie will still have very low market share post-MBA, she'll be cost competitive with larger groups and top OECD consultants, though less so than those from low-cost countries, she'll still be lousy at marketing herself, and she'll still be strong to very strong in basic consulting skills, track record, and communicating. Where her position will be slightly strengthened is in qualifications (up from a rating of 4 to 4.5—still no Ph.D., unlike some peers) and range (up from 3 to 4, now that she'll also be marketing her business strategy product).

Figure 6.1. Valerie's Competitive Position Post-MBA in the Segment: Economic Competitiveness to Direct Clients

Key Kapabilities: Competitiveness to Direct Clients	Weighting	Valerie	EconCo	A Top OECD Indept	A Top Low-Cost Indept
Relative Market Share	15%	1	4	1	1
Cost Factors: Overhead control, Scale economies	20%	4	2	3	5
Management Factors: Marketing	10%	2	5	3	3
Service Factors: Effectiveness—Analyse, Report, Present	10%	4.5	5	5	5
Effectiveness—Qualifications	10%	4.5	5	5	5
Effectiveness—Track record, Brand	15%	4	5	5	5
Efficiency—Availability, Work ethic, Delivery	5%	5	4	4	5
Relationship—Communication, Attitude	10%	5	4	4	3
Range	5%	4	5	4	4
Premises	0%				
Competitive Position	100%	3.6	4.1	3.6	4.0

Key to Rating: 1 = Weak, 2 = Below par, 3 = Favorable, 4 = Strong, 5 = Very strong

Overall Valerie's competitive position in the economic competitiveness/direct client segment will rise from 3.5 to 3.6 with the MBA (see Figure 6.1). She'll remain a favorable to strong player in her main segment, clearly without the muscle, depth, and breadth of market leader EconCo, but competitive with the best of fellow OECD independents (largely due to her readiness to under-price them to secure the right job) and not uncompetitive with the best of those from low-cost countries (against whom it is difficult to compete on price).

In another important segment, economic competitiveness to prime contractor clients, such as EconCo, Valerie finds she has a stronger position of 4.0, rising to 4.1 with an MBA, due to the higher weighting for efficiency and the lower one for market share and management we found in the last chapter (see Figure 5.2).

But in her target new segment, business strategy to direct clients, Valerie is disappointed to find that her competitive position emerges as an unspectacular 3.2 (Figure 6.2). She reasons, however, that this is inevitable, since she'll set out with little direct experience—little more, in fact, than the project work and summertime work experience gained during the MBA program itself.

Figure 6.2. Valerie's Competitive Position Post-MBA in the Segment: Business Strategy to Direct Clients

Key Kapabilities: Business Strategy to Direct Clients	Weighting	Valerie	EconCo	A Top OECD Indept	A Top Low-Cost Indept
Relative Market Share	15%	1	4	1	1
Cost Factors: Overhead control, Scale economies	20%	4	2	3	5
Management Factors: Marketing	10%	2	5	3	3
Service Factors: Effectiveness—Analyse, Report,	10%	3	5	5	5
Effectiveness—Qualifications	10%	4.5	5	5	5
Effectiveness—Track record, Brand	15%	2.5	5	5	5
Efficiency—Availability, Work ethic, Delivery	5%	5	4	4	5
Relationship—Communication, Attitude	10%	5	4	4	3
Range	5%	4	5	4	4
Premises	0%				
Competitive Position	**100%**	**3.2**	**4.1**	**3.6**	**4.0**

Key to Rating: 1 = Weak, 2 = Below par, 3 = Favorable, 4 = Strong, 5 = Very strong

She'll just have to build experience as she goes along. If she can try and incorporate some business strategy work in her economic competitiveness projects and win one or two small strategy contracts with private or public sector organizations, she should be able to raise her ratings against product capability and experience/track record over time, perhaps lifting her competitive position to a healthier 3.5 within three years in this segment.

Finally, Valerie thinks about risks to her competitive position over the next few years. Clearly her average rating in the business strategy segment represents a risk, but one that a backer should find tolerable, given her fall-back position: she will in parallel be bidding for other contracts in economic competitiveness, both direct and as a subcontractor, where she is well placed.

More worrying to a backer, Valerie ponders, is the market demand trend towards public administration projects, as set out in Chapter 2. In that segment, she has less product and process familiarity and not much experience. People at her main prime contractor client and former employer EconCo also know she's not overly enamored of this type of work, thereby denting her ratings against the K2s of delivery and attitude. Overall her subcontracting competitive position in public administration comes out at just under 3.0, well below that in economic competitiveness of 4.1.

But it could be even worse. Is attitude a must-have K2 in economic consulting? Valerie wonders. If a subcontractor doesn't have the right attitude, won't he or she be last to be invited to pitch? Might there be worse problems than having a low rating against the attitude K2? Might she become a *non-player* in this segment? If so, what would be her fall-back position if market demand for competitiveness work slowed, given that her position in business strategy is not that strong?

Just how backable is she? wonders Valerie. Next she'll put some numbers around these risks, in Chapter 7....

Thus Spake the Oracle

An economics graduate enrolled for a master's degree at Columbia Business School in 1950 because Benjamin Graham, author of one of his favorite books, *The Intelligent Investor*, was a lecturer there. In this student's own words, "The basic ideas of investing are to look at stocks as business, use the market's fluctuations to your advantage, and seek a margin of safety. That's what Ben Graham taught us. A hundred years from now they will still be the cornerstones of investing." After a few years' stockbroking in Omaha, he joined his former teacher's partnership in New York before setting out on his own when Graham retired two years later. By then he had resolutely set out the Key Kapabilities required for success in investment management. Tens of billions of dollars later, Warren Buffett may well have been right.

7

Will You Make Your Plan?

Laying Out Your Plan in a Market Context
Is it Achievable?
The Bottom-up Approach
Implications for Employees
Assessing Revenue or Profit Plans
Risks in Your Plan

We're approaching the end-game of Part I, where we find out if you're backable if you carry on with your current or return to your pre-MBA job or business. Your backer now has plenty of information on you and your job. He knows where market demand is headed, whether competition is going to heat up, and how you measure up to your competitors today and over the next few years. What's more, he has this information for each of your main business segments.

He's ready to pull it all together and assess if you're likely to achieve your planned return. That's what we'll look at in this chapter. In the next, we'll look at how your backer assesses the risks of you not making your plan, as well as the opportunities for you to beat them.

> *Once you have mastered time, you will understand how true it is that most people overestimate what they can accomplish in a year and underestimate what they can achieve in a decade.* –Anthony Robbins

Laying Out Your Plan In a Market Context

The secret to assessing whether you're likely to make your plan is to lay it out in a market context. This will give you a market-derived perspective on its achievability. It's a "top-down," market-driven approach. The "bottom-up" approach, where you look at all the specific initiatives you have for developing business in each of your segments, we'll look at in a later section.

The process for a top-down assessment of your business plan is straightforward, as long as you take one step at a time. You've already done virtually all the work, especially in Chapters 1, 2, and 6. All you have to do now is bring the strands together and review them from the perspective of your backer.

The flow set out below is a process of eight steps, each following logically from the previous step. Here it is:

1. *Business segments*—You look at one segment at a time.

2. *Your revenues or pay*—What revenues (for the self-employed) or pay (share of total pay for employees) are you expecting to achieve in each segment this year? If this year is untypical in some way, it would be sounder to put here your "normal" revenues or pay for the year. You already worked this out in Chapter 1.

3. *Market demand prospects*—How do you expect the market to grow each year over the next few years in each segment?—from Chapter 2.

4. *Your competitive position*—How do you measure up relative to the competition in each segment and how may this change over the next few years?—from Chapter 3.

5. *Planned revenues or pay*—What revenues (for the self-employed) or pay (share of total pay for employees) are you expecting to achieve in each segment in three years' time? Again, from Chapter 1.

6. *Planned revenue or pay growth*—What growth in revenues or pay each year does that represent over the next three years?

7. *How achievable?*—This is where you look at your plans from the perspective of your backer. Would he think you are likely to achieve your planned revenues or pay in this segment? His assessment will be based largely on how reasonable your revenue or pay forecasts seem in relation to market demand prospects and your competitive position—see later.

8. *More likely revenues or pay*—What your backer thinks is a *more* likely forecast of your revenues or pay in each segment in three years' time.

In this process, your backer puts your plans in a market context. He looks at how the market is likely to develop and whether you are likely to fare better, worse, or the same as your competitors. And *against that market background,* he judges whether your plans and forecast revenues or pay seem achievable.

Is It Achievable?

I am a slow walker, but I never walk backwards. –Abraham Lincoln

This top-down assessment of plan achievability works best in a chart. Eight entries in the process flow, so we take eight columns (see Figure 7.1).

Figure 7.1. Assessing How Achievable Are Your Planned Revenues or Pay

Your Business Segments	Your Revenues or Pay ($000)	Market Demand Growth (% per year)	Your Competitive Position (0-5)	Your Planned Revenues or Pay ($000)	Your Planned Revenue Growth (% per year)	How Achievable?	Likely Revenues or Pay ($000)
	This Year	Next Few Years	Next Few Years	In Three Years	Next Three Years		In Three Years
1	2	3	4	5	6	7	8
	Source: Chapter 1	Source: Chapter 2	Source: Chapter 6	Source: Chapter 1	Source: Chapter 1	Source: Here in Chapter 7	
A							
B							
C							
Others							
Total							

The first six columns are easy to fill in—you've already done the work! Columns 1, 2, and 5 are taken from the work you did in Chapter 1. There you allocated your current revenues (if self-employed) or pay (if an employee) into your most important business segments, both now and in three years' time. All you need to add here in column 6 are the average annual growth calculations.

Column 3 summarizes the conclusions of Chapter 2 on market demand prospects for each business segment. Likewise, column 4 summarizes the work on your competitive position in Chapter 6.

Note: You needn't bother filling in the totals for columns 3 and 4 in the chart. This is because the market and competitive analysis in Chapters 2 through 6 has been at the level of *each of your main business segments*. Each segment is represented in one row of the chart, and we work on one row at a time until we get to the end in column 8. Once we've worked on all the segments/rows, we'll then add up column 8 to get a total of likely revenues (or pay) and compare that with the total for planned revenues in column 6. Finally, we'll be able to assess how achievable your overall plan is in the bottom row of column 7—as highlighted with the explosion box!

Only columns 7 and 8 are new to this chapter, on how achievable your plan is and what outcome is more likely. These two columns will form the backbone of your backer's decision, along with the risk assessment in the next chapter.

Arriving at a conclusion on the achievability of your planned revenues (or pay, if you're an employee) in a business segment can sometimes be obvious. But often it can require a dose of sound judgment. Judgment comes with experience. I've made scores of such conclusions over the years—from businesses worth hundreds of millions of dollars to individuals worth a few tens of thousands. I can't expect you to share my experience, but I can give you a few tips. My limited aim is not to help you get it absolutely right but to help ensure *you don't get it absolutely wrong!*

The key to the assessment is *consistency*—whether your plans for the future are consistent with these two main areas of evidence:

> ▷   Column 3: Market demand prospects (as in Chapter 2).
> ▷   Column 4: Your competitive position, now and over the next few years (as in Chapter 6).

There are other pieces of evidence you should also bear in mind. These can be important and should arguably be included in the chart as extra columns. But a chart of a dozen or so columns becomes unwieldy. They are:

> ▷   Competitive intensity in the marketplace over the next few years (as in Chapter 3), although this can sometimes be just the inverse of column 3's market demand prospects—in other words, the faster the market growth, often the less competitive the workplace, and conversely, the slower the market growth, often the more competitive the workplace.

> ⬧   Your recent track record: your revenue or pay growth over the last couple of years in relation to growth in market demand over the same period (if you're self-employed) or in relation to fellow employees (if you're an employee).

Here's an example of consistency: If you find that the market in a business segment is set to grow steadily, and you assess yourself as having a favorable competitive position, then all else being equal, you should be able to grow your business at the same pace as the market in that segment. "All else being equal" may well include (a) your finding that the market isn't likely to become more competitive, and (b) the fact that you have a track record in recent years of being able to grow your business along with the market. If your plan over the next few years is merely to grow your business at the same pace as the market, then your backer should find it achievable. If, however, your plan is to grow way beyond that, he'll need to have convincing reasons on how you plan to beat the market.

Your backer won't necessarily be fazed by a high growth plan, as long as it's consistent. Suppose your competitive position in a business segment has been and should remain strong (around 4 on the 0 to 5 scale), and is demonstrated by your having outperformed the market in the past. If you're planning to continue to beat the market in the future, then your backer should find the assumptions consistent.

But suppose your competitive position in a segment is just okay-ish (around 2) and you've underperformed against the market in the past. Suppose too that your position isn't expected to show any significant improvement in the future. If your plans for this segment show you *beating* the market in the future, your backer's eyebrows will be raised. Your plans are *inconsistent* with both your future position and your previous performance.

Suppose, however, you've underperformed against the market in the past, but you've recently taken steps to improve your competitive position to favorable (around 3). If you're planning to grow with the market in the future, then your story will at least be consistent. All your backer will need to do is confirm that you have indeed sharpened up your act.

Remember, however, that this exercise offers a first cut at assessing achievability, no more. It assumes no discontinuities between the recent past and the near future, no specific, bottom-up initiatives. Discontinuities can often be the big exception to the above market-driven, "top-down" process, as we'll see in the next section.

A Test on Achieving Plan

Here's a set of examples on assessing whether plans seem achievable, purely from a market-driven, top-down perspective.

You're thinking of backing Ms. Random, who runs a business with six main segments. She's a sound manager, but her forecasting skills seem somewhat erratic. You take it one segment at a time, working your way across each row in Table 7.2. You need to take a view on the likelihood of Ms. Random achieving her plans in each segment. Which of the possible boxed answers should be slotted into the six cells of column 7?

Figure 7.2. A Test: How Achievable Are Ms. Random's Plans?

Ms Random's Business Segments	Her Revenues or Pay ($000) This Year	Market Demand Growth (% per year) Next Few Years	Her Competitive Position (0-5) Next Few Years	Her Planned Revenues or Pay ($000) In Three Years	Her Planned Revenue Growth (% per year) Next Three Years	How Achievable?	Which Answers Match Each Segment?
1	2	3	4	5	6	7	
A	10	5%	3.0	16	17%		1. Most likely
B	10	5%	3.0	12	5%		2. Likely
C	10	5%	3.0	10	0%		3. Likely
D	10	5%	2.0	13	9%		4. Unlikely
E	10	5%	3.5 to 4.0	14	12%		5. Unlikely
F	10	-2.5%	3.0	15	14%		6. Most unlikely

Answers: A:4, B:2, C:1, D:5, E:3, F:6

The answers are shown under the table, upside down. How well did you do? The reasoning behind the answers is as follows:

- ▷ Taking segment B to start with, Ms. Random plans to grow revenues at the same pace as the market and she's favorably positioned. Her plan seems *likely*.

- ▷ Tracking back to segment A, her competitive position is the same, yet she plans to grow much faster than the market, which seems *unlikely*.

- ▷ In segment C, her position is again favorable, but she plans to grow more slowly than the market. Her forecast seems conservative and *most likely* to be achieved.

- ▷ In segment D, her positioning is only okay-ish, and yet she plans to outgrow the market, which seems *unlikely*.

- ▷ In segment E, her competitive position is set to improve to strong and she plans to outperform the market, which seems *likely*.

- ▷ In segment F, market demand is set to decline and competition is likely to be tough. Ms. Random is favorably placed, yet she is planning to grow revenues strongly, beating the market by a wide margin. This seems *most unlikely*, even, in the absence of robust supporting evidence, wild.

Did you get all six right? A career in venture capital may await you...?!

The above answers are subject to a major warning. They assume that Ms. Random will continue to offer the *same* range of services to the *same* customer groups within the *same* business segments in the future as she did in the past. This may or may not be so. She may have *specific initiatives* up her sleeve to justify her planned earnings in each segment.

The Bottom-up Approach

One main reason why the "top-down" assessment of plan achievability may not tell the whole story is because of specific initiatives you may be planning *within* a particular business segment. These initiatives can work in either direction, enabling you to either beat or fall behind the market in that segment.

These "bottom-up" initiatives typically relate to a changed mix of services and/or customers within a business segment. You may be set to broaden, or conversely narrow, the precise mix of services you offer within a segment. Likewise to broaden (or limit) your range of customers there.

Another main area of discontinuity concerns changes in investment attention. You may feel that recent under-performance in a business segment may have been because of relative under-investment, whether in assets, marketing, product development, or training. So you are planning to invest more in that segment over the next couple of years. Conversely, you may feel that, having invested heavily in a segment over the last couple of years, it's time to ease off the throttle and reap some rewards.

These "bottom-up" initiatives, often highly specific to a business segment, need to be given careful consideration by your backer when assessing the achievability of your plans.

And what about *capacity?* This could be one good reason why you may not be able to grow your business along with the market, despite your favorable competitive position. Your utilization (average number of paid hours work per day) may be getting so high that you are approaching capacity. There may not be enough hours left in the day for you to serve more customers.

If so, lucky you! But you may want to consider nudging up your prices. That'll soon give you some more slack! Or you could try "bottom-slicing." This is when you rank all your customers by how profitable each one is to you. Then you start phasing out the least profitable and gradually replacing them with more profitable customers.

Our gardener did that to us a few years ago. He used to come once a week throughout the year before I started to take an interest and do bits and pieces myself. After a while, I scaled him down to once every other week spring through autumn, and once a month in winter. A year or so later, he became so busy that he bottom-sliced us and quit, sticking with customers who gave him more frequent (and less arduous!) work. Serves me right. It took us ages to find a replacement as good as he!

Implications for Employees

If you're an employee, it's possible that you've been skimming through this chapter so far and thinking what on earth all this has to do with you! Fair point. Especially if you were in the same job, with steadily growing pay, for a few years pre-MBA and are set to return to that or a similar job post-MBA.

The answer is that it could be important if you're planning any significant *change* in the balance of your job towards one or more of your addressed business segments. You could be doing the same job, in theory, with the same title, same office, same reporting structure, but the balance of your responsibilities and tasks may be different. Your backer will need to assess how achievable your plans are, given the market environment and your position in each segment.

We shall take a look at an exemplar, Gary, a manager-level employee before, during and after his MBA, in Chapter 8.

This chapter can also be useful to employees in highlighting any risk of you losing your job over the next few years. If market demand is set to contract in a key segment, if job competition is going to get tough and if your competitive position is insufficiently strong, your backer may assess the chances of you making your planned earnings as unlikely.

Assessing Revenue or Profit Plans

This section applies only to the self-employed. Employees can skip this unless you have plans on becoming self-employed!

So far, we've been assessing revenue performance and revenue prospects. This may not be sufficient for your backer.

Much depends on your cost structure. If there are significant differences in your cost structure for each business segment, then you may need to do a further stage of assessment. Many self-employed people won't need to. Their main cost is their time, and costs of materials or subcontractors may be similar in each segment.

If, however, differences are significant, then you'll need this second stage. Ultimately, your backer isn't that interested in what happens to revenues, your "top line." *It's what happens to profits, your "bottom line," that counts.*

This second stage is also best laid out initially in a market context. In the first stage, we focused on market growth prospects and changes in your competitive position. In this second stage, we focus on change in competitive intensity. The assessment process flows like this:

1. *Business segments*—Again, you look at one segment at a time.

Revenues and Profits*
2. *Revenues this year*—As before.
3. *Profit margin this year*—What percentage profit margin will you make in this business segment this year?
4. *Profit this year*—Revenue multiplied by profit margin.

Competitive environment
5. *Recent competitive intensity*—How tough is competition compared to other segments, high, medium or low (from Chapter 3)?
6. *Future competitive intensity*—roughly how tough is competition likely to be over the next few years compared to other segments, high, medium, or low (also from Chapter 3)?

Your profit plan
7. *Planned profit margin*—What percentage profit margin are you planning to make in this business segment in three years' time (also from Chapter 1)?

How achievable?

8. *How achievable?*—Here's the assessment of your backer on the achievability of your planned profit margin in this segment, taking into account changes in the competitive environment, in a range from most unlikely through to most likely.

Your backer's forecasts

9. *Likely profit margin*—What your backer thinks is a more likely percentage profit margin for this business segment in three years' time.

10. *Likely revenues*—What your backer thinks are likely revenues in this segment in three years' time (from the first stage chart).

11. *Likely profit*—Likely revenues multiplied by likely profit margin.

---

*We typically use "gross profit," which is revenues less costs of materials and other direct costs, such as subcontractors. Even better where you have data is to use "contribution to fixed overhead," which also takes into account variable overhead costs. In many self-employed businesses, marketing spend can differ greatly by business segment. If that's so for you, then you might choose to define marketing as a direct cost and your contribution margin as "revenues less costs of materials, other direct costs, *and* marketing costs."

Again, this assessment process works better in a chart. There are 11 entries in the process flow, so here's a chart with 11 columns (Figure 7.3).

Figure 7.3. **Assessing How Achievable Are Your Planned Profits**

Your Business Segments	Your Revenues ($000)	Your Profit Margin (%)	Your Profit ($000)	Competitive Intensity (Low-Med-High)		Your Planned Profit Margin (%)	How Achiev-able?	Likely Profit Margin (%)	Likely Revenues ($000)	Likely Profit ($000)
	This Year	This Year	This Year	This Year	In Three Years	In Three Years		In Three Years	In Three Years	In Three Years
1	2	3	4	5	6	7	8	9	10	11
		Source: Chapter 1		Source: Chapter 3		Source: Ch 1		Source: Here in Chapter 7		
A										
B										
C										
Others										
Total										

Most of the work needed to fill out this chart you have already done. In columns 3 and 7 you need to put in your profit margins by segment, current and planned. In columns 5 and 6, you put in indicators of how intense competition is today and how that is likely to change over the next few years—your conclusions from Chapter 3.

This stage just adds columns 8 and 9. How achievable are these profit margin forecasts and what is a more likely profit margin? Column 10 is lifted directly from the likely revenue forecasts from Figure 7.1 and column 11 falls into place.

There are three main factors that will determine how achievable your profit margin forecasts are, as follows:

- Pricing pressures from competitive forces in the marketplace ("top-down")
- Your initiatives to improve the cost effectiveness of your business ("bottom-up")
- Any initiatives you may have to invest in strengthening an existing line of business or in launching another ("investment")

As in the first stage, your backer is looking for *consistency* in the profit margin forecasts. If competition is going to get stiffer, pricing is likely to come under pressure, and he'll expect profit margins to be squeezed. If your plans show profit margins moving the other way—actually improving—you'll need to have some good "bottom-up" reasons why.

Conversely, if competition is set to ease up and your profit margins are planned to stay flat, or even shrink, your backer may think you're being rather conservative—unless there are "bottom-up" reasons why you feel the need to be adding cost.

You may have a number of bottom-up initiatives in mind to improve your cost effectiveness over the next few years. These could include:

▷ Reduced reliance on subcontractors, doing more of the service delivery yourself.

▷ More careful buying of materials, or buying in bulk to drive down unit costs.

▷ Better negotiating techniques on all your purchases, both subcontractors and materials.

▷ Tighter control over overhead, for example shifting to other telecoms or electricity providers, moving to more economical premises, or more targeted marketing.

We'll look more carefully at how to improve profit performance in Part II. The important thing at this stage is that whatever your plans for driving down cost and improving profit margin from the bottom up may be, they'll need to be consistent and convincing to your backer.

Finally, you may need to incur extra cost in investing in your business. This could be for strengthening your competitiveness in an existing business segment, for example in a refit of your premises or updating your IT capability. Or it could be for diversifying into an entirely new business segment. Either way, the investment will need to be justified by the prospect of suitably higher cash flow over the next few years.

Risks in Your Plan

You've already pulled out into three separate charts the main risks and opportunities relating to market demand (Chapter 2), competition (Chapter 3), and your competitive position (Chapter 6). Risks and opportunities associated with plans for your business or job are the fourth and final element in the Risk Jigsaw.

Here, therefore, you need to add those major risks and opportunities that relate to what you plan to do in your business, or with your job, over the next few years. How likely are those risks to occur, and if they do, what sort of impact would they have on your plan? Likewise for opportunities. Again, you may find the chart in Appendix A, Figure A.2 helpful.

You've now filled out all four of the components in the Risk Jigsaw. In the next chapter, you'll bring these four together and pull out those most important. You'll pinpoint those key risks or opportunities that determine whether you are, or are not, backable in your current job or business.

Are Valerie's Plans Achievable?

As we saw in Chapter 1, Valerie's plans, should she decide to return to her independent economic consulting business post-MBA, are two-fold: to sell more work direct to the end-client, with less reliance on subcontracting, and to focus on economic competitiveness and business strategy work, away from public administration.

She plans to grow average annual revenues from U.S. $100,000 per year to $150,000 in three years. How realistic is that?

She asks her fellow independent, David, to act as a hard-nosed investor and take an objective, critical look at her forecasts (see Figure 7.4).

Figure 7.4. **How Achievable Are Valerie's Revenue Plans in Economic Consulting Post-MBA?**

Valerie's Business Segments	Valerie's Revenues ($000)	Market Demand Growth (% per year)	Valerie's Competitive Position (0-5)	Valerie's Planned Revenues ($000)	Valerie's Planned Revenue Growth (% per year)	Her Backer's View: How Achievable?	More Likely Revenues ($000)
	This Year	Next Few Years	Next Few Years	In Three Years	Next Three Years		In Three Years
1	**2**	**3**	**4**	**5**	**6**	**7**	**8**
Competitiveness to Direct Clients	45	Steady (0-5?)	3.5 to 3.6	60	10%	Likely	55-65
Administration as Subcontractor	25	Medium (5-10?)	<3.0?	0	$-\infty$	Unlikely	>0 [15?]
Regulation to Direct Clients	15	Medium (5-10?)	3.3 to 3.5	30	26%	Possible	20-25
Business Strategy to Direct Clients	0	Fast (>10?)	3.2 to 3.5	50	∞	Challenging	20-40
Competitiveness as Subcontractor	15	Steady (0-5?)	4.1	10	-13%	Likely	>10
Total	**100**			**150**	**9%**	**Challenging**	**120-140**

David concludes that the $150,000 target is challenging, with revenues of $120–140,000 a more reasonable forecast. His views differ much by segment.

Given Valerie's favorable to strong position in competitiveness to direct clients, and despite the slowdown in growth in this segment, he finds her forecast achievable. But in the second most important segment, business strategy, also to direct clients, her forecast seems challenging. Market demand is growing faster, but Valerie's competitive position is only modestly favorable, and she would need some luck to make those numbers.

Investors try not to rely on luck. More likely, David thinks, she will need to do further subcontracting to make up the numbers—hopefully in her favored competitiveness or regulation products, conceivably in business strategy, but possibly in the faster growing administration segment—despite Valerie's poor position there.

David then casts his eye over Valerie's profit forecasts (Figure 7.5) and finds them also rather challenging. She assumes that she will need to do less traveling to win her direct client work, due to her growing name and brand recognition. Hence she has projected gross margin to increase from 85 to 90%. David thinks this unlikely, given that future opportunities in the maturing competitiveness product may well be in countries where she is less well known. Likewise, her forecast of an 85% margin in business strategy work may underestimate the amount of travel time needed to win business with private sector clients in developing countries.

Figure 7.5. **How Achievable Are Valerie's Profit Plans in Economic Consulting Post-MBA?**

Valerie's Business Segments	Valerie's Rev's ($000)	Valerie's Gross Profit Margin (%)	Valerie's Gross Profit ($000)	Competitive Intensity (Low-Med-High)		Valerie's Planned Profit Margin (%)	Her Backer's View: How Achievable?	Likely Gross Profit Margin (%)	Likely Rev's ($000)	Likely Gross Profit ($000)
	This Year	This Year	This Year	This Year	In Three Years	In Three Years		In Three Years	In Three Years	In Three Years
1	2	3	4	5	6	7	8	9	10	11
Competitiveness to Direct Clients	45	85%	38	M/H	High	90%	Possible	85-90%	55-65	52
Administration as Subcontractor	25	95%	24	Med	M/H	95%	Likely	95%	>0 [15?]	>0 [14?]
Regulation to Direct Clients	15	85%	13	Med	M/H	90%	Unlikely	85-90%	20-25	20
Strategy to Direct Clients	0	N/a	0	L/M	Med	85%	Challenging	75%	20-40	22
Competitiveness as Subcontractor	15	95%	13	M/H	High	95%	Possible	95%	10	10
Total	100	88%	88			89%	Challenging	85%	120-140	111

David slots in his own more conservative revenue and margin forecasts and finds that Valerie's overall gross margin is more likely to fall slightly from 88% today to 85% in three years' time than it is to improve to 89%, as forecast by Valerie.

Valerie and David then ponder the risks and opportunities beyond the plan. David is concerned about the lumpy nature of their business. Contracts won are often big and tend to last many months, but success owes much to timing and availability. If a contract comes up where Valerie has excellent contacts but is unavailable, she has no choice but to pass. If nothing else then comes up for a few months in areas where Valerie is strong, she might have to fall back on sub-contracting. That's fine, if it's in competitiveness, regulation, or even business strategy, but what if it's in administration?

Some of Valerie's prime contractor clients already know of Valerie's negative attitude to administration work, so her prospects there are not rosy. And if administration work is all that comes up for a while, long gaps could appear in Valerie's revenue stream.

This is a serious risk to the achievability of Valerie's business plan, to be weighed alongside other risks and balanced against notable opportunities in the next chapter.

A Diamond in the Rough

Upon graduating top of the year from his MBA course at the School of Business at the University of Connecticut in 1976, this New Englander stayed put, accepting the offer of a lectureship. It is questionable whether this career choice would have met his business plan aspirations. He lasted one year before moving to investment banking, where he rose rapidly through Morgan Stanley and CS First Boston. He went on to head Barclays Capital, ultimately fronting the acquisition of the core U.S. assets of Lehman Brothers, following its bankruptcy in 2008. Bob Diamond became one of the highest paid bankers in Britain—a world apart from his initial career choice of genteel academia.

8

How Risky Is Backing You?

The Suns & Clouds Chart
What the Chart Says about:
> » Extraordinary Risk
> » The Balance of Risk and Opportunity

Making Your Chart Sunnier
The Risks of Backing You

In the last chapter, you assessed whether plans in your current or pre-MBA job or business are likely to work out. You're almost there, but for one final stage. *How risky are you?* How likely is it that one or two or the risks you've met along the way will blow your plans? On the other hand, what are the odds of one or two of those opportunities helping you beat your plans?

We summarized the main market demand risks and opportunities at the end of Chapter 2. Likewise for industry competition in Chapter 3.

In Chapter 6 we moved away from the market as a whole and looked at the risks and opportunities around you and your competitive position. Finally, in the last chapter, we pulled together the main risks and opportunities associated with your business plan.

The risk jigsaw is complete. Now we view the assembled picture *as a whole.*

Once all the risks and opportunities have been assembled in one place, you'll be able to see whether the opportunities outshine the risks. You'll have the answer to the key question: Are you backable?

The Suns & Clouds Chart

I first created the Suns & Clouds chart in the early 1990s. Since then I've seen it reproduced in various forms in reports by my consulting competitors. They say imitation is the sincerest form of flattery, but I still kick myself that I didn't copyright it back then!

The reason it keeps getting pinched is that it works. It manages to encapsulate in one chart conclusions on the relative importance of all the main issues debated thus far. It shows, diagrammatically, whether the opportunities (the suns) outshine the risks (the clouds). Or vice-versa, when the clouds overshadow the suns. In short, in one chart, it tells you whether you're backable. Or not.

The chart (Figure 8.1) forces you to view each risk (and opportunity) from two perspectives: how likely it is to happen, and how big an impact it would have if it did.

The great news is that you've done all the work needed to fill in the chart. Every bit of it. At the back end of Chapters 2, 3, 6, and 7, you drew up charts highlighting all the main risks and opportunities. In these charts, you didn't just list each risk and opportunity. You also assessed their likelihood and impact. All you have to do now is portray those findings diagrammatically.

In the chart, risks are represented as clouds, opportunities as suns. The more likely a risk (or opportunity) is to happen, the further to the right you should place it along the horizontal axis. In Figure 8.1, risk D is the most likely to happen, and risk B the least.

Figure 8.1. The Suns & Clouds Chart

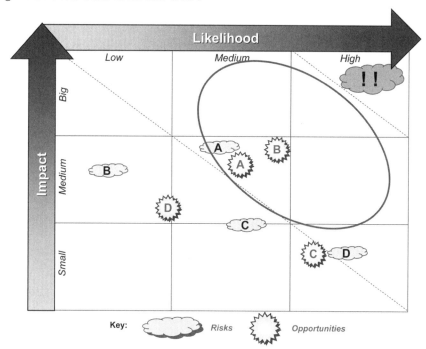

The bigger the impact a risk (or opportunity) would have if it were to happen, the higher you should place it up the vertical axis. In the same chart, opportunity B would have the largest impact, opportunity C the smallest.

For each risk (and opportunity), you need to place it in the appropriate position on the chart taking into account *both* factors—its likelihood *and* impact.

Don't worry if things don't make that much sense initially. This chart changes with further thought and discussion. *Always*. Arguably its greatest virtue is its stimulus to discussion. I have often given PowerPoint presentations of 100 slides or so, with no more than a couple of questions for clarification every now and then. Then when the Suns & Clouds chart comes up, toward the end of the presentation, it can remain on screen for a half-hour or more. It stimulates discussion and provokes amendment. A client may choose to debate for 10, 15 minutes the precise positioning of one risk, or opportunity, *and what can be done to shift its position favorably*.

Remember, you can not be exact in this chart. Nor do you need to be. It is a pictorial representation of risk and opportunity, designed to give you a *feel* for the balance of risk and opportunity in your business.

What the Chart Says

The Suns & Clouds chart tells you two main things about your backability: whether there are any *extraordinary* risks (or opportunities), and whether the overall *balance* of risk and opportunity renders you backable.

Extraordinary risk

Take a look at the top right-hand corner of the chart. There's a heavy thundercloud in there, with two exclamation marks. That's a risk that is both very likely *and* very big. It's a showstopper risk. If your backer finds one of them in your business or job, then that's it. You're unbackable where you are.

The closer a cloud gets to that thundercloud, the worse news it is. Risks that hover around the diagonal (from the top left to the bottom right corners) can be handled, as long as they are balanced by opportunities. But as soon as a cloud starts creeping toward that thundercloud, for example to around where opportunity B is placed, that's when your backer starts to get itchy feet.

But imagine a bright shining sun in that spot where the thundercloud is. That's terrific news, and your backer will be falling over himself to invest in you.

It's not unusual for a backer to find a showstopper risk. There's an excellent TV program on the BBC called "Dragon's Den," where five millionaire "dragons" listen to a 10-minute presentation on a budding entrepreneur's plans and consider whether to back him or her. Most leave with no investment. Often it's just one risk that turns off the dragons. It may be incredulity that anyone would buy such a product or service. Or that the entrepreneur has been trying for so long, or has invested so much, for such little result. Or the product is too costly to yield a profit. Each is a risk that the dragons see as highly likely and with big impact. Each is a top right hand corner thundercloud, a show-stopper.

Some risks are huge, but most unlikely to happen. That's not to say that they won't happen. The unlikely can happen. But these are not show-stopper risks. They are top *left* hand corner risks. If we worried about the unlikely happening we would never cross the road. Certainly no backer would ever invest a cent!

In fall 2001, my colleagues and I were advising a client on whether to back a company involved in airport operations. After the first week of work, we produced an interim report and a first-cut Suns & Clouds chart. In the top left-hand corner box, we placed a risk entitled "major air incident." We were thinking of a serious air crash that might lead to the prolonged grounding of a common class of aircraft. It seemed unlikely, but would have a very large impact if it happened. 9/11 came just a few days later. We never envisaged anything so catastrophic, so inconceivably evil, but at least we had alerted our client to the extreme risks involved in the air industry. The deal was renegotiated and successfully completed.

The balance of risk and opportunity

In general, for most investment decisions, particularly for individuals, there's no showstopper risk. The main purpose of the Suns & Clouds chart will then be to present the *balance* of risk and opportunity. Do the opportunities surpass the risks? Given the overall picture, are the suns more favorably placed than the clouds? Or do the clouds overshadow the suns?

The way to assess a Suns & Clouds chart is to look first at the general area above the diagonal and in the direction of the thundercloud. This is the area covered in Figure 8.1 by the parabola. Any risk (or opportunity) there is worthy of note: It's at least reasonably likely to occur *and* would have at least a reasonable impact.

Those risks and opportunities below the diagonal are less important. They are either of low to medium likelihood *and* of low to medium impact. Or they're not big enough, or not likely enough, to be of major concern.

A backer will look at the pattern of suns in this area of the parabola and compare it with the pattern of clouds. The closer each sun and cloud to the thundercloud, the more important it is. If the pattern of suns seems better placed than the pattern of clouds, he will be comforted. If the clouds overshadow the suns, he will be concerned.

In the chart above, there are two clouds and two suns above the diagonal. But risk D lies outside the parabola. The best placed is opportunity B. Risk A and opportunity A more or less balance each other out, likewise other risks and opportunities. Opportunity B seems distinctly clear of the pack. The opportunities seem to surpass the risks. The business looks backable.

Would You Have Backed the Beatles?

If you were a music producer at Parlophone in the first few months of 1962, would you have backed the Beatles?

Let's have some context. In Britain of the early 1960s, Parlophone was a distinguished record company that had never previously backed any rock 'n' roll artists. At the time, there were dozens of young rock 'n' roll groups with persistent promoters doing the rounds of the studios. One such group, the Beatles, had been turned down by all other recording studios.

Their leader, John Lennon, had been fronting groups for five years. He'd formed the Quarrymen in 1956, when he was 16, and within a couple of years fellow members had come to include Paul McCartney and George Harrison. They evolved into Johnny and the Moondogs and then, inspired by Buddy Holly and the Crickets, into Long John and the Silver Beetles. With Lennon's love of the pun, that soon morphed into the Beatles. (I am grateful to Suzanne Smiley's *A Brief History of the Beatles: From Their Humble Beginnings in Liverpool to the Birth of Beatlemania in America*, published in May 2000, for this interesting background.)

The group was one of many playing the Liverpool club scene. Their break came when they secured a gig to play in Hamburg, then a city crazy over U.S.-style rock 'n' roll. Their first trip proved short-lived. After a nightclub prank and a night in jail, they were packed off back home. Undeterred, they were back again the following year and it was there that they made their first recording, a cover of the traditional Scottish folk song "My Bonnie," arranged by fellow rock 'n' roller Tony Sheridan. It was on their return that the curiosity of a Liverpudlian record store owner, Brian Epstein, became aroused. Three customers came into his shop in just a few days and asked for a copy of "My Bonnie." He had heard of the Beatles from the local music magazine, *Mersey Beat*, but had had no previous interest in seeing them. He went to see them at The Cavern club. He wasn't hugely impressed with their music, but thought they had charisma. He signed up as their manager, arranged for a demo tape, and set off to hawk it around the record companies.

If you'd been George Martin, a producer at Parlophone, would you have backed these guys? You knew that one other record company, Decca, had shown some interest but had turned them down in favor of a similar group, Brian Poole and the Tremeloes. Some Decca executives also believed—in a now classic quote—that "guitar groups are on the way out." For your company's first venture into rock 'n' roll, would you have chosen these four lads from Liverpool? Let's look at their Suns & Clouds in Figure 8.2.

Figure 8.2. Early 1962: Would You Have Backed the Beatles?

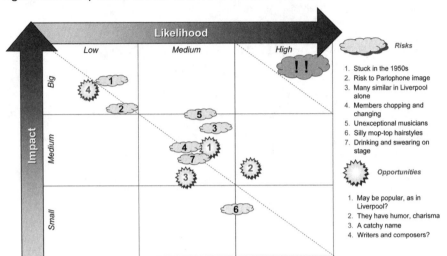

It couldn't have been an easy decision for George Martin. On the one hand, there were so many wannabe groups around (risk 3) and the Beatles seemed unexceptional musically (risk 5). On the other hand, they seemed to have charisma and humor (opportunity 2). And, on the back of their Hamburg experience, they had built a loyal following among club-goers in Liverpool (opportunity 1). These may have been the four issues that stood out, two risks and two opportunities, above the diagonal, within the parabola.

No one would blame him, he must have thought, if he turned these guys down. Yet he had a hunch. They seemed to have something. Maybe they could improve their musical abilities. Maybe they could be marketed. He backed them. What would you have done?

Making Your Chart Sunnier

One of the best features of the Suns & Clouds chart is that you can make it dynamic. If you don't like the balance of risk and opportunity shown on the chart, you can do something about it. You can improve your backability—and the chart shows this clearly.

For every risk, there are mitigating factors. Many, especially those related to the market and competition, will be beyond your control. Those related to your competitive position, however, you may well be able to influence. There may be initiatives you can undertake to improve your competitiveness and lower your risk. Some risks, indeed, may be wholly within your control. You may even be able to eliminate them from the chart.

Likewise, there may be opportunities where your chances of realizing them can be enhanced through some initiative. Later in this chapter we'll see how our self-employed exemplar Valerie will improve her chart by addressing her chronic weakness for self-promotion. And how our employee exemplar, Gary, will do likewise by tackling his phobia for public speaking.

Risk mitigation or opportunity enhancement in the Suns & Clouds chart can be illuminated with arrows and target signs. They'll show you where to aim for and remind you that it's a target. You can improve the overall balance of risk in backing you. As we'll see in Part II, you'll become more backable.

Making the Beatles More Backable

As a music producer at Parlophone in early 1962, you decided to back the Beatles. But how could you have improved their chances of success? You could have encouraged them to develop their own musical and songwriting capabilities. And to differentiate themselves further from other Liverpudlian groups—you might even have accepted that their mop-tops should stay, rather than revert to rock 'n' roll pompadour. And that they should wear more distinctive clothing, even collarless jackets! You'd also have insisted, contractually, that they cut out the drinking and swearing on stage.

How would that have impacted on the Suns & Clouds and your backing decision?

Figure 8.3. Early 1962: How Could You Have Improved the Beatles' Chances?

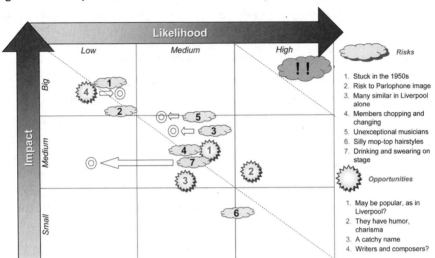

Figure 8.3 might have helped you. Risks 3 and 5 could have been nudged to the left, with risk 7 shifted contractually all the way to the left. Meanwhile, opportunity 4 might be able to be nudged to the right. The overall balance of risk and opportunity in the chart has improved. It might have made your decision to back the Beatles a bit simpler.

As a postscript to this tale, let's see how the backing decision would have changed one year later, in spring 1963. After the release of their first album, would you have backed the Beatles? You know the answer, but it's fun to see what the Suns & Clouds chart would now look like.

One year later, the Beatles' first single "Love Me Do" had reached the U.K. Top 20. Their second single, "Please Please Me," and their first album, of the same name, were riding high as number ones in both the single and album charts. Was this a flash in the pan? Were these guys to come and go with little trace like many before them?

You weren't to know then that their album would stay at number one for 30 weeks, before being replaced by, yes, their second album! That their fourth single, "She Loves You," would become the biggest seller of all time, topping hits by their role model, Elvis Presley, and would remain so for more than a decade.

What you did know was that you'd sure made the right decision the year before. You'd also greatly underestimated them as musicians. They could write and compose catchy songs. The Suns & Clouds chart was transformed (see Figure 8.4).

Figure 8.4. Spring 1963: Now Would You Back the Beatles?!

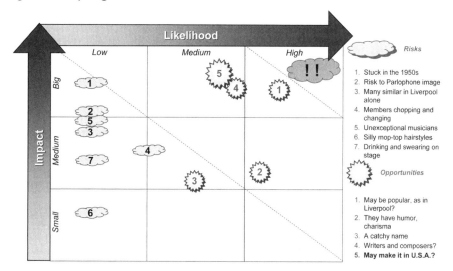

All the risks in the earlier Suns & Clouds chart had retreated leftward into insignificance. Even the risk of the four members splitting up was greatly reduced. Meanwhile the opportunities were dazzling. Their popularity as performers had soared. Their potential as songwriters was astonishing. And to cap it all, a new, huge opportunity had arisen (number five). Could they conceivably become the first British group to wow a U.S. audience?

Would you have backed the Beatles in the spring of 1963? The Suns & Clouds says it all. Would you play the lottery if you knew what number was coming up?

Would You Have Backed Oprah?

Here's one more example. This is an individual rather than a group and she's more contemporary. She is the phenomenon that is Oprah.

Back in 1983, Ms. Winfrey was a talk show host at a local TV station in Baltimore, Maryland. She had done well and seemed to be on a steadily upward career progression. Having graduated in communications at Tennessee State University, she went on to become the youngest and first black female news anchor at a local TV station in Nashville. She moved to Baltimore to present the evening news but later switched to a talk show slot.

This was a young woman going places. And yet her early years had hardly been promising. Born in Kosciusko, Mississippi, to unmarried, teenage parents, her mother a housemaid, her father a soldier turned coalminer and barber, she was raised initially by her grandmother in modest rural environs and then by her welfare-dependent mother in an inner city neighborhood in Milwaukee, Wisconsin. She has stated that she suffered abuse there from the age of nine. She rebelled. She became pregnant at 14 but lost the child soon after birth. She was sent to her father in Nashville, where his strict attention to schoolwork helped her gain a scholarship to Tennessee State University.

Suppose Oprah now needed some backing, and she came to you, an investor, to tell you she had been offered a job in Chicago to host WLS-TV's low-rated, half-hour, morning talk show, *AM Chicago*. Suppose she needed cash to pay off, say, credit card debts incurred in Baltimore or to put down a deposit on a two-bedroom apartment in a trendy part of downtown Chicago.

She was optimistic that this show would do well. It had slipped down in the ratings in recent years and needed some new vigor. She thought she had what it needed. She was confident that she could raise ratings in Chicago, maybe compete with the doyen of daytime talk shows, *Donahue*. She thought her formula could even one day go national. Would you have backed her?

Figure 8.5. 1983: Would You Have Backed Oprah's Move to Chicago?

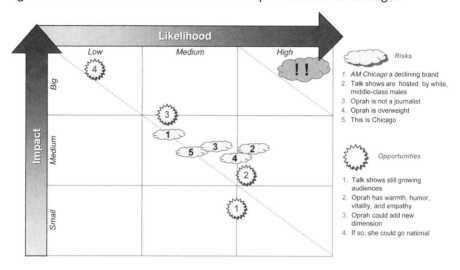

You may not have done. Oprah's Suns & Clouds would not have looked too promising (see Figure 8.5). Successful talk shows were hosted by white, middle-class males, many with years of experience in journalism and/or TV reporting. They had interviewing skills that were seen as integral to the talk show format.

Oprah was black, female, working class, and overweight. Above all, she had little foundation in journalism or reporting; she was a presenter. These were big risks, with high likelihood, high impact.

On the other hand, you may have seen something in her. Her prospects on paper may not have looked too good, but there was something exceptional about her personality. She—her warmth, humor, vitality, empathy—may have been the big opportunity.

You may have backed her.

If you had, it would have been a good call. Within months, her show went to the top of the Chicago talk show ratings, surpassing *Donahue*. It was relabeled under her name and extended to one hour. Opportunity 3 in the chart had shifted far to the right. Three years later the show went national, shifting opportunity 4 into the top right-hand box.

The rest is history. She's the highest paid entertainer on TV ever and the first black female billionaire. She's also a leading philanthropist. She has donated hundreds of millions of dollars to charity and has fronted fundraising campaigns to raise yet more. She has been rated as one of the most influential women in the world.

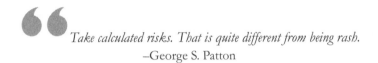

Take calculated risks. That is quite different from being rash.
–George S. Patton

The Risks of Backing You

It's time for you to position *your* suns, *your* clouds.

You already know what the main risks and opportunities facing you are. You've already pinpointed them for your backer in Chapters 2, 3, 6, and 7. All you need to do now is place each of the main risks or opportunities in the appropriate spot in the Suns & Clouds chart.

Is there a showstopper risk? Is your backer is going to run a mile? Hopefully not.

Is there any risk approaching the showstopper area? Will your backer have to think about it very carefully indeed? Can you do anything to mitigate its impact? Would you be able to demonstrate this to your backer, with supporting evidence?

What about the overall balance of risk and opportunity? Do your suns outshine the clouds?

Do you have any initiatives in the pipeline to shift any clouds to the left, or suns to the right?

Would you back you in your current or pre-MBA business or job?

There's one more thing we need to check before we leave this chapter. Is there any chance that your attitude is, or could become, a showstopper risk?

Could your attitude blow your plans?

We examined this in Chapter 6 (see Any Chance You Won't Get Past First Base?). If you're at business school because you were getting fed up with your former job, or aspects of it, then your attitude may be a risk if you return.

Let's remind ourselves of Zig Ziglar's quote that we came across in Chapter 4: "It is not your aptitude, but your attitude, that determines your altitude." To what extent could your attitude get in the way of your altitude?

If your attitude is a risk, where should it be placed on the Suns & Clouds chart?

Is your attitude a minor factor in lowering your competitive position in a job where attitude is nice to have but not a must have? Fine. Then the risk of you losing your job (or promotion) because of your attitude is of low likelihood, high impact.

If, however, attitude is a must-have K2 and yours is not what it should be, is there any chance of you losing your job because of your attitude? Is there a strong chance? May you become unbackable?

If we return to the original Suns & Clouds example, suppose risk A represents the risk of you losing your job because of your attitude. Your attitude is not great but not dire, so you assess the current risk as of low likelihood, high impact.

But suppose two things seem likely to happen. Your incoming boss sees things in a different light and wants to put customer service top priority, with attitude becoming a must-have K2 for all his team members. Meanwhile, your enthusiasm for the job continues to wane and your attitude deteriorates.

Could the risk of you losing your job become a showstopper, as shown by the arrow in Figure 8.6?

Figure 8.6. **Could Your Attitude Become Too Great a Risk?**

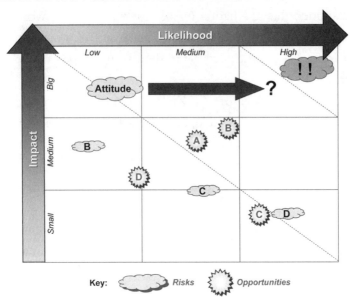

If so, your attitude could become a serious constraint on your back-ability.

The backing decision is almost made. You reviewed your plans in the last chapter and assessed risks and opportunities in this one. All that remains is the overall storyline of Chapter 9.

How Risky is Valerie?

Valerie eagerly draws up her Suns & Clouds chart for a return to independent economic consulting post-MBA (see Figure 8.7). At first glance, she thinks it would look well balanced to a prospective backer.

She has taken care to assess the impact of all risks and opportunities in relation to their impact on *her backer's* profit forecasts, not her own. Had she done the latter, risks would have edged upwards and opportunities downwards, making her look much less backable.

Figure 8.7. Valerie's Risks and Opportunities in a Return to Economic Consulting Post-MBA

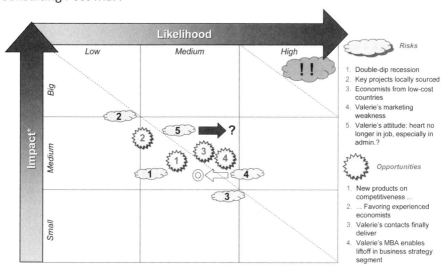

As a result, risks 4 and 5 seem adequately balanced by opportunities 3 and 4. Surely she looks backable?

She again tries out her former colleague David as a notional backer. He soon spots the flaw in the analysis. It is too static and needs to have dynamic elements thrown in.

In particular, risk 5 is a concern. He has long known of Valerie's lack of affection for work in public administration and governance, but that is the way the market is heading. If she is to reach her backer's revenue expectations of $120–140,000 per year, she may have to do some of this work. Yet some prime contractor clients already know of her lack of enthusiasm in this sphere and won't be calling her.

It's not perhaps a showstopper risk, but David suspects it could move to the right over time, as Valerie's frustration with having to accept administration work grows.

On the other hand, there is a risk that Valerie could perhaps mitigate. She is a self-effacing individual and dislikes self-promotion, which is why she has placed risk number 4 to the right of the diagonal. But there are things she could do, courses to take, that could help her to market herself in discrete and unostentatious, yet effective, ways. This option will be developed further in Part II, but the presence of such an initiative suggests the cloud can be shunted to the left of the diagonal.

As for so many investment decisions, the answer is not clear-cut. Perhaps the development of a storyline will help, as we shall see in the next chapter....

How Risky is Gary?

We met Gary in the introduction to this book. He has a background as different from Valerie's as is imaginable. Born, brought up, educated, and employed in North Chicago, he is now doing his MBA in...yes, North Chicago. And he has every intention of returning to his former company, UtiliCo, post-MBA in...you guessed it, North Chicago. But is he backable?

Gary is an employee, Valerie self-employed. Yet all the tools used by Valerie in Chapters 1 to 8 above are directly applicable to an employee. We used Valerie as the prime exemplar because the self-employed *have to* use these business analysis tools to survive. But it is the contention of this book that it also greatly benefits the employee to think of him/herself as a business and to use these same tools to clarify career development or change issues.

Indeed, Gary has used the tools faithfully—and we'll see his conclusions from each chapter in his storyline in Chapter 9. He has also drawn up key risks and opportunities at the end of Chapters 2, 3, 6, and 7, just as Valerie did, and has slotted them into his own Suns & Clouds chart (see Figure 8.8).

Figure 8.8. Gary's Risks and Opportunities in a Return to UtiliCo Post-MBA

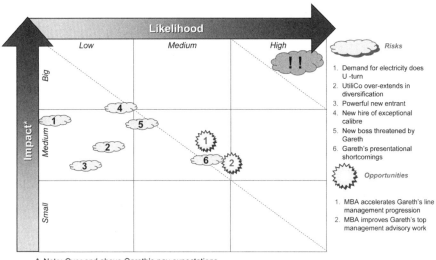

* Note: Over and above Gareth's pay expectations

Gary's chart shows that he is highly backable in a return to his former job. Market demand and industry competition risks (numbers 1 to 3) are negligible. Personnel competition and managerial risks (4 and 5) seem controllable. The main opportunities of accelerated line management progression and improved top management advisory work seem indisputable.

The only blip on the horizon is Gary's presentational skills. He is a quiet, reticent, family man, happy to chat or debate with anyone, peer or manager. But put him on his feet, in front of an audience of 10, even two, and he tightens up. Vitality dissipates, volume drops, words get swallowed, and unintended pauses become uncomfortably elongated.

Business school has, if anything, worsened his speaking phobia. He compares himself to those in his school who are like Valerie, peppering their presentations with anecdotes, or Hari, whom we shall meet again in Chapter 13, arguing forcefully, or Jennifer (Part III), so confident and articulate...and he dries up.

Gary suspects that his presentational shortcomings are a serious constraint on his career development at Utilico. He will need to address this in Part II....

More Suns than Clouds in Texas

When this Texan left Yale with his bachelor's degree, he wasn't looking for a career. He viewed his "first decade after college as a time to explore." After a few years' assorted jobs and military service, his father encouraged him to go to Harvard Business School to "broaden [his] horizons." When he emerged he still had no idea what he was going to do. He had been an unexceptional student at both universities, but Harvard gave him not just "a better understanding of management," but "the confidence to pursue my entrepreneurial urge." His home town in Texas was booming—the Arab oil embargo two years earlier had quadrupled the global price of oil. He launched his own oil and gas exploration company, financed by his education trust fund surplus and external investors.

His Suns & Clouds chart would have been intriguing—significant risks of business sensitivity to oil prices, his own inexperience, and (perhaps) temperament, but outshone by the then exceptional profitability of Texan oil fields, once discovered. He had unwittingly followed the guideline of Chapter 2: *It's better to be in a market with the wind behind than in your face.* His company prospered until the oil price squeeze of the early 1980s, at which point he sold out to another player as the industry consolidated. George W. Bush moved on to the baseball business and politics, becoming the first and only MBA President of the United States of America.

9

What's the Story?

Developing a Storyline
My Storyline: Why I Wrote This Book
Writing Your Own Storyline

*It's not the size of the dog in the fight, it's the size of the
fight in the dog.* –Mark Twain

In Chapter 8 you assessed whether the risks of you not achieving your business plan, in your current or pre-MBA job or business, were surpassed by the opportunities of beating it. You're all but ready to conclude whether you, armed with an MBA, are backable in that job. All that's needed now is a coherent storyline to underpin and justify your conclusion.

Developing a Storyline

This is the fun bit. All, yes, *all* the hard work has already been done. In each chapter you've had to do some serious research and thinking—about market demand (Chapter 2), competition (Chapter 3), your competitive position (Chapters 4 to 6), the achievability of your plans (Chapter 7), and the risks and opportunities around those plans (Chapter 8).

All you need to do now is take your headline conclusions from each of those chapters and weave them into a coherent storyline. One that puts the backing decision in full context.

And that storyline will lead you to answer the key question behind Part I: *Would you back you in your current or pre-MBA business or job?* You need to compose a series of conclusions, which when put together form the overall conclusion, the answer to the key question.

You should set the storyline out as follows:

The overall conclusion on why you are or aren't backable (in which you summarize in bold the findings from the headlines below):

- ▷ *Market demand prospects:* Your conclusions on what's going to happen to market demand, by key business segment (Chapter 2).

- ▷ *Competition:* Your conclusions on whether competition is tough and going to get tougher, by key segment (Chapter 3).

- ▷ *Your competitive position:* Your conclusions on how you stack up to the competition, now and over the next few years, by key segment (Chapter 6).

- ▷ *Your plan:* Your conclusions on whether your plans are achievable (Chapter 7).

- ▷ *Risks and opportunities:* Your conclusions on what main risks and opportunities are likely to affect your plan (Chapter 8).

This storyline must be concise. You must force yourself to get right to the point. *Each bullet point should be no more than one sentence.* It can have a couple of commas, with some backup qualifying phrases, if necessary, maybe even a dash or a colon. But just the one sentence.

The more long-winded you make this storyline, the more difficult it will be to derive your overall conclusion. The conclusion itself should also be just the one sentence. It should answer the question: *Would you back you?*

A Storyline for Backing Sharon Stone Pre-*Basic Instinct***?**

Suppose a then little-known Hollywood actress, Sharon Stone, was in need of some financial backing in 1992. She has just been cast for the role of crime novelist Catherine Trammel in the movie *Basic Instinct*. Many of Hollywood's leading ladies have turned down the role, perhaps because of the risqué, occasionally violent sex scenes. Let's imagine that the funding Sharon is seeking, perhaps for a move up the property ladder, depends on the success of this new movie.

Her backer's conclusions may have been along these lines:

Sharon seems set to shine in what could well be a high-grossing movie, enhancing her Hollywood marketability and enabling her to meet, even exceed, her plans:

- ▷ *Market demand prospects:* Demand for lead female actresses in Hollywood thrillers is buoyant, although hits in the steamy, femme fatale, *Body Heat* genre are infrequent.

- ▷ *Competition:* Competition for lead female roles gets stiffer by the year, but has been limited for this movie, with many stars turned off by its explicitness.

- ▷ *Sharon's competitive position:* Sharon's career has been patchy, with forays into B movies, but this movie could make her highly marketable—her producers say her auditions were sensational, conveying smoldering sensuality and *sang froid*.

- ▷ *Sharon's plan:* Sharon's financial plans should be met if she acts on a par with her co-star, Michael Douglas, and greatly exceeded if the movie does well.

- ▷ *Risks and opportunities:* The opportunity for this movie to be a hit, with its blend of intrigue, lust and Californian splendor, seems to outweigh the risk of it flopping due to Sharon's current lack of star pull.

Note that each bulleted sentence represents the conclusion of one chapter, and that the overall conclusion, which sits firmly at the top, summarizes all the bullets below it. Based on that overall conclusion, would Sharon have secured backing? You bet!

A Storyline for Backing the Beatles

We saw in the last chapter a couple of Suns & Clouds charts that may have helped Parlophone producer George Martin make his decision on backing the Beatles in early 1962. Let's look at the full storyline.

The Beatles don't seem musically outstanding, but they have charisma and could extend their popularity beyond Liverpool:

> ▷ *Market demand prospects:* Demand for Buddy Holly-style beat groups seems set to remain and could reach a wider audience.

> ▷ *Competition:* There are a dozen or more beat groups in Liverpool alone, and countrywide it'll be difficult to differentiate one from another.

> ▷ *The Beatles' competitive position:* The Beatles don't seem musically gifted, they look silly and behave badly, but their humor and charisma could extend their popularity beyond their home town.

> ▷ *The Beatles' plan:* Their financial targets aren't unreasonable and could readily be met with some hit covers—much more so if they could write their own tracks.

> ▷ *Risks and opportunities:* Risks seem to overshadow opportunities, but they've got something and may be worth a shot.

With that storyline, should he have backed the Beatles? It was a bit of a punt. But if you were Paul McCartney in early 1962, would you have backed you in your current business? Of course. You were in the right business. You believed you were gifted at it, you loved it, and the sky was the limit.

My Storyline: Why I Wrote This Book

In the next section, you will write your own storyline to answer Part I's key question: Would you back you in your current or pre-MBA job or business?

It's only fair that I be prepared to do what I'll be asking you to do. In short, would I back *me* in my current business?

Here's some background. I trained as an economist and spent the first dozen years of my career working in various idyllic tropical locations such as the West Indies, Borneo, Thailand, and Fiji—a lifestyle not dissimilar to Valerie's. I figured that care-free times couldn't last forever, so I went to business school and ended up incarcerated in a London investment bank. I belatedly escaped and, after a brief foray into politics, worked with a terrific U.S.-based management and technology consulting firm for 10 years. Sadly, the firm went under, and now I'm an independent consultant, working with a network of fellow freelancers under the banner of Vaughan Evans & Partners (VEP). I specialize in advising companies and financiers on the strategic risks and opportunities of investing in businesses, in other words, Strategic Due Diligence (SDD).

Here's the storyline I developed in 2005 on whether I would back me:

VEP's offering is distinctive, but leads to fluctuating utilization, so downtime needs to be better used to diversify into areas such as writing:

> ▸ *Market demand prospects:* Demand for SDD recovered in 2005 after its deep recession of 2002–2004 and should remain buoyant over the next few years. (Yes, I too failed to spot the looming credit crunch!)

> ▸ *Competition:* Competition has intensified greatly in the 2000s, with top-tier providers more aggressive on pricing and low-cost providers upping their game.
>
> ▸ *VEP's competitive position:* VEP's SDD offering (top-tier quality @ low overhead pricing = exceptional value added to client) is distinctive, but lack of critical mass constrains regular flow of work.
>
> ▸ *VEP's plan:* VEP's SDD activity levels and revenues fluctuate widely, so downtime should be used more productively to assure financial targets.
>
> ▸ *Risks and opportunities:* VEP is overly exposed to the volatility of SDD work and should diversify into areas such as writing and speaking.

Hence the *Backing You* series of books. Would I back *me* in my current business? Tricky one. My revenues from SDD go up and down like a yoyo. One quarter they're hot, the next they're not. They're like London buses—none comes for ages, then three arrive at the same time (and you can only jump onto one!). Spread over the year, they're okay, but an investor would prefer less volatility, more predictability. It took me a while to recognize that the VEP model could only ever be like that. If I were to better use downtime to diversify earnings—for example through writing then speaking about this book—then I might back me.

Writing Your Own Storyline

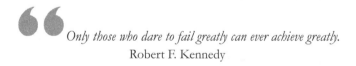

Only those who dare to fail greatly can ever achieve greatly.
Robert F. Kennedy

I've done it. Now it's your turn. But here's a warning: It may not be pretty.

There's one thing I've learned. It's better to be honest and *dispassionate* in assessing your backability. When I launched my consulting business a few years ago, my analysis was crammed throughout with wishful thinking. Perhaps it served a purpose in boosting my confidence—it can be lonely working from home. But I was fooling myself.

Worse, it pushed back the dawn of realization by a couple of years. It then took two years (of downtime) to write my first book, and a further year and a half for publishing, so my diversification arrived much later than it need have done.

So, try to be objective. Think what an investor would conclude. *Not what you'd want him to conclude.* Develop a fair and balanced storyline, but make sure it's independent, hard-hitting, and conclusive.

You never achieve real success unless you like what you are doing.
–Dale Carnegie

And be direct. Are you or are you not backable as an MBA graduate in your current or pre-MBA business or job? Would you back you? *Yes,* or *no.* Or perhaps, *yes, if…* Or even, *no, but …*

If the answer has a *Yes* in it, then you should find Part II helpful. This will show how you can perform even better in your current job.

If the answer if *No,* or *No, but…,* then you should turn to Part III (see Figure 9.1). You need to find a business or job where you stand a better chance of succeeding. Part III will show you how to find a career where you aspire to be, one that inspires you, *and* where you'll be backable.

It will show you how to back the passion in you.

Figure 9.1. Moving on to Part II or Part III...

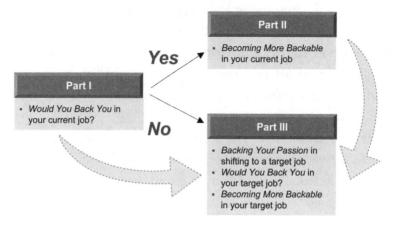

Valerie's Storyline

We've looked in detail, segment by segment, at Valerie's pre-MBA business, markets, competition, competitive position, plans, risks, and opportunities. Is she backable?

Here's the hard-hitting storyline Valerie works up for a return to independent economic consulting post-MBA:

Valerie's strategic position, strong in steady segments and average in growing segments, seems vulnerable, and backing will be conditional upon improved marketing and attitude:

- *Market demand prospects:* Demand for independent economic consulting to developing countries seems set to grow steadily, despite the global recession, more so in public administration than economic competitiveness work.

- *Competition:* Competition is medium/high and intensifying moderately, largely due to low-cost entrants and local substitution.

- *Valerie's competitive position:* Valerie is well placed in economic competitiveness to direct clients, even more so as a subcontractor, but less so in public administration and her planned new segment of business strategy.

- *Valerie's plan:* Valerie's plan seems challenging, given the likely need to fall back on public administration work, for which she is less well placed and enthusiastic.

- *Risks and opportunities:* Valerie has upside in her contacts and business strategy work, especially if she improves her marketing, but the risk of needing to do public administration work outweighs the opportunities.

The above comes as quite a shock to Valerie. How can it be that someone who was so successful for so many years in her former career, and who is doing just as well in business school, possibly in line for honors, may not be backable in a return to her former business?

The reason is two-fold:

- Market demand is shifting in a direction unfavorable to her.
- She is intent on entering a new segment in which she won't be especially competitive.

As is the solution:

- Adopt a more positive attitude to public administration work, recognizing its importance in ensuring more effective distribution of aid and economic assistance.
- Transform her marketing capabilities to attack the segments where she wants to work.

Valerie resolves to study Part II of this book carefully to help her become more backable in a return to independent economic consulting. But she will also have a go at Part III and see whether or not she should be focusing her efforts in an area where her passion truly lies....

Gary's Storyline

Gary's storyline for a return to UtiliCo post-MBA has little of the riskiness of Valerie's:

Gary is strongly placed in a company with sound prospects, but should improve his presentation skills if he wants to maximize his potential:

- *Market demand prospects:* Demand for electrical power should continue to grow steadily in Illinois, with modest fluctuations in growth rates according to the economic cycle and/or conservation initiatives barely affecting demand for good engineering-qualified managers in leading companies.
- *Competition:* Competition is low/medium and should intensify only modestly, unless a competitor strong elsewhere in the U.S. enters, while competition for managerial jobs from within UtiliCo or from outside should be no tougher than before.
- *Gary's competitive position:* Gary has an excellent managerial track record at UtiliCo, and will be even more strongly placed with his MBA, but his presentational shortcomings may constrain his prospects of making it to board level.
- *Gary's plan:* Gary's plans are modest and seem readily achievable.
- *Risks and opportunities:* Gary's MBA should ensure continued upward progression at UtiliCo, but he should improve his presentation skills to exceed his plan and get to the top.

Gary is highly backable. He is returning to an organization with which he is familiar and a job he is good at. His earnings prospects are sound and low risk.

But if his notional backer wants to maximize returns—if Gary would like to maximize his promotional prospects, responsibility, and earning power in the company—he will need to address his presentational weakness.

Gary knows what he wants to do, where he wants to go. There is no need for him to read Part III of this book. But he would benefit from studying Part II on how he can make himself more backable in a return to his former job. We'll catch up with him again in Chapter 14.

Part II

Becoming More Backable

Envisioning the Ideal Provider
Identifying the Capability Gap
Selecting Your Strategy to Bridge the Gap
Backing YouCo
Are You More Backable?

Introduction

Part II is for you if you concluded in Part I that you would back you in your current or pre-MBA job or business. Your earnings target is likely to be met. Opportunities seem to outshine the risks.

It shows you how to design a strategy to make yourself *more* backable.

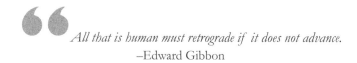

All that is human must retrograde if it does not advance.
–Edward Gibbon

It does this in a sequence of steps, similar to those used in business strategy. They are:

- ▶ Envisioning the ideal provider (Chapter 10).
- ▶ Identifying the capability gap (Chapter 11).
- ▶ Selecting your strategy to bridge the gap (Chapter 12).

Chapter 10 envisions the future and the ideal provider of the services you offer. It encourages you to think out of the box about how things may evolve in the markets and customers you serve. It suggests that you build scenarios about the future and consider what would be the capabilities of the ideal provider of services under each scenario. You then deduce what capabilities would be common to these providers in all or most of the scenarios. These could become target capabilities for you to aim for.

Chapter 11 starts by reviewing your overall strategic position, by means of the Strategic Bubble Bath chart. You'll map how well placed you are in your main business segments, ranked by how attractive each segment is. You can then reconsider where you aim to be in three to five years' time. If your plans do indeed seem achievable, as concluded in Part I, are you sure you have set sufficiently challenging goals for yourself? Should you stay with these business segments, or venture into new ones? To what extent should you attempt to close the gap with the ideal provider? Should you be stretching your sights and making your plans more ambitious? Should you be "going for the goal"?

The chapter then suggests that you revisit the assessment of your strengths and weaknesses in Chapter 6 for each of your main business segments. You'll do this in the light of the scenarios you've developed and your newly reset sights. This will lead you to identify the shortfall between your current capabilities and those to which you aspire—the K2 gap.

In Chapter 12, you'll select a strategy on how to bridge the K2 gap. You'll be introduced to the three main generic strategies, which we call *Stand Out!*, *easyU!*, and *Sharpen Act!* We'll look at Madonna's distinctive and highly successful strategy. You'll be shown how to develop your strategic options, which may include investment in marketing and training if you're an employee, possibly self-financed. If you're self-employed, further areas of investment may include premises, equipment, staff, or partnership. You'll be shown how to evaluate these options and how to build a realistic action plan.

In Chapter 13, Backing YouCo, we look at the possibility of you as an employee becoming self-employed. One alternative that may have emerged in Part I is for you to carry on doing the same job, initially for your same company, but independently, running your own business. In other words, you outsource yourself. Your form your own company, typically called

NewCo in the world of corporate finance, and in this case YouCo. This chapter sets out the main pros and cons of going independent. And it offers a host of tips, especially in the crucial area of sales and marketing, where so many of the newly self-employed founder.

Chapter 14, Are You More Backable?, reviews where you could end up having followed the initiatives set out in Chapters 10 through 13. Having envisioned the ideal provider, reset your sights, identified the gaps, built on your strengths and worked on your weaknesses, and possibly having launched YouCo, you should now be better placed against your peers.

How would that impact on your competitive position of Chapter 6? Will your Suns & Clouds chart have become sunnier? Will the balance of risks and opportunities have shifted in your favor?

Will you have become *more* backable? That's the intention.

First let's do some brainstorming.

10

Envisioning the Ideal Provider

Envisioning Future Scenarios
Profiling the Ideal Provider in Each Scenario
Identifying Common Capabilities

Chapter 10 envisions the future marketplace and the ideal provider of the type of services you offer. It suggests that you build scenarios about the future and consider what would be the capabilities of the ideal provider of services under each scenario. Then you can deduce what capabilities are common to these providers in all or most of the scenarios. These may become the capabilities you should aim for in the next chapter.

Envisioning Future Scenarios

The first step in making yourself more backable is to envision the future of the marketplace in which you work. Will it be more competitive? Will customers have different expectations? Will providers need to develop different capabilities?

To answer these questions, you need to do some brainstorming, thinking a bit more creatively and laterally than you may have done in Chapters 2 to 4. You need to go through and beyond those chapters. You need to get the right-hand side of the brain working.

Different folks have different strokes for thinking laterally. Some think most creatively in bed, some in front of a log fire, others in a place of worship. Some visualize, some meditate, others soak in a flotation tank. Me? I walk. The setting has to be green, preferably with plenty of blue. The cliff paths of the West Wales coastline are perfect, with fields, hedgerows, and baaing sheep to one side, the Cambrian Sea, rocks and squawking cormorants to the other. If I can't be there, a park or a golf course will have to do, preferably with a lake or pond, and some wildfowl waddling around.

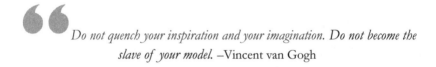

Do not quench your inspiration and your imagination. Do not become the slave of your model. –Vincent van Gogh

Wherever and however you do it, you need to stimulate those gray cells to think creatively. In Chapter 2, you looked at market demand drivers in each of your main business segments and how they may change, thereby influencing demand for your services in the future. In essence you were more or less extrapolating the past into the future.

Seven, eight, nine times out of ten, perhaps, such extrapolation should suffice. The most likely tends to happen. But what if the unexpected happens? To one or more demand drivers in a business segment? What if a previously unconsidered driver becomes important? What if demand lifts off in a related segment? What if market demand in one of your segments should start to blur with that in another segment? Perhaps one where you are worse (or better) placed than in the initial segment?

Likewise for competition and customer needs. To what extent did your thinking in Chapters 3 and 4 reflect an extrapolation of the past into the future? Sure, you had to come up with the most likely developments in the competitive environment, or in customer needs. That's what your backer needed to know. But what about other less likely but possible developments?

Try to brainstorm a range of scenarios on what may happen in your marketplace. Venture beyond the more likely outcomes—you've already drawn those up. Think of those that are less expected but still *quite* likely to occur. Stay clear of fanciful outcomes with only a remote chance of happening. Go for scenarios that could actually happen.

Apply the reasonability test: "Is it reasonable for me to assume that such and such an outcome could take place over the next five years? Sure it may be less likely to happen than the other outcome, but looking back five years from now would I be surprised that it actually happened?"

You may well have identified some of these scenarios in Part I, perhaps translating them into risks and opportunities in your Suns & Clouds chart of Chapter 8. Now is your chance to develop them a bit further, seeing how they pan out and examining the implications.

Other scenarios, especially on the opportunity side, could be new. They'll be incremental to those shown on your Suns & Clouds chart. They should hopefully reflect the "out of the box" nature of your brainstorming. They may steer you in a new and promising direction.

Settle on *two to four scenarios*. Give each a name, something that brings the scenario to life.

Profiling the Ideal Provider in Each Scenario

You already assessed the Key Kapabilities (K2s) required for service providers in your field to meet the needs of customers—see Chapter 5. Now you should consider what K2s are required to meet possibly changed future customer needs, under each of the scenarios you have envisioned.

Some K2s may become more important in one scenario, with therefore a higher weighting. The converse may be true for other K2s.

Some K2s may become more important in one scenario, but less important in another.

Some K2s may be brand new.

The old, new and re-weighted K2s need to be drawn up for each scenario. The ideal provider in that scenario will be the person with the highest achievable rating against each of the K2s.

You should do this for each of the two to four scenarios you have brainstormed.

The man who has no imagination has no wings. –Muhammad Ali

Identifying Common Capabilities

The final step in envisioning the ideal provider is to identify what capabilities are common to each of the scenarios.

Some will be pertinent to only one scenario, others to more than one. One or two may be applicable to all scenarios.

You mustn't forget here your original, most likely scenario, the one developed in Part I. The capabilities that were identified and weighted there remain the most important, since they are the ones *most likely* to be needed. These you are now adding or reconsidering may represent just the icing on the cake.

Lack of commonality doesn't necessarily mean that isolated K2s are unimportant. But it does mean that, in the next chapter, you may choose not to take a particular K2 into account. You won't have the time or resources to prepare for every eventuality. Choices will have to be made. You'll need to formulate a strategy and pursue it.

If one or two K2s are common to most, even all, scenarios, they could become target capabilities on which you can set your sights.

You're drawing a picture of the ideal provider in your marketplace over the next few years. In the next chapter, you'll judge to what extent you should aim to acquire the capabilities of the ideal provider.

Valerie's Envisioning

Valerie knows exactly how best to do some brainstorming. She's a serial jogger and has jogged in every country where she has lived—from up and down the Blue Mountains of Jamaica to aside Lake Victoria in Uganda. Any time she wants some serious get-away-from-it-all contemplation, all she has to do is stop midway on one of her 10- or 20-mile circular jogs. On this occasion, she's too busy to go anywhere distant, so she jogs once round the perimeter of the spring-blossoming Regent's Park, right opposite her business school, and finds a relatively peaceful spot by a pond to sit and envision the future.

She comes up with three scenarios on independent economic consulting, to each of which she attaches a descriptive name:

- *Adminophilia!*—public administration and organizational efficiency come to dominate resourcing requirements on aid-financed projects over the next few years.
- *Brand Power!*—governments become ever more conscious of using branded suppliers.
- *Strategy4Us2!*—Not only are many client organizations in need of advice, but so too some of their providers, the economic consulting groups!

Valerie then profiles the ideal provider in each of these scenarios. She figures that these capabilities will be needed over and above those set out earlier in Chapter 5:

- *Adminophilia!*—nothing new here, just that understanding of approach, experience, and attitude in this segment will become more important; for those providers less interested in this work, marketing for the lesser amount of work available in other segments would become a more important K2.

- *Brand Power!*—marketing again becomes a more important K2.
- *Strategy4Us2!*—strategy, marketing, and general management skills will become more important in driving future growth and profitability in economic consulting groups as the industry continues maturing and consolidating.

Finally, Valerie examines the scenarios for commonality of K2s. The answer is apparent: marketing seems set to become a more important K2 for providers of independent economic consulting services over the years ahead. Given her acknowledged weakness in this area, Valerie approaches the next chapter with some trepidation....

11

Identifying the Capability Gap

Stretching Your Sights
Your Strategic Position
Aiming towards the Ideal Provider
The K2 gap

In Chapter 10 you envisioned the ideal provider of the services you offer in your current or pre-MBA job. You identified capabilities for successfully competing in that marketplace over the next few years.

This chapter identifies the gap between your capabilities and those to which you aspire. It starts by mapping your strategic position—how well placed you are in your main business segments, ranked by how attractive each segment is. It then asks you to reconsider where you aim to be in three/five years' time. If your plans do indeed seem achievable, as concluded in Part I, are you sure you've set sufficiently challenging goals?

Should you stay with these business segments, or venture into new ones?

Should you be stretching your sights and making your plans more ambitious? Should you aim to become the ideal provider in your type of service? Should you be "going for the goal"?

You then revisit the assessment of your strengths and weaknesses in Chapter 6 in the light of the scenarios you've developed and your newly reset sights. And you identify the shortfall between your current capabilities and those to which you aspire. This is the K2 gap. In the next chapter, you'll select a strategy on how realistically to bridge this gap.

Stretching Your Sights

Where do you want to be in your current job or business in three, five years' time? What's your vision of yourself? Do you envision being more or less where you are today, doing more or less the same things, serving more or less the same customers?

If the answer is a yes, or a rather less committal "I suppose so," that's fine. You're backable anyway. That's why you're reading Part II of this book.

If, however, you're of a more ambitious nature, you may want to raise those sights. Sure, you're backable now, but how about becoming more backable? How about raising the bar on your potential achievements? How about raising the return on your investment in yourself?

If you're an employee, try thinking of yourself as a business. Your backer has already agreed to invest in your pre-MBA career. He figures he'll get an acceptable rate of return from you. But think how pleased he would be if you managed to give him an annual rate of return 1%, 2%, even 5% higher than expected? And if he's going to get a higher return, think how much higher yours would be!

That's just one side of the coin, I know. The other side is the non-monetary, which may be more important to you. Especially if financial circumstances seem reasonably under control. Caring for or helping other people may be your main driver of job satisfaction, letting the money side of things go hang. That's fine and admirable. As long as the bills get paid.

However you take these non-monetary factors into account, you may still benefit from coming up with an answer. Where do you want to be in three or five years' time? Do your sights need raising?

> *Achievement is largely the product of steadily raising one's levels of aspiration…and expectation.* –Jack Nicklaus

There are three main aspects of setting and possibly raising your sights:

- ▷ Which business segments should you address? The same as now, or others with promise?
- ▷ In which business segments should you become more competitive?
- ▷ How close to the ideal provider should you become in the segments of your choice?

Deciding on the first two of these can be facilitated with the *Strategic Bubble Bath* chart. For the third, we'll meet the *Going for the Goal* chart.

Your Strategic Position

In Part I you declared yourself backable in your current or pre-MBA career. That's why you're reading Part II. This implies that the main business segments you address are in at least reasonably attractive markets (Chapters 1 through 3) and that you are at least reasonably placed in those segments (Chapter 6).

In setting your sights for the next few years, however, would you like to reset them to address another business segment (or segments) that are in *more* attractive markets than the ones you currently address? If so, do you have grounds for believing that you would be at least reasonably placed in this new segment? Or that you could readily become so?

Meanwhile, are there any less attractive business segments you should consider withdrawing from? Or where your competitive position is not that good?

Furthermore, isn't it time we redefined what we mean by an attractive business segment? In the business world, the definition is relatively straightforward. Market attractiveness is typically taken to be a blend of these four factors:

> Market size
> Market demand growth
> Competitive intensity
> Market risk

These factors remain valid for an individual as well. But they're not sufficient. They make no allowance for the soul, for the subjective, something that's often treated as an irrelevance in the corporate world.

We need to add at least a fifth factor, which we can term *enjoyment* (or *fulfillment*, if you prefer). This should give the definition of attractiveness a better balance.

If you're thinking of resetting your sights to address a more attractive business segment, you should look before you leap. Figure 11.1 shows an example of someone who is in four segments and is contemplating getting into a fifth. She has landed a backer, so we can assume she has an attractive business mix.

Segment D emerges as the most attractive, followed by new segment E. B is rather unattractive. In assessing overall attractiveness, she has gone for a simple average of the ratings against each factor. She could instead have opted for a weighting system, yielding a weighted average. Or she could, say, have double counted one of the factors, say Enjoyment. More accurate, perhaps, but she went for simplicity.

Figure 11.1. **Attractiveness of Business Segments: An Example**

Business Segments	Market Size	Market Growth	Competitive Intensity	Market Risk	Enjoyment	Average Attract-iveness
A	3	1	2	3	5	2.8
B	2	2	2	3	2	2.2
C	2	3	3	4	4	3.2
D	3	5	4	2	4	3.6
E (New)	3	4	5	2	2	3.2

Key to Rating: 1 = Unattractive, 3 = Reasonably Attractive, 5 = Highly Attractive
[For competitive intensity, remember that the more intense the competition, the *less* attractive the market.
Likewise for Market Risk: the riskier the market, the **less** attractive]

One word of warning! When assigning a rating to competitive intensity, remember that the more intense the competition, the *less* attractive the segment. A highly competitive segment would get an attractiveness rating of 1 (not 5!). It's the same for market risk. The riskier the market, the *less* attractive it is, so the lower the rating. The other factors are more straightforward—the larger the market, the faster it's growing or the more enjoyable it is for you, the higher the rating.

The next step is to pull out the competitive positions she would have drawn up in Chapter 6 for each of her main business segments. For example, she may have found a competitive position of 4.0 for segment A, 2.6 for B, 3.4 for C and 3.7 for D. E is a new segment, but she figures she could become reasonably competitive within a year and achieve a rating of 3.0.

She's now ready to draw up a Strategic Bubble Bath chart. Each business segment is represented by a bubble. Its position will reflect competitive position (along the bottom of the bath) against the attractiveness of the segment (up the side of the bath). The size of each bubble should be roughly proportional to the scale of revenues currently derived from a segment.

Figure 11.2. **Strategic Bubble Bath: An Example**

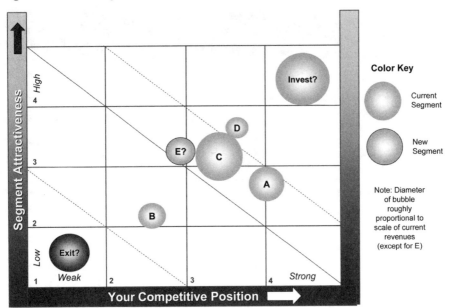

The closer your segment bubbles float to the top right-hand corner the better placed you are. Above the top right dotted diagonal, you should be thinking of investing further in that segment. Should your bubble sink to below the bottom left dotted diagonal, however, you should seriously consider exiting that segment.

The strategic position shown in Figure 11.2 is sound. It shows favorable strength in the biggest and reasonably attractive segment, C, and an excellent position in the somewhat less attractive segment A. Segment D is highly promising and demands more attention, given the currently low level of revenues. Segment B should perhaps be exited—it's a rather unattractive segment, and she's not that well placed. The new segment E seems reasonably promising.

In setting her sights, this exemplar may consider the following worth pursuing, subject to evaluation of her strategic options in the next chapter (see Figure 11.3):

> ❯ Continued development in segments A and C.

> ❯ Investment in segment D (see arrow showing the resultant improved competitive position).

> ❯ Entry to segment E (with her competitive position improving with experience).

> ❯ Exit from segment B (see the cross).

Figure 11.3. **Strategic Bubble Bath and Sight Setting: An Example.**

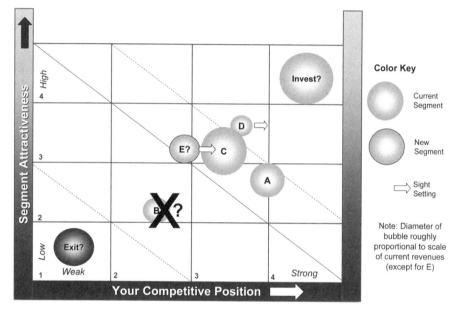

Try setting out your own Strategic Bubble Bath. It should look good. You found that you were backable in Part I, so your strategic position should be sound. Your *main* segments, from which you derive most revenues, should find themselves positioned above the main diagonal.

Do you have any new segments in mind? How attractive are they? How well placed would you be?

Are there any segments you should be thinking of getting out of?

Which segments are so important that you would derive greatest benefit from improving your competitive position? Where should you concentrate your efforts?

Those are your sights. Should they be stretched? How close to the ideal provider of services in one or more of those key business segments do you aim to become?

Aiming Towards the Ideal Provider

In Part I, you identified your strengths and weaknesses and rated them against the Key Kapabilities required to compete in each of your main business segments. You found that there was a gap between your overall rating and that of the ideal provider, who realistically would have gained a rating of between 4 and 5 against each K2.

In the last chapter, you envisioned scenarios where new K2s may be required or existing K2s gain in prominence. These could further widen the K2 gap—if you were to sit still.

Where do you want to be in tomorrow's marketplace? Are your sights currently set on bridging the K2 gap found in Part I? Or should you consider raising your sights toward bridging the possibly wider K2 gap of Chapter 10?

Do you want to become a good player in tomorrow's marketplace? A strong player?

> *If you want to be successful, find someone who has achieved the results you want and copy what they do and you'll achieve the same results.*
> –Anthony Robbins

Or do you want to go for the goal and *lead* in tomorrow's marketplace?

Do you want to get as far as you can toward becoming Ms. (or Mr.) Ideal Provider Tomorrow?

Why not? The fact that you're reading this book indicates you're serious about self-development. Why not stretch your sights the whole way and go for the goal?

If so, however, remember that the goalposts may well have shifted by the time you're ready to shoot. Time moves on, and the ideal provider in five years' time will have a different mix of capabilities to her equivalent today. Perhaps only with slight differences in nuance, perhaps radically different. You may find the Going for the Goal chart in Figure 11.4 helpful.

Figure 11.4. Going for the Goal

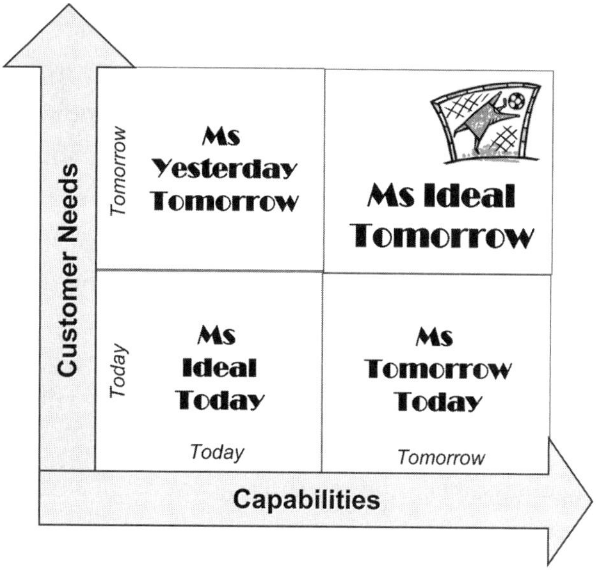

The Going for the Goal chart highlights three important points:

- ▷ It's fine being Ms. Ideal Provider today, but today only lasts one day.

- ▷ If you don't develop the extra capabilities required to meet the customer needs of tomorrow, you'll become Ms. Yesterday Tomorrow.

- ▷ There's little point in developing extra capabilities today unless customers need them, or you'll become Ms. Tomorrow Today.

If you've raised your sights to the very top and are aiming to become Ms. Ideal Provider Tomorrow, you need to plan carefully how you are going to bridge the K2 gap, and when.

The K2 Gap

In Chapter 6, you set out your ratings against the K2s you assessed in Chapter 5 for each of your main business segments. These K2s were in turn largely based on customer needs you identified and ranked in Chapter 4.

Your Chapter 6 work was not a purely static exercise. You were encouraged to take a dynamic perspective. You looked not just at customer needs and K2s today, but how they might change over the next few years. You also considered how you might improve your standing against one or more of the K2s over the next few years. *And* you gave some thought as to how your competitors could enhance *their* standing in the future.

You need to revisit those charts. You should check for any change in customer needs, K2s, your competitive position, or that of a competitor, as a result of change in:

- The external marketplace, given the scenario development you undertook in Chapter 10.
- Your aims, given the resetting of your sights earlier in this chapter.

You can now identify the K2 gap. You've revisited your competitive position in each of your main business segments, set your sights on which new segments to enter and established to what extent you wish to bridge the gap with the Ideal Provider.

That's the gap. In the next chapter, you'll develop a strategy on how to bridge it.

Valerie's K2 Gap

Valerie is unequivocal. If she's going to return to independent economic consulting, she'll do so only as an ideal provider. Otherwise, the investment of tens of thousands of dollars and two years of her life at business school will have been in vain.

She will raise her sights to the highest. She will be Ms. Ideal Provider Tomorrow.

Not only will she aim to be a top independent consultant, but a top manager too. She will raise her skills to a level where she would become a serious candidate for a top managerial job in a top economic consulting group.

All three scenarios she developed during the brainstorming of Chapter 10, *Adminophilia!, Brand Power!,* and *Strategy4Us2!,* highlighted one capability that would be the future key to success: sales and marketing.

But it was Valerie's weakest suit. When it came to other K2s, analysis, report writing, presentation, qualifications, track record, work ethic, communication, she was up there with the best of them.

But with sales and marketing, she wasn't. She didn't enjoy it and had always felt uncomfortable selling herself.

Figure 11.5. Valerie's Strategic Bubble Bath and Sight Setting

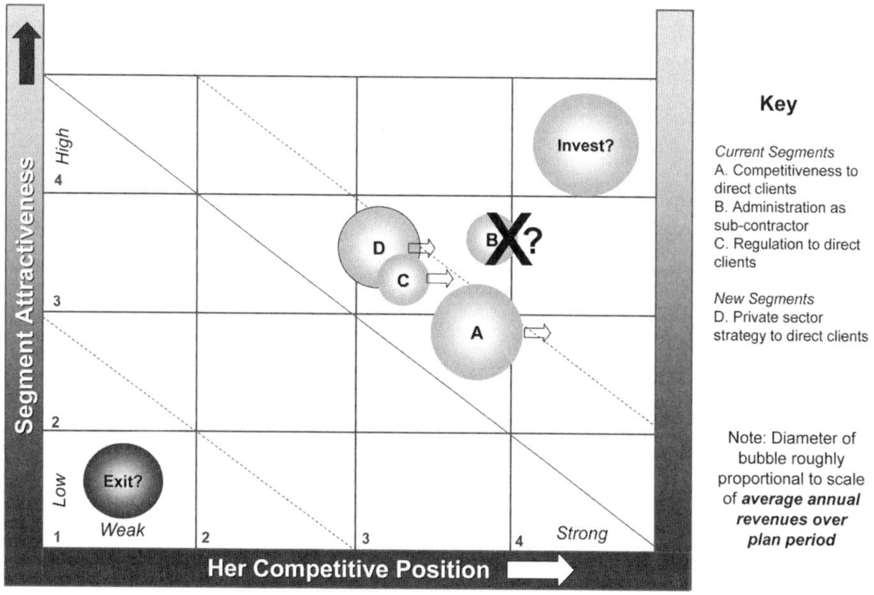

Business school would be of some but limited help. She would now be a bit clearer about the 4Ps. But it would barely raise her rating against that K2 from 2 to 2.5. It would not suffice. She needed to significantly improve her overall competitive position in her main segments—moving those bubbles noticeably to the right in Figure 11.5.

To be an ideal provider, she would need to get to a rating of 4 at least—a 5 would be a ridiculous target, since she would never be a natural salesperson. But surely a 4 was within reach?

How? —That's for Chapter 12...

12

Selecting Your Strategy

Strategy for the Individual
Three Generic Strategies
>> Stand Out!
>> easyU!
>> Sharpen Act!
Strategic Alternatives
Evaluating the Alternatives
Laying out an Action Plan

In the last chapter, you identified the K2 gap—the shortfall between your current capabilities and those you aim to have in your current or pre-MBA job or business. In this chapter, you'll select a strategy on how to bridge this gap. You'll be introduced to the three main generic strategies, and shown how to develop your strategic alternatives. These may include investment in training or marketing if you're an employee—possibly self-financed. If you're self-employed, other areas of investment may be in premises, equipment, staff or partnership. You'll be shown how to evaluate these alternatives and build a realistic action plan.

> " *Vision is not enough, it must be combined with venture. It is not enough to stare up the steps, we must step up the stairs.*
> —Vaclav Havel

Strategy for the Individual

You're at business school, so you know there are plenty of definitions of strategy, ranging from General Sun Tzu's military strategy to Kenichi Ohnae's competitive advantage. You may have developed one of your own.

I'm an economist, so I believe that we should bring the words "scarce" and "resources" into the definition. Just as economics can be defined as the optimal allocation of a nation's scarce resources, so too can a company's, or indeed an individual's, strategy be defined thus: Strategy is how you deploy your scarce resources to gain a sustainable advantage over the competition.

What resources do you have? You've already examined them in Chapter 6 when you were assessing your capabilities and competitive position. And again in Chapter 11 when you were identifying the K2 gap. You've already done most of the groundwork needed to draw up your strategy.

When a company formulates its strategy, it considers how best to allocate its available resources to meet its goals. These resources are essentially its assets—its people, physical assets (for example, buildings, equipment, inventory) and cash (and borrowing capacity). It has to decide on how it should allocate—or invest—these resources to optimal effect.

For an individual, it's no different. You need to deploy your resources to their most telling effect. Except that the number of people involved is often in the singular. It's you! The most obvious of your resources are *your* capabilities, *your* physical assets (if any), and *your* cash (and/or overdraft potential).

We shall either find a way or make one. –Hannibal

Your most precious resource, however, may be time. And that could be your secret weapon. You may be able to find time during working hours where you could invest in training to improve your skills. Or you may have to think about carving a segment out of leisure time.

"Time is money" is an old cliché, but that makes it no less valid. It's especially so when your plans to make yourself more backable involve a substantial investment in precious time.

If you're self-employed, a day off for training could mean the loss of a day's earnings. If you're an employee, and you can't get your employer to agree it's in the company's interests as well as yours, it can mean the forfeiting of a day's vacation. Any day invested in self-improvement tends to have both an *actual cost*, what you have to pay out in cash (although this may be free, like a day in the public library), and an *opportunity cost*—the forfeiting of what else you could be doing. That could be time spent on pursuing an alternative strategy. Or it might just be the sacrifice of your leisure time. That has an opportunity cost too—it's time that could otherwise be spent on the golf course, or with your feet up.

So, in summary, you need to develop a strategy to bridge the K2 gap. That strategy will exploit your capabilities and will typically entail investment in cash and/or time.

Robert M. Grant, in his excellent book on business strategy, now in its sixth edition and a must-read for business school students, *Contemporary Strategy Analysis,* invites readers to think about how business strategy is relevant also to the individual. He cites the extraordinary case of an entertainer in her mid-forties with the family name of Ciccone but known to many across the world by her Christian name alone: "In the summer of 1978, aged 19, Madonna arrived in New York with $35 to her name. After five years of struggle she landed a recording contract… "Madonna" [her first album, 1983] ultimately sold 10 million copies worldwide… Twenty years later, Madonna was still the world's highest earning female entertainer and one of the best-known women on the planet." (Blackwell Publishing, Malden, MA, 2008)

Grant wonders how on earth this unprecedented feat has been possible, given the entertainer's evident limitations: "What is the basis of her incredible and lasting success? Certainly not outstanding natural talent. As a vocalist, musician, songwriter, or actress, Madonna's talents seem modest. Few would regard her as a natural beauty."

One answer, according to Grant, has been the clarity of her ambition, her going for the goal: "her dedication to a single goal: the quest for superstar status." She also possesses "relentless drive" and has been adept at "drawing on the talents of others—writers, musicians, choreographers, designers." But he spies one consistent strategy throughout her career: "Most striking has been her continuous reinvention of her image—from the street-kid look in the early 1980s, to hard-core sexuality in the 1990s, and the spiritual image that accompanied motherhood."

There is one further element to her strategy that has been key to success: "As a self-publicist, she is without equal. In using sex as a marketing tool, she has courted controversy through nudity, pornographic imagery, suggestions of sexual deviance and the juxtaposition of sexual and religious themes. But she is also astute at walking the fine line between the shocking and the unacceptable."

Only a diehard fan would disagree with Grant's assessment. Madonna is an entertainer of unexceptional musical or dramatic resources, yet successful to an astonishing and unprecedented degree. She has been an inspiration not just to her natural successors, like Kylie or Britney, who can also sing and dance a bit, but to countless other pop music and reality TV wannabes. Many of the latter possess plenty of Madonna's resources of determination and self-publicity, but seem blissfully unaware that you need a modicum of talent on which to base the marketing hype.

We know that Madonna's goal was to be a superstar. What was her strategy? How did she allocate her scarce resources to meet that goal? In one sentence, which is what a strategy should fit in, how about this? *To build on her capabilities in the performing arts through sustained investment of cash, time and energy in image reinvention and self-publicity.*

We'll come back to Madonna later in this chapter. But what's your strategy? How will you deploy your scarce resources to gain a sustainable competitive advantage? In one sentence?

First, let's look at the generic strategies.

Three Generic Strategies

There are three main generic strategies for an individual to select to achieve his or her goals. The first two are based on generic business strategies. To develop a sustainable competitive advantage, and to enjoy profitable growth, companies generally follow one of two generic strategies: (1) a differentiation strategy, or (2) a low-cost strategy.

To simplify, they either do something distinctive and well, or do more or less the same as the others but at lower cost. What they would be well advised *not* to do is the same as other companies do, the so-called *me-too* recipe for lack of success.

For an individual, whether employed or self-employed, these generic business strategies are directly transferable. Let's call the differentiation strategy the *Stand Out!* strategy, since we can all get a handle on the importance of standing out, being special to someone or some group of people (customers). It's making your offering different, special, distinctive from others. It's Madonna's strategy.

For the low-cost strategy, let's call it the *easyU!* strategy. European readers will be familiar with the astonishing success of the low-cost airline easyJet (similar to that of Southwest Airlines in the United States), which later diversified into other low-cost offerings in sectors such as easyCar, easyMoney, easyMobile, and so forth. If you're going to make your offering the lowest cost on the market, then easyU! just about sums it up.

But for individuals, there's a third generic strategy that is hugely important. That's where circumstances combine to constrain your pursuit of the other two strategies. You may not be able to differentiate sufficiently, you may not choose to become the lowest cost provider, but you *do* need to improve your competitiveness or you may find yourself in trouble. We'll call that the *Sharpen Act!* strategy.

To summarize, there are three generic strategies for individuals to achieve their goals:

1. Stand Out!—differentiate for success
2. easyU!—become low cost for success
3. Sharpen Act!—improve your competitiveness for partial success

Let's look at each in turn.

Stand Out!

Think about how well-known, successful companies differentiate themselves. Rolls Royce in the majesty of car design, Dell in custom-built laptops, Sony in high-quality graphics on game machines. Or on a less lofty plane, McDonald's in burger quality consistency, Ben & Jerry's in homemade ice cream, Quizno's (or Prêt-A-Manger in Britain) for fresh, quality ingredient sandwiches.

In each case, this differentiation will come at an extra cost. But that will be more than made up by the volume of business sold, and typically, the extra grand, dollar, or even dime able to be added to pricing over and above competitors' offerings due to the differentiation.

It's the same with individuals. Madonna has been around for over 20 years, yet her concerts have become no cheaper to get into. Likewise for the Rolling Stones, whose differentiation (the bad boy image, created from the outset and maintained painstakingly through the decades) has kept them a premium act for closing on half a century.

Think of comedians. All successful comedians, in whatever country, have readily recognizable persona. Charlie Chaplin had perhaps the most identifiable differentiation in Hollywood history: a tramp in an ill-fitting suit, with a bowler hat and an umbrella. Chaplin fell into that role while auditioning as a drunk. It went down well enough to land the role and the rest is history.

I'm not suggesting you go down to the nearest charity shop and buy a suit three sizes too small and a silly hat. But it is worth considering in what ways you differentiate yourself from other providers of your services.

You have of course looked at many aspects of your differentiation in earlier chapters, namely Chapter 6 on your competitive position and Chapter 11 on your K2 gap. But it's worth having a rethink because it may influence your choice of strategy.

Differentiation is all about building on your strengths. It's taking what you're good at, those K2s where you rate highly, and doing them even better. It's typically not about working on your weaknesses, which is more associated with the third generic strategy, Sharpen Act!

Madonna's is a Stand Out! strategy, one of image reinvention and self-publicity. Yet even she has not shirked from applying aspects of the Sharpen Act! strategy over the years. Can you think what they are? What weaknesses has she worked on over the years? We'll return to these questions when we look at the Sharpen Act! strategy below.

The Stand Out! strategy is essentially that promoted by Marcus Buckingham and Donald O. Clifton in their stimulating bestseller, *Now, Discover Your Strengths*. Their thesis is that organizations that encourage employees to iron out weaknesses to become stronger have been misguided. They fail to identify each individual's unique pattern of strengths and build on them.

The authors worked with the Gallup Organization for many years. In one large survey, employees were asked this question: "At work, do you have the opportunity to do what you do best every day?" They found that those answering "strongly agree" to this question worked in business units with higher customer satisfaction ratings, greater productivity and lower employee turnover. Yet the "strongly agree" respondents were only 20% of those surveyed. If only a fraction of the remaining 80% could be encouraged to work to their strengths, the authors argue, just imagine the resultant uplift in productivity and profitability, let alone employee satisfaction.

The authors identify two principles that should guide the world's best managers: (1) Each person's talents are enduring and unique, and (2) each person's greatest room for improvement is in the area of his or her greatest strength. The book then shows how you as an individual can capitalize on your strengths, and how you as a manager can manage the strength-building process of your employees and of the organization as a whole.

Buckingham and Clifton perhaps exaggerate to make a point, certainly a forceful point. Differentiation through playing to your strengths can for sure be a strategy for success, and is almost certainly the best route. But the low-cost strategy is also a well proven strategy for success. And their dismissal of what we call here the Sharpen Act! strategy is not wholly fair. Individuals may not find themselves in the right circumstances to play wholly to their strengths. They may have little practical choice but to work on their weaknesses. This may not yield them stunning success, but it could well enable them to keep their job and improve their lot. It can be a strategy for partial success. It can make them more backable.

easyU!

It's easy enough to visualize how the likes of JetBlue in the United States and Ryanair in Europe have been successful. These low-cost airlines have grown rapidly and profitably, despite seeming to give away so many of their tickets. The trick is in load factor. Their planes are usually full. And if a passenger only contributes to the costs of landing charges and taxes, that's still better for the bottom line than an empty seat.

How can this apply to an individual? How can an easyU! strategy work for you?

Simple. It's all about utilization. If you're a self-employed professional, your earnings are typically a reflection of your charges on the one hand and utilization on the other. If your time charged is low, there's no point in having high charges. Your earnings at the end of the year will be low.

easyJet makes money because of high utilization. Perhaps you could too?

The easyU! strategy can succeed at any point in the pay scale. One of my former management consulting colleagues retired as a director, but wanted to keep active. So he offered to continue to work for the company on a freelance basis at a much discounted daily rate—a fraction of what the company could bill the client for his time. Suffice to say that he found himself busier in "retirement" than he had been in full-time employment!

Is this a strategy that could work for you? If you're an employee, would you be prepared to take a pay freeze or cut, and tighten the belt at home, in order to retain your job? You may have no option if your company is restructuring. But even if your company is in fine shape, is it worth considering this strategy to secure your position?

If you're self-employed, how's your utilization? How price sensitive are your customers? Would your utilization be improved if you shaved your prices? Would that boost the bottom line?

Sharpen Act!

We've discussed the differentiation and low-cost strategies. For individuals there's a third generic strategy to be considered. It's not the optimal, perhaps. But it could well be better than no strategy at all. It's the Sharpen Act! strategy. It's where you build on your strengths to the extent that you're able to in the circumstances, but meanwhile you work on some of the weaknesses that are holding you down. You set out to improve your competitive position.

This is a strategy that Buckingham and Clifton (above) would not approve of, but you may have little choice. Individuals are unlike companies. In a market economy, companies can buy or sell business units, open or close down production units, hire or lay off personnel, outsource operations, possibly to offshore, low-cost economies, relocate headquarters to lower cost towns. They play to their strengths, whether following a differentiation or a low-cost strategy. They deploy their scarce resources to maximize shareholder value.

Individuals can't always do that. They may have personal commitments. To their children, perhaps, in continuity of schooling. To caring for their aged parents. To the needs of their spouse. To their communities—the other people, societies, charities, and organizations they support. These commitments impose constraints, very often welcome constraints, on freedom of action.

MBA students may well have fewer personal constraints than other professionals or managers, simply due to age. But it is just as well to think about whether there are any personal constraints limiting you from carrying out a full-blooded Stand-Out! or easyU! strategy.

Individuals also have financial commitments. To the loan provider for your business school fees. To the mortgage provider. To the credit card company. To the health insurer. To the private school. These commitments also impose constraints, typically less welcome than those above, on freedom of action.

Individuals also have desires. Suppose they desire to be doing some form of work that they're really not that well placed to address? Should they play to their strengths, stick to the work they're good at and abandon their dreams? Or should they improve on some of their weaknesses and have a go? It's surely an option, a possible strategy.

There are some elements of the Sharpen Act! even in Madonna's strategy. Her overriding strategy is of course one of Stand Out!, but over the years she has also worked on some of her weaknesses and sharpened up her act—for example:

> Voice training, improving her pitch, range, and control to the extent that she auditioned for, and won, the role of Evita, the leading lady in the movie based on the musical by Tim Rice and Andrew Lloyd Webber.

> Body toning, famously, through harsh yoga regimes and even giving consideration (*Sunday Mail,* October 2006) to going under the knife: "Never say never! I sure don't rule it out, although I don't want to be made up of silicone, plastic and man-made fibre."

Does the Sharpen Act! strategy apply to you? Either on its own, or in conjunction with Stand Out!? Or does easyU! make more sense? Let's look at the alternatives you may choose to consider within these generic strategies.

Strategic Alternatives

You know where you want to get to. You know how you want to travel there. But which route do you take? The answers are, of course, as many and diverse as getting from your home to the office, from London to Timbuktu, or from Las Vegas to heaven!

There are any number of possible strategic alternatives. Any number of permutations of investment in effort, cash, and time. Your challenge is to narrow down the universe of alternatives into those two or three most strategically consistent and viable.

If you're self-employed, there are six main areas you may need to invest in, namely marketing, training, equipment, premises, staff, and partnering. If you're an employee, the latter four are unlikely to be relevant. For employees, investment in training is typically the most important, but investment in marketing should not be dismissed. Let's take a look at these two first, since they apply to all of us.

Investment in marketing

There are hundreds of thousands of self-employed people out there, like—I have to admit—myself, who don't devote enough time, effort, and cash to marketing. Then we complain when the phone doesn't ring.

It's not where our interest lies. We prefer to spend our time doing our job, not selling ourselves to potential customers. We'll take a deeper look at this in the next chapter on the pros and cons of setting up your own business.

Suffice to say that if no one knows you're there you won't get any business.

Every dollar, euro, or zloty spent on marketing is an investment. Not all will be well spent. Some will turn out to be lousy investments. But you won't know until you try. And some spending may pay big dividends.

Not so long ago I met up with a former contact I had lost touch with over a roast beef sandwich, a beer and a coffee. It set me back around U.S. $60. I saw it as a networking investment. I had no expectations of any direct work, but I thought he might give me some tips on what was going on and who was doing what. And maybe a referral or two. I was wrong. His company was contemplating changing its policy on the use of outside consultants. Two months later I landed my first engagement with them. A handsome return on investment.

Would that other lunches, coffees, letters, phone calls, and emails were as productive! In truth, you just don't know. The vast majority are dead ends. But you don't know that at the time. You've just got to keep at it.

Does your business need further investment in marketing as one component of your strategy to achieve your goal?

What if you're an employee? Is investment in marketing applicable? Very much so. Again, you're not going to get far being good at your job if no one in your organization knows about it. Much as you may dislike it, especially if you're a modest character, you do need to let your boss, and his boss too, know how you're contributing to the company's success.

> 66 *The fact is, everyone is in sales. Whatever area you work in, you do have clients and you do need to sell... You need to sell you and your ideas in order to advance your career, gain more respect, and increase your success, influence and income.*
> –Jay Abraham

This doesn't mean you have to be a creep. We've all seen them at the office. They time their visits to the water cooler to coincide with the boss's. They laugh uproariously at the boss's feeble jokes (think of the atrocious David Brent character in the BBC sitcom *The Office*, or Michael Scott in the U.S. adaptation). If the boss is a fan of the New York Yankees or Liverpool Football Club, guess what? —so are they!

Sometimes such creeps win, though. I've known some who have got to the very top. Good luck to them. But good managers generally see through such creepery. Of course they'll appreciate an employee being courteous, even humorous, but most of all they want to know that the job is being done well. And it's up to you to let your boss know just that. That may require a conscious and sustained effort in self-promotion. An investment in marketing.

Investment in training

You know all about investment in training. You're doing it right now, investing many thousands of dollars in an all embracing program of self-improvement.

The MBA is the epitome of dedicated training. It offers a broad range of skills and knowledge to make you better equipped in for the world of work, from corporate management and public administration to finance, consulting, and enterprise. But it's a huge investment, the biggest investment in self-improvement you'll make in your life.

And it may not be sufficient. You may know where you want to be in five years' time. You know what the K2 gap is. You know that yours is primarily a Stand Out! strategy, with a touch of Sharpen Act!. But you know too that further training may be needed to bridge that K2 gap and meet your goal.

Training in general can be on-the-job or dedicated. It can refine your skills or develop new, related skills. It can aim at a modest honing of capabilities, or at developing new, life changing capabilities. It can be anything from a one-day blitz in speed-reading to the MBA you're doing now.

Whatever the training options you consider, they should satisfy two fundamental criteria:

- They should be consistent with your strategy.
- They should seem like a sound investment.

The first criterion is self-evident. We're talking here about training for the workplace. Training in tennis skills is fine, but unless you're a pro, it's beyond the scope of this book. If you're training for work, it should be consistent with your strategy of investing your scarce resources to bridge the K2 gap assessed above in Chapter 11.

The second criterion is more intriguing. If you're an employee, there should be areas of training available to you provided by the company. The HR function in larger organizations has become highly sophisticated over the last couple of decades. There is typically a provision made for each grade of employee for some element of training each year. This is not always the case with smaller companies.

But what if what the training courses provided by the company don't coincide with the K2 enhancement needed to achieve your personal goals? Then you have three choices. You can try to persuade your boss that it is in the company's interests for you to broaden your capabilities through undertaking this training. Or you can leave the company for a similar company where that training will form part of the employment package. Or you can finance it yourself in your spare time.

If you do have to finance the training yourself, then you should be reasonably confident that it will prove a sound investment.

If you're self-employed, training can be just as important. You may need further training in your field of specialization, or to diversify into a related field. Or some serious training or coaching in an area of deficiency, such as selling skills.

But for the self-employed, any cash costs for training are usually to your account. There's no boss for you to persuade. You're the boss and you must convince yourself. The training investment will need careful evaluating and it had better yield a good return.

There may be occasions when you can get your customers to cover the costs of training. This is not an unethical suggestion. Now and again, you may pitch for work where your current capabilities cover most of the work required, but not all. If the customer cannot find a provider with the full range of capabilities at an appropriate price, she may be willing to contract with you on the understanding that you will upgrade your capabilities during the course of the engagement to complete the work satisfactorily. Your customer won't pay for any cash costs of training, but she's effectively covering them by paying you for the work you'll carry out during and after training.

Investment in premises or equipment

If you're self-employed, investment in premises or equipment may be required to bridge the K2 gap identified in Chapter 11.

There is never just the one solution to such investment. Think of buying a house. You develop your criteria for the ideal house: four bedrooms, three baths, three-car garage, fenced backyard, a green and peaceful neighborhood, and located in a particular school district. You'll find plenty of houses that fit some of these criteria but few that fit all. One or two may fit the criteria so well they'll be outside your price range.

It's similar with selecting business premises. You'll need to select your criteria carefully, screen and rank the available options, and narrow them down to a manageable two or three.

Think too of buying a digital camera or an MP3 player. You'll have your criteria, but there are so many to choose from, each differing in specifications, design, and price, that you despair of ever being able to make up your mind!

It can be almost as daunting with business equipment. Which laptop? Which drill? Which pick-up? On the plus side, the range to choose from is typically narrower than in consumer goods. On the minus side, business equipment is generally more expensive, so it's important to make the right decision.

Again, you need to select your criteria carefully, screen the options available, and narrow down to those most promising.

Investment in staff

This is potentially the most exciting of the investment options available to you. If you're a self-employed business person, investment in an employee tends to mean one thing: you're growing! It means that you're making the transition from being self-employed to an employer. There's no halfway house. You're either an employer in the eyes of the tax authorities, or you're not. If you employ one person today, you could be employing half a dozen tomorrow. Or a dozen? Two dozen? One hundred?!

Again, you need to ensure that the engagement of staff is consistent with your strategy for bridging the K2 gap and has every chance of achieving a sound financial return. In general, you'll need to feel comfortable that the extra revenues you can generate with an employee on board are greater than the total extra costs incurred from engaging the employee—including wages, benefits, social security, insurance, and extra overhead. This may not always be the case, however. You may choose to engage an employee to take some of the load off you, make life more tolerable and acknowledge the trade-off between extra cost and improved quality of life.

Investment in partnership

This is another exciting investment option. Again it implies growth, although partnerships can sometimes be used as a defensive measure to ward off aggressive competition.

Partnerships among the self-employed can range from the wholly informal to the contractually formal. At the least formal end of the scale, it can mean a simple arrangement of mutual referral. You ask your plasterer if he knows a good electrician, and he gives the name of his "partner," using the word in its broadest sense. Likewise, he'll pass on the names of carpenters, plumbers, and roofers in whom he has confidence. And they'll do the same for him. No formal contracts, no sales commissions. Just an understanding: You scratch my back, I'll scratch yours. And a pint or three of beer in the pub later on!

Partnerships can be made more formal for the benefit of all parties. This is especially true where a joint investment in premises, equipment, or both needs to be made. A partnership shares the risk. Many professional practices are partnerships, whether lawyers, doctors, dentists, vets, alternative therapists.

Formal partnerships are a means of reducing the financial risk of an investment, but they represent an entirely new area of risk, namely dependence on others. Before signing on the dotted line, it's crucial to minimize that risk by finding out as much as you can about your prospective partners. One word of caution: Try to make sure that your partners share the same core values and ethics as you. These, more so perhaps than compatibility of skills and experience, are what will hold the partnership together. And make the parting tolerable when the partnership splits up, as most do.

Marketing, training, equipment, premises, staff, and partnering are the main areas of strategic investment for you to consider, within the context of one of the three generic strategies discussed above.

You now need to develop two or three strategic alternatives. Each will represent a defined and coherent strategy for bridging your K2 gap. They may reflect investment in one area alone, or investment in a combination of areas. Alternative A, for example, may involve further training in marketing skills, while alternative B may be more ambitious, involving relocation of premises and partnership with someone with proven marketing skills.

Evaluating the Alternatives

You have derived two or three strategic alternatives. But you can't do both or all of them. How do you choose which to pursue?

The answer is straightforward. You should choose the alternative that gives you *the highest return for the lowest risk.*

How you get there is a tad more complex. Ideally, you'll do a full discounted cash flow (DCF) analysis on each alternative. You'll project future cash flows, assess their value in today's money (NPV, or net present value) and compute the return on investment of each alternative (IRR, or internal rate of return). You'll then tweak the underlying assumptions to see how sensitive the NPVs and IRRs are to things not working out as expected.

But DCF analysis is never as straightforward as that. What discount rate should you use? For how many years should you project? How to calculate terminal value, how to treat corporation tax?

My advice is to either do DCF analysis properly, or not at all. I have seen it done poorly so many times, leading to wildly off the mark valuations and wayward investment decisions. To do it properly, study a dedicated text such as *Valuation: Measuring and Managing the Value of Companies* by McKinsey & Co. Inc. (Wiley, 2010) or *Principles of Corporate Finance* by Richard Brealey, Stuart Myers and Franklin Allen (McGraw Hill, 2007).

If not at all, there are other simple ways to evaluate investment alternatives. As long as you remember three fundamentals.

The first is the nature of making an investment. It usually means a cash outlay today that should give you cash, or other benefits, coming in for years to come. Investment tends to be a one-time, up-front cost, leading to recurring annual benefits.

Second is "sunken costs." When you're comparing the viability of strategic alternatives, any cash you've already spent has to be forgotten about. Tough, but it's gone. It's history. You must only take into account what *extra* cash you need to spend on an alternative from this day forward to generate the benefits expected.

The final fundamental is the difference between money of today and money of tomorrow. You have no doubt had this hammered into you at business school, but it does bear repetition: cash invested today in a strategic alternative has a higher value than cash generated in future years as a result of that investment.

Here's a simple* way to evaluate a strategic alternative. Work out the cost of the investment, say $I. Assess the annual benefits from the investment, or the difference between the extra cash inflow (from revenues) and the extra cash outflow (from expenses) generated each year as a result of the investment. If the annual benefits are different each year, take their average over the first five years, $B/year. Divide B into I, and this gives you the "payback," the number of years taken for the cash costs of the investment to be recouped.

---

*Simple or simplistic? The payback approach to evaluating investment alternatives has its drawbacks. It doesn't properly take into account the time value of money, nor the possible lumpiness or risk of annual cash flows, and it ignores cash flows beyond the payback period, thereby favoring investments with short-term returns. But it is undeniably the simplest approach.

If payback is *four years* or less, that could well be a sound investment**. But don't jump on it. Work out the payback on the other strategic alternatives as well. Who knows? They may have an even lower payback.

**That is equivalent to a 9%/year rate of return over a five year period, assuming—conservatively—no benefits beyond five years, due to obsolescence, competitive response, etc.

If you believe your investment is going to give you a longer-term advantage, and could last all of ten years, then an investment with a longer payback may still be beneficial. You might give serious consideration to an investment with a payback of six to seven years. It'll be riskier, of course, because all sorts of things could happen to your competitive situation over that time period.

Next you need to work out the "net benefits" of the strategic alternative. Here, strictly speaking, you should discount the value of benefits received in later years, because of the time value of money discussed above—especially if annual benefits in, say, year 5 are much larger than in year 1. But for many investments made by individuals, as opposed to those by companies, it should be a good enough *first approximation* to assess net benefits by adding up the sum of the annual benefits in the first five years and subtracting the investment costs.

If your strategic alternative represents an investment with a much longer-term horizon, like doing your MBA, then you should work out net benefits properly, using DCF analysis.

The above assumes that benefits are readily measurable. Often the benefits will be more obscure. The main benefit of a strategic alternative may, for instance, be an improvement in your competitive position, making you more competitive and better placed to respond to competitors' initiatives. The trick then is to compare scenarios *with* and *without* the investment. The *with* scenario is what your earnings would be if you make the investment. The *without* scenario is what your earnings would be if you do nothing. The difference in annual benefits between the two scenarios can then be attributed to the investment.

There are, however, other elements that have not been taken into account. The above has focused on one side of the story, the financial, whether readily measurable or not. What are the other, non-financial bene-fits of pursuing one alternative compared to the others? A greater sense of fulfillment, or higher status in the community, for example? Are there any negatives in pursuing the alternative, such as a more stressful peer group, longer working hours? All these need to be factored into the evaluation.

Finally, and crucially, as ever in this book, there's risk. Each alternative will be more or less risky than the other. The alternative that promises the highest returns for the lowest investment outlay may be unacceptably risky. Another alternative that offers modest payback for a modest outlay may be virtually risk-free. How risky are your proposed alternatives?

Now you're ready for the evaluation itself. It may be helpful for you to lay out the strategic alternatives in a table, along with their investment cost, annual benefits, payback, net benefits, non-financial benefits, and risk, as shown in Figure 12.1.

Figure 12.1. **The Payback Approach to Evaluating Strategic Alternatives**

	Unit	A	B	C
Cash Benefits Investment Costs (= I)	$			
Average Annual Cash Benefits over 5 years (= B)	$/Year			
Payback (= I /B)	Years			
Total Cash Benefits over 5 years (= TB = B x 5)	$			
Net Benefits (= TB − I)	$			
Risk	L/M/H			
Non-Cash Benefits		➤ .... ➤ .... ➤	➤ .... ➤ .... ➤	➤ .... ➤ .... ➤ ....
Non-Cash Dis-Benefits		➤ .... ➤ .... ➤	➤ .... ➤ .... ➤	➤ .... ➤ .... ➤ ....

N.B. The payback approach can be misleading: you may need to adjust to reflect the **time value of money**, the **lumpiness** of cash flows, or cash flows **beyond** the forecast period

The table will guide you on which of the three alternatives is the most *financially* beneficial. It should be the one with the highest net benefits and with an acceptable payback. *And* with acceptable risk. Note that the alternative with the fastest payback is not necessarily the best—net benefits may be too small, even though they are the most rapidly achieved. But if the alternative with the fastest payback is not mutually exclusive with the one that has the highest net benefits, perhaps you could do both?

!!!Warning!!!

Investment appraisal can be complex. If you are uncertain of the evaluation methods or unclear about the results of your evaluation, you should seek professional advice!

The most financially beneficial alternative may not, of course, be the most beneficial to you overall. You need to compare the cash benefits in the table with the non-cash benefits. This is highly subjective. One alternative may be the most financially beneficial, but have the most negative implications on your quality of life. That's when evaluation becomes tricky. It's up to you, and how you balance your earnings aspirations with other aspects of your life. There's always a trade-off.

It's up to each of us to figure out for ourselves the work-life balance that best suits us.

Laying out an Action Plan

So you've selected the most appropriate strategic alternative to narrow the K2 gap and achieve your goals. That's the easy bit! The tricky bit is in carrying it through, in implementing the strategy.

For that you'll need to draw up an action plan. This will be a chart of all the activities you need to undertake to achieve your strategy, including a start date and a target completion date. Figure 12.2 gives a format you might find useful:

Figure 12.2. **Drawing Up an Action Plan**

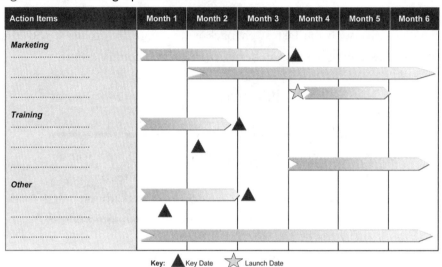

Action Items	Month 1	Month 2	Month 3	Month 4	Month 5	Month 6

Marketing

Training

Other

Key: ▲ Key Date ☆ Launch Date

The key to getting things done is to revisit your action plan regularly, say once a month. Chastise yourself if you've fallen behind. Insist on giving yourself sound, supportable reasons if you have.

The problem with implementing a strategy is that if you fall behind with one action in the plan, it often has a bearing on another. If you're not careful you'll find you're unable to launch one strategic thrust because of delay in another. Prolonged delay can mean having to abandon that thrust. You may even have to bin the whole strategy.

What's going to be in your action plan? When should each task start? By when should you have finished it? How realistic is that? Will you really be able to do that task by the end of that month? Make it as realistically achievable as you can. Then go out and achieve it.

You now have a strategy and an action plan. What if your winning strategy is to carry on doing what you were doing pre-MBA, but on your own, breaking free from your former employer and setting up as an independent operator? That's for Chapter 13…

Valerie's Strategy

Valerie is in no doubt. Hers is to be a Stand-Out! strategy. If she is to return to independent economic consulting post-MBA, it'll be as a top performer. A highly differentiated player. Nothing less will do.

Yet it will also have elements of a Sharpen Act! Strategy, for one central plank will be to address what to date has been Valerie's main weakness—sales and marketing.

In a sentence, Valerie's strategy will be: To build on her competitive position in economic consulting through sustained investment of cash, time, and energy in quality delivery and marketing, especially in the target segment of business strategy.

This will be a tough challenge. Clients, actual and prospective, are by definition spread across the globe. They will be hard and costly to reach.

She identifies three strategic alternatives, all designed to transform her sales and marketing capabilities:

- Take a one-year part-time course and become a Chartered Marketer with the Chartered Institute of Marketing
- Engage a business coach highly experienced in sales and marketing, preferably to developing countries— possibly a retired executive from a competing economic consulting group
- Form an alliance with a marketing-oriented, non-competing consulting group (or groups)

Valerie soon rules out A—she will have had enough of studying and case studies after two years of business school. C is a possibility—low investment costs in cash, though perhaps not in time. B will be expensive—business coaches don't come cheap, not if they are any good.

Yet B seems to offer the most attractive returns. Once the initial investment in a few days of the coach's time is spent, beyond that it should just be the odd hour or two of advice, as and when required. Just having someone there to fall back on, someone to challenge her, to probe, to guide, to encourage, should be a great help over time. It can be lonely being an independent and difficult to find the motivation to pick up the phone (see the next chapter) where having a coach to prod you along can not be a bad thing, Valerie figures.

She resolves to start the process of finding the right person....

13

Backing YouCo

The Self-employed Workforce
The Issue of Credibility
Going it Alone: Six Tough Cons and Four Major Pros
What's Your Service?
The Importance of Sales and Marketing
Seven Tips on Selling YouCo
Four More Tips on Managing YouCo

In Chapter 11 you were encouraged to stretch your sights and reset your goals. You evaluated a number of strategic alternatives for attaining those goals in Chapter 12. One such radical alternative may have been of going it alone, of providing more or less the same services as you do now, or you did in your pre-MBA job, but under your own banner. Running your own business.

This chapter is for those who are considering becoming self-employed. You may have been employees before entering business school, or you may have come direct from university. You'll form your own company, typically called NewCo in the world of corporate finance, but for you: YouCo. You'll sell your services independently, perhaps initially to your former colleagues, now your customers, and subsequently to new customers. Or you may be entering into competition, whether direct or indirect, with your former company. What are the pros and cons, the pitfalls, the risks, the opportunities, of YouCo?

The Self-employed Workforce

When I was at business school in the early 1980s, there was much academic debate on what the workforce would look like at end of the century. Many believed that the nature of work was fundamentally changing. One of my lecturers, Professor Charles Handy, a spellbinding communicator and author of many path-breaking books on the nature of organizations, envisaged that the workforce would become more atomized (see *The Age of Unreason* or *The Elephant and the Flea*). Technology—and this was largely the telephone, the answering machine (then with magnetic tape technology), and the fax machine, well before dial-up Internet, email and, later, broadband—would enable people to work either independently from home or in loose networks of like-minded individuals. The need for large organizations, for large companies of people, would diminish.

It hasn't quite turned out like that. Sure, we all know lots of self-employed people, working out of small offices or from home (the so-called *soho* workforce). We all know self-employed people who work within networks, usually informal. I work as an independent, based in my *soho* (that is, my loft) and with my own offering in management consulting reinforced by a network of associates. They too are fellow independents, all with complementary areas of specialization.

Yet the proportion of the self-employed in the U.S. workforce has stayed strangely flat. Growth has been negligible. They represent around 10.5% of the non-agricultural workforce (half of the agricultural workforce is self-employed), within just one decimal point of the rate in the mid-1980s (10.4%).

The self-employed are mainly male (roughly 13.5% of the male workforce, compared with 8% for women), white (12% of the white workforce, compared to 11% for Asian, 7% for Latino and 5.5% for blacks) and experienced (18% of 55- to 64-year-olds, compared with just 2.5% of 25 to 34 year olds). (Data from *Self-Employment in the United States: An Update*, Monthly Labor Review, July 2004.)

After farmers, the self-employed are found mainly among those in management, business and financial occupations (22%), construction (21%), other services (20%), and sales (16%). In "other services," highest rates of self-employment are in personal care (barbers, hair salons, nail salons) and household repairs and maintenance. In professional services, self-employment is generally low (9%), but with higher rates in fields such as health care, design, education, landscaping, and child daycare. But the highest rates are for artists (47%), writers (47%), musicians and singers (43%), and photographers (38%).

Why haven't these rates grown over the last two decades? The answer is complex and may lie within some large scale trends in the workplace. On the one hand, globalization and transnational mergers have led remorselessly to larger and larger corporations worldwide. On the other, the generally applied corporate strategy of sticking to what you are good at and selling off or outsourcing non-core activities has served to restrain employment growth in larger organizations.

The trend to outsourcing does not, however, seem to have had much impact on the self-employed. When a large company outsources, it tends to do so to a specialized outsourcing provider, typically a company, not an individual. Outsourcing has propelled the growth of thousands of small and medium sized businesses, but seems to have had little effect on the self-employed. The industries and occupations where self-employment rates are high are little different from what they were 20 years ago. Some exceptions spring to mind, such as IT services, and film and TV production services, but they are relatively few and have yet to make a major statistical impact.

The Issue of Credibility

One major constraint limiting growth in self-employment is credibility. When a reasonably large organization buys in services, it needs to feel comfortable that the service will be delivered to the appropriate standard and on time. If that doesn't happen, it expects the supplier to face some sort of penalty. In the worst case, this could be court action. If the provider is an individual, the organization may be reticent to impose a penalty, let alone sue her.

Thus the buyer is taking on an element of risk that would not be present if he bought from a company. Should things go wrong, his boss could well turn round and ask him why he used this individual. What was so distinctive about her offering that made it worth taking on the risk that she would not perform?

Take a simple example. The manager of a medium-sized insurance broker's firm decides that the offices are looking a bit drab. Some carefully selected greenery should brighten things up. Rather than request each department to put up its own plants, he asks his PA to contract a plant display provider to design, install, and look after the lot. The PA has three main options. She could either go to a nationally or regionally branded plant display firm, to a local firm, or to an independent, self-employed individual specializing in the field, like Pansy.

The advantages to the PA of going with Pansy's Plants are significant. She's likely to be more conscientious, enthusiastic, and committed, since this is her livelihood. She will also be cheaper since she has few corporate overheads. But there may be perceived disadvantages. The PA will be reliant on Pansy and her alone, not just for regular maintenance, but for sorting out the paperwork. And what happens when Pansy is on holiday, or sick? What happens if she gets so busy that she can't show up when needed?

Some of the PA's concerns would be addressed if Pansy had a partner. The two of them would be able to stagger their holidays and cover for each other when sick. When it comes to the final decision, the PA may choose Pansy, and more likely perhaps if Pansy had a partner, but she may conclude that life would be simpler if she went with Office Greenhouse, the local firm that many other companies in the office block use. That way it would all be less personal and more commercial, and there would always be a receptionist to speak to when something needed sorting out.

Thinking back to our analysis in Part I of this book, guarantee of supply is typically an important customer need (Chapter 4) and credibility often a Key Kapability (Chapter 5). It may or may not be a must-have factor, depending on the nature of the service provided.

The issue of credibility is seldom one of competence in doing the job. For the self-employed, the issue can often be one of *being available* to meet the needs of the client at the precise time the client wants those needs met. It is this issue that may offer a partial explanation as to why the economy-wide trend to outsourcing has led to such little growth in the rate of self-employment.

This issue applies primarily in business to business, or B2B, services. It applies less in B2C, or business to consumer, services. The householder often prefers an independent plumber or gardener to an employee of a small plumbing or gardening firm. Many householders value the one-to-one relationship, and yes, it usually works out cheaper.

Nobody talks of entrepreneurship as survival, but that's exactly what it is and what nurtures creative thinking. –Anita Roddick

Going It Alone: Six Tough Cons and Four Big Pros

For a chapter about setting off on your own and forming YouCo, you may think the above section comprises a rather gloomy start. Credibility is going to be an issue, especially in B2B work, it says. And the rate of self-employed has barely changed since the 1980s.

Good. It's just as well to take such an important step with your eyes open. I'm self-employed, and it ain't easy. If any reader thinks otherwise, you're in for a rude awakening. Self-employment can be rewarding. It can help you achieve the work/life balance you seek. But don't make the mistake of thinking it's easy.

Let me give you more of the bad news, then I'll balance that with some good. Here are six reasons why setting up YouCo will be tough:

> It's not easy to win business
> You have to do everything yourself
> There ain't no security
> Work blurs into home time
> It can be lonely
> Don't do it for the money

Then there's the balance: four major reasons why YouCo could well be good news:

> You're your own boss
> You'll grow *your* business
> You can select your own free time
> You'll see more of the family

Let's first face up to the bad news. These are some of the arguments against.

It's not easy to win business

Most newly self-employed people have little experience of winning business. At their former company, they were handed work to do on a plate. Business won by the firm was promoted by the marketing team and clinched by the sales team, on the back of a brand that conferred some degree of credibility in the sales process. They may not have been on either team. They were service deliverers after the business had been won.

They were order-takers, not order-makers.

Some newly self-employed come out of government or another non-profit-making organization. They have even less idea of what it takes to market and sell a successful enterprise. One with no brand name and no track record other than your own resume.

There are thousands of self-employed people out there offering a service that too few people know about. That's unfortunate, but a few choice tips in the next section (*It's All About Selling and Marketing*) may help.

You have to do everything yourself

When you're self-employed, running YouCo, who do you ask to type a letter? Then post it? Or answer the phone? Make the coffee? Keep the books? Wine and dine a key client? Chat up the local journalist? Design the business cards? Write the brochure? Provide content for the website? Choose the laptop? And the ISP? Delete the spam? Fix the abominable pop-ups? Slot in a new ink cartridge to the printer? *And* having done all that, provide the service and do the job?

The answer is scary: You!

You're not just the CEO, CFO, and COO. You're also the CGO— chief gofing officer.

If you're going to back YouCo, face it. You'll have to do most everything yourself. Much of it will be fun. Some of it will be pure grind. All will need to be done. And the buck stops with you.

Time allocation is a key prerequisite of a successful self-employed person. There are so many tasks to be done. How to fit it all in? Again there will be some tips later in the chapter (*Then There's the Admin*).

There ain't no security

If you're an employee and you're feeling dreadful, with the flu, or perhaps something worse, what do you do? You call the boss and suggest, croakily, that you stay home for the day. You'll still receive your salary. Likewise if one of the kids is unwell, your spouse is unavailable, and you need to take the child to the doctor, your bank account will still be credited at the end of the month.

Sure, we've all come across ogre bosses who can be unsympathetic, or downright heartless, but most managers accept the situation and cause little fuss—as long as they feel that the employee is genuinely trying to keep time away from work to a minimum.

Likewise, when you're on holiday. For an employee, it may be quite comforting to think of your paycheck landing in the bank while you relax on a Caribbean beach on New Year's Eve. You may even contemplate the contribution your company is making to your pension fund as you sip your rum punch and gear yourself up for the limbo.

Above all, an employee feels she has some sort of job security. Not as much these days as in earlier decades, perhaps. Not so much in the United States as Britain. Not so much in Britain as continental Europe. But some. It's human nature. No matter how easy it is to make staff redundant, no manager likes doing it. No more than they like firing employees for incompetence. As long as you're doing your job conscientiously, and as long as the company is ticking over profitably, you have a reasonable degree of job security.

There's none of that when you're self-employed. None at all. When you're sick, or when you have to care for sick relatives, there's no pay. Same when you're on holiday. The cost of the holiday is not just what you pay to the tour operator, but the earnings you are foregoing by being there. There's no pension, other than what you take out from profit and pay into your own personal pension fund.

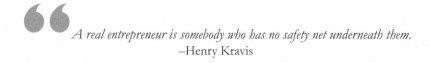

A real entrepreneur is somebody who has no safety net underneath them.
–Henry Kravis

And there's no security when the market gets tough. Unlike for an employee, who may hold on to the job and hopefully salary as the company tightens its belt, the self-employed have to take the revenue downturn on the chin. For the self-employed, you eat what you catch. You are as we all once were: a hunter-gatherer.

Work blurs into home time

Another disadvantage self-employed people admit to when pressed is that there becomes a finer distinction between when work stops and play starts. Work can infiltrate leisure time.

This is especially true if you work from home. It can be difficult to turn off the laptop or put down your tools and play with the kids when there's work remaining undone.

Take the most extreme example of this, the politician. I was a full-time politician for a couple of years in the early 1990s. I loved it, but it put huge pressure on my then young family. The work is never-ending. Political issues pay no heed to the time of the day. There's as likely to be an issue arising at 9 P.M. as at 9 A.M. The pressure starts at dawn when you prepare to answer calls from the local (or national) radio or TV stations. And after attending whatever events you need to in the evening, work finishes only after you've caught the news reviews late into the night. The diary in between will be filled to the brim by your agent and activists. Slots have to be consciously set aside for the family, but even when you manage to make these slots your mind can be, sadly, elsewhere. And that's assuming no crisis. When there's a political emergency of any kind, and they are frequent, all diary events are rubbed out, and the needs of the family again put on hold.

Sure, the politician's life is a grotesque extreme of the pressures of the home-based self-employed, but I've known some to be so obsessed with their businesses that they too live a version of this lifestyle. Fine if that's their sole goal. But some only realize the impact on their family when it's too late.

There will be further tips on how to counter this disadvantage later in *Then There's the Admin.*

▬ It can be lonely

As CEO of YouCo, you're likely to be pretty isolated for much of the time. That comes with the territory. Worse, when things go badly, it can be lonely.

When I worked with an international firm of management consultants, it was always a blow when the team lost a pitch for a coveted piece of business. Fortunately, the winning happened more frequently than the losing, so it was relatively easy to shake off the bad news. The team would retire to the pub, have a quick post-mortem, down a beer or two, crack some jokes, and go home. The next day, we'd move on to the next challenge.

Things are different when you're self-employed. Bad news like a lost pitch can be hard to take. It gets more personal. It's not your company the client is rejecting in favor of another provider. It's you. It's your skills, your track record, your storyline, your pricing, your personality, your face, your armpits (?!), your everything. In a word, *you*. It can be tough. That's when it can be lonely. (Ironically, while drafting this very paragraph a few years ago on a predecessor book, a phone call came in to tell me that I had lost a pitch. It was the largest piece of business I'd pitched since being self-employed! I had been working to land it on and off for over six months. It was a body blow. I felt dispirited, drained of confidence, lonely. Again. But it could have been worse. I didn't lose to a competitor. That's when it really hurts. On that occasion, the company just changed its mind, maddeningly, about going ahead with the project. At least I was able to spend more time writing…!)

But again that comes with the territory. A self-employed person *will* receive bad news now and again. Whether it's a lost pitch, a demanding client, a disappointing subcontractor, a prolonged delay, a dispute in payment, bad times will happen. You need to develop a support network to see you through the bad times. There are some tips later in *Where's Your Support?*

Don't do it for the money

It's a common fallacy that self-employed people make more than employees. It's not generally the case.

It's easy to see how the misconception arises. When you look at the hourly or daily rate charged by a self-employed service provider it can seem outrageously high. Mentally, you multiply by eight hours a day, five days a week and 52 weeks a year, and you end up with investment banker numbers. But once you build in a factor to allow for her utilization, you find that the annual takings come crashing down. Depending on the type of business, she'll be doing well if she can sell three days per week on average, very well indeed if she can average four days per week, after allowing for marketing, pitching, admin, and sheer down time. And who's going to pay her when she's on holidays or sick with the flu?

Then think of all the extras she'll have to pay for herself, benefits that employees often take for granted. There are pensions and insurances (for example, life, health, dental) that may have to come out of her takings, outgoings that could account for 10 to 15% of her revenues.

Then there's another factor, especially for those of us in B2B services. Some clients seem to begrudge paying the self-employed the kind of daily rate we feel we need to pay our bills. Why? Because they feel we have so many benefits already from working from home. We don't have to pay an office rental or other overhead. We have no hyper-stressful commuting journey, and we can supposedly take time off whenever we feel like it for a round of golf…so why should they pay us a commercial rate? Most have no comprehension of the trials of self-employment. Nor should we expect them to have.

A word of advice: If you're contemplating launching YouCo because you see it as a way of making more money, think twice. That may turn out to be the case; if so, lucky you. But when you present your plan to a backer, be aware that he won't expect you to make more money than before. He'll look very carefully indeed at your assumptions on pricing and utilization.

Phew! So much for the disadvantages, now let's try to redress the balance. Here are some of the major advantages of being self-employed, of being the head honcho of YouCo!

 ## You're your own boss

This is the most obvious advantage. No reporting, no asking for permission, no annual reviews, no internal politics, no need to account to anyone but you! To those of us with little patience for bosses of limited capability other than playing the corporate game of snakes and ladders, this is a big plus.

 ## You'll grow *your* business

Each time you win a new customer, that's *your* precious customer. Each time you receive payment, that's *your* bank account you'll be dropping the check into. Each time you prepare your annual accounts, hopefully you'll be tracking the growth of *your* company, *your* enterprise, *your* initiative, *your* energy. *Your* baby. It feels good.

 ## You can plan your own free time

This is the flip side to the disadvantage above of work slipping into leisure time. Leisure can also slip into work time more easily when you're self-employed. You're bashing away at the laptop and the lad comes home from school. "Dad, how long are you going to be?" "Oh, just a couple of hours, son." "But, Dad, you're always working. And look, it's sunny outside. It might rain later on. We need some exercise. Come on, Dad, let's go to the park *now?*" Why not?!

Ask a London taxi driver what he likes about his job. He'll tell you it's the flexibility of the hours. That's why so many golf courses in the counties around London are full of taxi drivers in the middle of the week. "Once I've made my numbers, I head off for the course," said one to me recently. I bet his doctor approves of that attitude to life!

It's easy to get distracted, however. We all have our weak spots. I'm particularly vulnerable when the Wimbledon tennis is on the TV. Or the Ryder Cup. Or West Indian cricket. Fortunately, Welsh (or Fijian) rugby tends to be at weekends. Likewise, Liverpool (or Brazilian) soccer. Otherwise temptation would be overpowering. It's just as well I can't fathom what's going on in American football, baseball, or basketball. I'd never get any work done!

The self-employed person needs time discipline, for sure (see *What about the Admin?* later on). But the opportunity now and again to be able to break out, without having to answer to anyone other than your own self and your own business, is to be treasured.

 ## You'll see more of the family

Few self-employed people have long commutes. Many are based from home or from nearby offices, maybe on the Main Street down the road. Many visit other people's homes within a reasonable radius of theirs. Time saved in commuting should mean more time with the family. When you see both parents of a child at an after lunch performance of the school's jazz band, what's the betting that the working parent is self-employed?

So there you have it. Some fantastic advantages to being self-employed, balanced by some rather grim disadvantages.

It's a lifestyle choice. Over to you!

If you do decide to go for it, here are some tips on how to make YouCo a success.

What's Your Service?

What service do you offer? This may sound rather obvious, but you need to be clear about what YouCo is to offer, and to whom.

There are four typical situations where an employee makes the transition to self-employed:

1. *Outsourced:* She works for a company (or nonprofit organization), providing clearly defined services within the company, and she leaves to supply the same services to her former company, and perhaps to other companies in due course, but as a self-employed contractor.

2. *Competing for clients:* He works for a company that supplies services to other companies (B2B) and he leaves to compete with his former company in providing those services to the same and other clients.

3. *Competing for custom:* She works for a company that supplies services to consumers (B2C) and she leaves to set up a business supplying the same or similar services to consumers, perhaps in competition with her former company or perhaps targeting other consumers (for instance, in a different area).

4. *A fresh start:* He leaves his company to start his own business, little or nothing to do with his former job or his former company.

It's important to be clear as to which of these routes applies to you. Your sales and marketing strategy—in the next section—will depend on it.

In Part I, where you assessed whether you were backable in your current or pre-MBA job, you were asked to think of yourself as a business, as being outsourced, the first typical route to self-employment noted above. This was to help clarify your markets, competitors, customer needs etc. Now your hypothetical customers may become real.

The second and third routes also require much forethought. Will you be competing against your former employer? How will you rate against the required K2s? How will you handle the credibility issue? Or will you be dodging direct competition and targeting a niche where your former employer has little interest? The latter may be more attractive to a backer.

Or is yours the fourth of the routes, a fresh start? If so, you need to be sure that the market demand for your new offering is buoyant, that competition is not becoming tougher and that you'll rate favorably against the requisite K2s. This will be very much the theme of Part III of this book.

Another way of looking at the fresh start route is to consider whether your intended offering addresses some "unmet needs" in the marketplace. This is one of the secrets to a new venture's success highlighted by William Bridges, a leading authority on organizational transitions, in his esteemed work, *Creating You & Co*. He suggests that an "unmet need" could be uncovered by spotting signs such as a missing piece in a pattern, an unrecognized opportunity, an underused resource, a signal event, an unacknowledged change, a supposedly impossible situation, a nonexistent but needed service, a new or emerging problem, a bottleneck, an interface, or other similar signs.

The Importance of Sales and Marketing

I said it earlier, but I'll say it again. It can't be stressed enough. Believe me, I've found out the hard way (and I'm still learning). Here it is. If no one knows you're there, you won't get any business. No matter how good you are at what you do.

If you're from a sales background, you'll have a head start on forming YouCo. Even if there are others out there much better at executing the work, you could well do better than they. You'll know how to make customers aware of your offering, and how it differs from the others.

One of the most successful professional speakers in Britain is Frank Furness (www.frankfurness.com). When he started out, he readily admits that he wasn't the most charismatic of speakers. But he had been in sales and marketing all his life and he set about applying all this experience on himself and his business. Through a strategy of relentless marketing, coupled with a sideline bootcamp business in coaching starter speakers to do the same, he has built a thriving business worldwide—and meanwhile has developed into a speaker capable of delivering inspirational content.

If, however, you're like most of us who have gone it alone, and you've had very little experience in selling and marketing, then please take one thing away from this section: *Seek help!*

Consider postponing any plans you may have had to further develop your offering. Learn instead how to sell. It'll open your eyes. Learn the most effective ways to market your type of service.

The first step is to buy some books. You've already invested in this book. That's just the start. You should invest in two or three books on how to sell and market your service as well. Some of them may be fat and pricey. Buy them anyway. You don't have to read every word. Skim through, hunt for the bits that seem appropriate to your situation. If there's *one tip* in that book that helps you make *one sale,* your investment could be recouped many times over.

Here are a couple of books that have helped me. *Getting Business to Come to You*, by Paul and Sarah Edwards and Laura Clampitt Douglas, is a comprehensive guide. They show how you can stand out from the crowd, through focusing, niching, and demonstrating why you're the best provider. And how to create a winning marketing message and develop a promotional package. Finally they help you design tailor-made marketing methods just for you. It's all in there, in almost 700 pages.

Slimmer is *Get Clients Now*, by C. J. Hayden, a book that's tailored to management consultants and professionals. That's the business I'm in, and it's more relevant to me than other more general marketing books. Hayden shows how to develop a marketing strategy and features a 28-day marketing program aimed at locating, landing, and keeping clients.

Try putting your occupation and the words "sales, marketing" into Google or Amazon and see what's been written that's targeted directly at your business. There probably won't be many, but buy one or two. They may not be brilliant, but just one or two nuggets could justify the purchase price a hundred fold.

Another small book I found useful is *Rapid Referral Results* by Roy Sheppard, which highlights the importance of referrals, one of the key tools in the armory of the self-employed—see below under *Don't be shy about asking for referrals.*

If reading these and similar books doesn't do the trick, consider enrolling on a course. There are plenty around, whether at local further education colleges, business schools, or ad hoc seminars by sales professionals.

The latter can be quite expensive, so look carefully for someone who's experienced in your field and do thorough web research on her before you pay up and attend.

Seven Tips on Selling YouCo

Here are seven tips I've learned along the way. They may not be comprehensive, like in larger tomes on sales and marketing, but do these and you'll be well on your way:

1. Perfect your elevator speech.
2. Reinforce your message.
3. Try 10-touch marketing.
4. Pick up that phone.
5. Don't be shy about asking for referrals and testimonials.
6. Don't be greedy.
7. If you have to, use an agent.

Perfect your elevator speech!

You need to be absolutely clear about what it is you offer and why it delivers distinctive benefits to your clients. All in one simple sentence. It should be able to be delivered, if necessary, when meeting a stranger in an elevator between the first and third floors!

Here's an example. Pansy visits many office blocks and frequently finds herself giving her elevator speech, literally. Not surprising, really. Her elevator companion will be dressed for the office, whether suit and tie or smart casual, depending on the office dress code. But Pansy will be in her usual baggy green T shirt, with the Pansy's Plants logo embossed in yellow, and her denim cutoffs. She looks different and intriguing and this often sparks a chat. Here's her line: "Yeah, I'm Pansy, and I run my own plant display company. I'm passionate about how the right plants can create a sense of well-being in an office environment." Short and sweet, it communicates precisely what she does, and focuses on a feel-good benefit to a potential customer.

Reinforce your message!

Don't just send a client a letter, a leaflet, or a business card. Certainly don't just zap her an email. Call her. Knock on her door. Get yourself in a newspaper or journal she reads talking about your business and its benefits. Bump into her at networking events. Get your clients to speak highly of you to her.

Let her receive a simple message by hearing it from many different sources.

The message can be further reinforced if she hears from these varied sources at round about the same time. If in the space of a week, she has met you at a conference, read about you in a journal and been recommended to you by a peer, your message will be that much greater than the sum of the three individual messages. This is the Holy Grail of the PR world: simultaneous bombardment of the client with a simple message from multiple sources.

Try 10-touch marketing!

I can't remember where I heard this from, probably from some web surfing, but it lodged in my mind and I find it most helpful—if only to remind me how my own woeful marketing efforts fall way behind target every year. You need to develop a 10-touch marketing campaign for your key clients. In other words, your client needs to be reminded of your existence and your message 10 times during each year—that's more or less once a month, excluding the summer holidays. The touches can range from sending a Christmas card to a two-hour PowerPoint presentation, from a catch-up call to a liquid lunch on a Friday, from an email with an interesting attachment to a piece of business. But try to make it a 10-touch year for each key client.

Think of your message as a Post-it note. At the first contact, you slap it on her shoulder. After a while it starts to lose its stickiness. It needs another slap, most effectively from a different angle, another source. And so on. Your goal is to have that Post-it sticking on her shoulder week in, week out, so when the moment arrives that she needs your service, she reaches up to her shoulder, extracts the Post-it, and calls you first.

Don't let the client forget about you. Don't let the competition sneak in behind you with their own Post-it notes because you fail to get in touch with a client for three, six months. Don't lose work without even being asked to pitch. That really sucks! Keep slapping that Post-it! Try 10-touch marketing.

Pick up that phone!

Why are so many self-employed people so shy of picking up the phone? Like me. I would do anything rather than call a client and ask him how business is going (and— hint—whether there's any opportunity for me to be of help). I'll suddenly discover that bills need to be paid, letters written, computer scanned for viruses, garbage taken out—whatever, other than pick up the phone. I'd prefer to have a tooth pulled or make a speech in front of a thousand people with my pants down.

The problem is that we know only too well how much we hate receiving unsolicited telephone calls ourselves. Late Sunday afternoon and the phone rings. No, not your mom, sister or a family friend, but some hapless caller from an overseas call center trying to get you to upgrade your cell phone. Or worse, a tape recording congratulating you on winning some phony timeshare vacation. We worry that our client may find our call no less an annoyance.

Too bad. We have to do it. Especially for those of us in B2B services. Phoning is much more effective than the cop-out of emailing. An email can get buried in a client's inbox in seconds. If you hate calling as much as I do, here are some tips that have helped me:

> *Prepare your pitch.* Have your pitch on a piece of paper in front of you, with the opening line or lines typed out, word for word, and the rest in bullet points.

> *Psych yourself up.* It may be 11 A.M. and the phone has been silent all morning. You haven't opened your mouth since the kids went out of the door at 8:30. Clear your throat.

Look at your achievements around the office. Assert your right to make contact by telephone. Remember, you're great! A friend of mine who is a self-employed life coach has a Post-it note on his telephone on which he has written in red ink: You're the dog's bxxxxxks!* It seems to work! (Note: This is a humorous, British slang expression, referring to a prominent part of a dog's anatomy and meaning "simply the best," or the "bees knees." It (perhaps rudely, for which I apologize) illustrates the point that you should find your own way of boosting your confidence before you pick up the phone.

▷ *Stand up!* If there's one thing to remember, it's this. You will be communicating only with your voice. Your face, your eyes, your hands, the other main tools for communication, are unseen. Your voice will carry so much more conviction, authority *and energy* if you're standing. Imagine going to the theater and seeing all the actors deliver their lines seated. You'd soon be yawning. It's the same with the phone. Stand up! Don't let your client nod off!

▷ *Don't waste her time.* Have something of interest or use or amusement to discuss with her, something she's going to remember once the phone has been put down. Give her some tidbits on what's happening in the market, for example on what her competitors are up to. Don't just call her and ask if there's any work for you.

▷ *Remind her of what you have in common.* From previous meetings, hopefully you'll have found something, anything, that you and she have in common—live in the same part of town, brother went to same school, mutual friend, worked for similar companies, kids the same age, play the same sport, share the same hobby, support the same team, whatever. Try to tap into that commonality every time you speak to her. The personal touch is appreciated more and remembered longer than the impersonal, no matter how informative or articulate the pitch.

> ▸ *Angle for a follow-up.* Try to steer for some follow-up action, enabling you to contact her again the next day or week. You may refer her to some interesting article during the conversation, then email it to her later.

Another thought: Find a partner. If you're on your own, it's so much more difficult to get the difficult things done, especially client calling. With a partner, he'll give you no choice. Likewise, you'll give him no choice. The clients have to be called, so call them you will. You'll split the list between the two of you. And you'll compare notes at the end of the day. That's partner pressure to perform.

One final tip about the phone. Invest in a high-quality answering machine cum speakerphone. The hands-free speakerphone can be invaluable when you need to speak and make notes at the same time, although it's best not to use it when cold calling, when you should be standing up. The answering machine (or voicemail) is a godsend. You make a call, you get your client's voicemail, and you await the call back. Finally it comes, right at the end of the day. The kids are back from school, you've had a long, unrewarding day, you're tired, a little down. *Don't take it!* Leave it to your chirpy answering message.

Then you have two choices. You can either go through the whole process again—psyching yourself up, checking your script, standing up—and call her back. Or you can wait until you're feeling less tired, more affirmative, and more optimistic the following morning. The answering machine gives you the option.

Don't be shy about asking for referrals and testimonials!

There is no better way of getting an introduction to a new prospective client than being referred to him by an existing, satisfied client. That's a referral, and it's the lifeblood of the self-employed. Best of all is when your client will actually call up the new client, or mention you next time he sees him. Next best is when your client suggests you should contact this prospective client and gives you an agreed testimonial about your capabilities. This you can put into a letter and follow it up with a phone call a few days later. Still good is when your client just says "Sure, you can use my name" and you call the prospective client, saying, "So-and-so suggested I give you a call."

Right now we have a problem with a smelly drain. The emergency drainage guy has been here and told us that it's definitely not a sewerage problem, that all seems to be working fine. It's probably an old surface water drain that wasn't closed off properly when the garage was converted to a side extension by the previous owner five years ago. The laminated floor boards will have to be ripped up, so it's a job for a builder with a sound understanding of drainage and who's not too heavy handed in the carpentry department. Who to go to? We have no idea. If only someone could refer us to someone who'd be just right for sorting this out. If only we had a referral.

It's the same with your clients. They always have a choice of provider. That's the marketplace. But they'd feel a lot more comfortable using a provider that's been recommended to them by someone they know and trust, rather than taking pot luck with the yellow pages. They'd feel safer using a referral.

Don't be shy asking for referrals. You should ask every client for them. Here's a tip from Roy Sheppard's book. He recommends you try something like this: "Referrals are the lifeline in our business. That means we have to work so much harder ensuring clients like you are totally satisfied with our work. That way you'll hopefully recommend us to others."

Your client should agree with that. He'll like the fact that you are trying harder for his benefit. Then you can nudge the conversation on to some actual referrals—who else should you be talking to, would he be prepared to contact them, could you use his name, and would he be prepared to give you a testimonial?

Don't be greedy!

This is a simple tip in completing the sale. When you realize you're in pole position to win a piece of work, don't blow it by being greedy. Remember it's better to be utilized and earning something than unutilized and earning nothing. It's as simple as that.

I fell into this trap early in my self-employed career. I contacted a former client about an opportunity I thought he might be interested in, and where an associate and I were unusually well placed to help him. He emailed me back with just two words: "How much?" This client has deep pockets. I knew he could opt for a top tier consulting firm and get similar advice, but at twice, even thrice, my price. So I thought I'd go halfway, at 50% above my usual rates. Bargain for him, bonus for me. Wrong again. He didn't reply. I was under-utilized for the next couple of months. I could have done 10, maybe 20 days' work for that client at my usual rate, or even at 10 to 15% above. Instead I blew it. I hope I've learned that lesson.

Don't blow business by being greedy. Give good service at a good price. That'll be doubly good value to the customer. And he'll use you again.

If you have to, use an agent!

If you've read the books on sales and marketing, been to a seminar or two and tried out some of the tips above, and you still aren't selling as much as someone of your capabilities should be delivering, try an agent. Find someone who's a professional salesperson and well placed to help you. Someone with some good contacts, preferably. Someone with plenty of energy and a passion for selling. Such people do exist! Payment of 10%, even 15% commission on sales should more than repay itself, compared with the alternative of you remaining under-utilized.

The final word on selling and marketing yourself should rest, perhaps slightly out of context, with the inimitable Ms. West…

It's better to be looked over than overlooked. –Mae West

Four More Tips on Managing YouCo

Sales and marketing will be the most important function in YouCo. But it's not the only one. You also have to deliver the goods, run a tight, profitable business, and stash the cash. And you need to build your support network. Here are some more tips.

Don't forget the delivery

It goes without saying that you must be especially good at your job if you're going to be self employed. Unlike for an employee, there's no one to hide behind. You're on your own, totally exposed.

Ideally, you'll be demonstrably better at your job than most employees at competing companies. Unlike them, you'll have no brand name when you start up. Unless you're going to compete on cost, you'll have to offer a better or a distinctive service to win custom.

Although you must certainly place most emphasis in the early days on selling and marketing, don't forget to keep sharpening your tools in delivering the service.

It may be a timing issue. If you're thinking of leaving your company in six months' time and launching your own business a couple of months' later, you should think about whether you need to get in any further training or development *now*, rather than wait until you leave your present company.

Ideally you'll be ready for top-notch service delivery from the day you launch. Then all you need to do is bring the business in and deliver quality work.

Stay on top of the admin

Unfortunately there's more to running your own business than selling, marketing, and delivering. Remember, you're not just managing director, sales and marketing director and operations director. You're also finance director, receivables manager, bookkeeper, and clerk.

YouCo, like all small businesses, will have its fair share of red tape. Are you going to set up a company or a partnership, or just put your earnings through you? What bank accounts should you use? Do you need to register for a sales or value added tax? You should get advice on these and other startup financial decisions from an accountant.

Then there's also the regular admin work. You'll need to learn about book-keeping, filling in your sales tax forms and 101 other things needed to keep the business ticking over. It's over to you, for example, to pay the electricity bill on time, thereby saving the embarrassment of being cut off while serving the client—imagine you're a hair stylist and the power cuts off with your customer in curlers under the drier!

You may find some government-sponsored courses in your area focusing on the red tape of running your own business. Go to them. They may be dull, but they could save you grief later on.

Some companies set aside time for employees to catch up with their expenses and other admin, termed "laundry days," say one Monday morning each month. That's fine, it you like things scheduled. Personally, I like to stagger things. I know that I have to set aside two or three days each October to do my annual accounts and tax return. And an hour or so each quarter for the value added tax return. The rest I tackle when the in-basket rises above 6 inches!

However you address it, admin work must be kept under control, yet not eat into too much work time. It's a delicate balance, one that will come with experience, and the odd mistake.

Stash the cash!

There's one admin task, however, which takes precedence over all others. Revenue on your P&L account is great, profit even better. But that's all paperwork. Profit doesn't go into the bank. Only cash does, and it needs collecting. By you.

Cash management is often quoted in surveys as one of the main reasons why most small businesses fail. Entrepreneurs are so busy selling and managing the delivery of work, they fail to pay sufficient attention to the building up of receivables (trade debtors). Meanwhile they often have little choice but to meet their payables (trade creditors) on time or they won't be able to deliver. If they're not careful, they'll run out of cash.

No matter how marvelous the market, how brilliant the business concept, how excellent the entrepreneur, if she runs out of cash, the business is bust.

It can be difficult for a small businessperson to insist that a customer pays up on time. You don't want to make too much fuss, because you want his custom again. Tough. You have no choice. You have to explain to your customer that whatever service you provide does not include acting as his banker.

Ken Blanchard, Don Hutson and Ethan Willis, in their excellent little book, *The One Minute Entrepreneur*, remind us that "making it in business requires three very important things…CASH, CASH, CASH." You'd do well to bear all three in mind.

Tee up your support

We saw earlier that lack of support of colleagues is a major disadvantage of being self-employed. So we self-employed must have some support system in place to compensate. What will yours be in YouCo?

Consider these situations. I had a pretty good start to 2004 and set off with the family for a long summer holiday contentedly ahead of budget. By the middle of October I was still feeling good about the year. I had eight "leads" in my pipeline, one or two of which at least were bound to land in the final quarter, I thought, so sealing a good year. I was wrong. In the space of seven days, seven of the leads evaporated. One I lost in a fair fight with a competitor and in each of the others my clients were unable to proceed, or chose not to. It was rough. The eighth lead floated away a week later. It wasn't until early December that I picked up another piece of work.

So between August and November 2004, I earned not one penny. The highest earning member of my household was my 15-year-old daughter, who'd been doing two hours every Saturday morning teaching little ones at math class! And that was on minimum wage!

It could have been worse. Another freelance consultant I know, Dick, managed to sell just 15 days' paid work in 15 months. He went weeks without the telephone going. Imagine not just a silent morning, or a silent day, but a silent week. How about a silent month? It wasn't just disheartening, it was morale-sapping, confidence-shattering. Dick persevered, however, and is now thriving with the very same business proposition he was offering during that awful year. In retrospect, he seems to have gone through just a prolonged bout of bad luck.

Suppose such hard times were to happen to you. How would you cope? What would be your support mechanism? Mine, when I went through those wretched couple of weeks of vanishing business, was my family. Less work meant more time to play with the lad, so that couldn't be a bad thing, I reasoned.

Dick also relied on his family for support, along with sympathetic fellow freelancers. But he also had one other form of support that really helps in maintaining sanity if you're self-employed. He had a bank balance that was robust enough to withstand *one year's worth of zero business*. It's a sound philosophy to have. No one enters the world of self-employment expecting to earn nothing for a whole year. But if you know that if everything goes wrong, if work dries up for a full 12 months and yet you can still survive, that can be a huge dose of comfort during the bad times. It can help you sleep at night.

My advice? Before launching into self-employment, make sure you have your lines of support teed up. They include not just your family, friends, and associates, but also your bank account, or a bank manager prepared to extend adequate credit.

Still thinking of starting your own business? Be aware that's it's not a bed of roses. But then nowhere is. YouCo, on balance, is the place for me. How about you?

> *I wanted to be an editor or a journalist. I wasn't really interested in being an entrepreneur, but I soon found I had to become an entrepreneur in order to keep my magazine going.*
> —Richard Branson

Valerie's Outsourcing YouCo

Valerie enjoyed reading this chapter. When she set up her own business in independent economic consulting four years before business school, the Backing You! series of books did not exist. It would have helped. So much of Chapter 13 seems relevant to Valerie, not just in retrospect, but in reminding her of what still needs to be done to run a successful business.

These things stand out for her:

- Hers was a curious combination of the outsourcing and competing routes to self-employment. She left EconCo to set up her YouCo, but her first two projects were with her former employer, with her former colleagues becoming her new clients. The contracts she signed did not prohibit her from competing directly with EconCo for future projects and indeed her third and biggest ever engagement was a direct client commission by the Government of Uganda. EconCo did not actually pitch for that work, but they could have done—if they had known about it! So Valerie had from the outset two very different routes to market—subcontracting to her former employer (and its competitors) and directly to the end-user. This presented marketing challenges.
- Her utilization over the four years had been okay but not great and could have been improved by more targeted sales and marketing. The tips above would have been

of much help, but, having now read Chapters 10 to 12, Valerie has decided to engage a business coach post-MBA to guide her sales and marketing efforts.

- Valerie isn't greedy, but she is choosy. She could have upped utilization if she had been less particular in which countries she was prepared to work. But life is short, she knows exactly where she wants to live, and will remain content to lower her charges (and/or her utilization) to get there.

- Sometimes the cash was late in getting stashed. One direct client seemed to think that 12 to 18 months' receivables for all suppliers was par for the course, unless the supplier were prepared to accelerate matters under the table—and Valerie most certainly was not!

- Valerie enjoys great support from her family and a healthy bank balance—at 34, she does not even own a house—and she knows that such support has been the bedrock for the globe-trotting lifestyle she has enjoyed to date

"It's all about selling and marketing," she reads again. Yes, she has gotten away with it so far. But if she is to break into the new segment of business strategy, she'll need to make sales and marketing the lynch pin of her YouCo strategy.

Hari's Fresh Start YouCo

It's time to catch up with Hari, whom we also met in the introduction to this book. Hari's background to date has been more akin to that of Gary than Valerie as he went straight from university into an electronics manufacturing company as a trainee manager. But, unlike Gary, his main motivation for doing an MBA is to explore new career directions. In particular, he has long been enthused at the idea of starting his own business. His role models are less the CEOs of corporate giants than those who started and developed their own businesses—not necessarily to Bill Gatesian heights, but into vibrant, sustainable, profitable $100 million-plus businesses. Hari eagerly enrolled in the second year elective course in Entrepreneurship. And he has an idea. This idea germinated during the final assignment in this elective, one where he and fellow student, now wife, Concha were tasked to put together everything they had learned into a coherent, potentially viable business venture. They came up with a proposition that wowed the class and the lecturer in the final presentation.

Hari's former job had involved much travel, too much of it. Concha likewise, a former IT consultant, had travelled endlessly. For this assignment they did some brainstorming on ways to make business travel less of a hassle , more fun. They came up with a load of ideas, from the dull to the whacky. But Hari's was special, and Concha added the extra touch.

Hari figured that wherever he travelled in the world of business he saw the same thing, especially in financial districts and airport lounges: elegant women sporting hundreds of dollars' worth of designer clothing on their bodies, designer shoes on their feet, designer handbag in their hands, but tacky $20 laptop cases slung over their shoulders! Businessmen too, though usually without the handbag. They all sported bland, shapeless, functional polyester cases enclosing an object of miraculous technological sophistication. Could there be a viable market for quality, leather, design-led laptop cases for men? asked Hari. And one coordinated with designer handbags for women? added Concha?

They certainly convinced the class, and the lecturer. They look at this chapter. Of the four typical situations for an employee to shift to self-employed, theirs is indisputably the fourth—it's a fresh start.

And they seem to have found a niche. There were no designer laptop cases on the market, period. This could either be one of Bill Bridges's "unmet needs" or an unwanted need. But even if it were the former, could the need be met at a profit?

One thing is for sure. Hari and Concha are now so fired up by this new venture prospect, there can be no returning to their former jobs. Their hearts will not be in them. They will be unbackable.

They resolve to become entrepreneurs, to switch careers. They will move on to Part III of this book, but skipping Chapters 15 and 16. They know where their passion lies. They have already screened out other jobs; in fact they haven't even bothered to think about them. They know where they want to go, they have a shortlist of one and only one job, so they move straight to Chapter 17 on where best to back....

YouCo's Runaway Success

This Oregonian was a keen middle-distance runner at the University of Oregon in Eugene, joined the Army for one year's active duty, and then enrolled at Stanford Graduate School of Business. He attended a Small Business class: "That class was an 'aha!' moment" .... Frank Shallenberger defined the type of person who was an entrepreneur—and I realized he was talking to me. I remember after saying to myself: 'This is really what I would like to do.' " He wrote a paper for the class, "Can Japanese Sports Shoes Do to German Sports Shoes What Japanese Cameras Did to German Cameras?" They were to do just that, or rather he was. After graduation, he travelled to Japan, discovered some high quality, low-cost sports shoes, and returned home with a sample. He sent them to his former coach at the University of Oregon, who was so impressed that they formed a company together. Initially selling from the back of a truck at track meets, Phil Knight backed his YouCo hands-on. His Nike went on to become the largest sports shoe and apparel supplier in the world.

14

Are You More Backable?

Do things Look Sunnier?
Your Suns & Clouds Chart Revisited

Let's recap. Part II is all about making you more backable. So far you have envisioned the ideal provider, reset your sights, and identified the capability gap. You have built a strategy to bridge it, possibly focused on the launching of YouCo, and developed an action plan.

Has your Suns & Clouds chart of Chapter 8 become sunnier? Has the balance of risk and opportunity shifted in your favor?

Have you become more backable in your current or pre-MBA job or business?

The answer, hopefully, should be a resounding *yes!* That, after all, is the purpose of Part II.

Do things look sunnier?

The strategy you developed in Chapter 12, which set out to address the K2 gap you identified in Chapter 11, originated from the brainstorming and scenario development you undertook in Chapter 10. This in turn took as its starting point the risks and opportunities you assessed in Chapter 8 of Part I.

Hopefully, therefore, your strategy will have been centered around either reducing the likelihood and/or the impact of the risks identified in Part I, or improving the likelihood and/or the impact of the opportunities.

Take a look at the risks and opportunities you assessed in Part I. How will they have changed as a result of your new strategy, assuming it is implemented successfully? What if your strategy is implemented with only partial success?

Are some of the risks now less likely? Or, if not, then with lesser impact? Have new risks been introduced by pursuing your new strategy? If so, are they containable?

What about the opportunities? Are they now more likely? Or, if not, then with bigger impact? Has your new strategy identified new opportunities? How promising? How likely, how big?

How has this impacted on your Suns & Clouds chart? Are the risks and opportunities now better balanced? Is your chart overall more sunny? It should be. That's what your strategy was designed to do.

Would You Have Backed the Early Madonna?

We took in Chapter 12 Madonna as an example of someone whose crystal clear strategy has propelled her to the top of her industry's earnings league year after year. Let's see how that strategy may have affected her Suns & Clouds chart over time.

Suppose you're a prospective investor, it's 1982, and you show up at a grubby studio in downtown Manhattan to meet a young woman with grandiose aspirations of stardom. Ms. Ciccone is a dancer who can sing a bit. She's a hard worker, but she's hard up. She's been scraping a living in New York City for five years, through a succession of low paid jobs, including modeling in the nude (as subsequently featured in glossy magazines).

She has, however, made some progress as an entertainer. She has worked with a number of modern dance companies, been a backing dancer on a world tour and played vocals and drums with a rock band, the *Breakfast Club*. She has written and produced a number of solo disco and dance songs. These brought her to the attention of Sire Records, with whom she has signed a singles deal. Her first single, *Everybody*, written by herself and for which she received $5,000, has just come out and is proving a hit on the dance charts and in the clubs. However, it has made no impact on the Billboard Hot 100.

Suppose she needs backing, whether for personal reasons or to invest in some promotional activity. She thinks an album deal is imminent. And stardom just around the corner. You see her as high risk (see Figure 14.1).

Figure 14.1. Would You Have Backed Madonna in 1982?

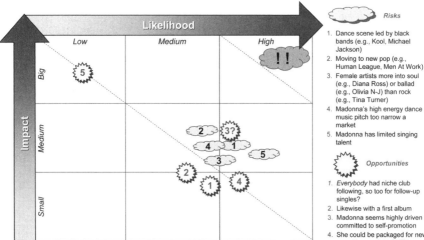

Would you have backed her? On the basis of the Suns & Clouds alone, possibly not. Music trends seemed to have been moving in other directions. *Everybody* was successful only in the small niche of club music. She might have followed that up with another single or two, even an album. But they too might have found just a niche following. She was a good dancer but a rather screechy singer. She dressed and looked sexy but so did loads of other dancers.

But you may have seen something else. One opportunity (sun 3) may have stood out. You would have spent some time with her and may have caught a glimpse of what many later came to recognize. A relentless drive, evidenced perhaps by her life over the previous few years as she painstakingly built up her performing experience. A steely professionalism. An extrovertism bordering on the exhibitionist, with a readiness to blend her very person with her image. Boundless ambition. This was special. You may well have decided to back her.

One year on and her Suns & Clouds (in Figure 14.2) will have changed out of recognition. Her first album, *Madonna*, reached the top 10 on the U.S. album charts and five of its singles became hits. One of them, *Holiday*, went on to sell 12 million copies. The main risks concerning the breadth of her appeal would have evaporated. The main opportunity—of her being able to carve out a new genre of white, female dance-rock music with huge popular appeal—was now looking not just conceivable but likely.

Figure 14.2. **Would You Have Backed Madonna One Year Later?!**

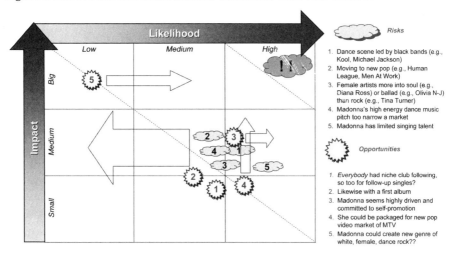

If you hadn't backed her the year before, you wouldn't be able to afford to now. Opportunities were unbounded.

After *Sex*?

Madonna's Suns & Clouds would have stayed more or less as described above through the 1980s. Albums such as *Like a Virgin, True Blue,* and *Like a Prayer* kept her at the top of the charts. Meanwhile she also received critical acclaim in the movie, *Desperately Seeking Susan*, although roles in other movies didn't earn such plaudits.

Then in 1992 came *Sex*, an extraordinary, coffee table book of photographs featuring Madonna in an array of sexually explicit poses. The book was largely damned by the media as being narcissistic, some said pornographic. It was followed by an album called *Erotica*, which met with similar criticism. The video accompanying the (successful) lead single was withdrawn from MTV. Not long afterwards, Madonna took the leading female role in a movie, *Body of Evidence*, a smuttier take on *Basic Instinct*. The movie flopped, further denting Madonna's appeal. Had she blown it? Had her star waned? Were these ventures into sexual explicitness just a sad, final fling for an entertainer who had passed her sell-by date?

Suppose that she had needed some backing then. Sure, she already had her millions of dollars stacked away in property and investments. But suppose she wanted more. Suppose she needed cash to buy another spectacular property, a virtual palace for $25 million? Would you have backed her? Would you have thought her capable of continuing to generate the kind of multimillion dollar income stream every year she had achieved in the 1980s?

Back in 1993, would you have thought that Madonna would recover from such a critical mauling, from an apparent obliteration of her fan base? That she would have gone on to produce further platinum-selling albums (like *Ray of Light* in 1998)? To star in a top-grossing movie (like *Evita* in 1996)?

You may well have done. For all the risks, the dominant feature in Madonna's Suns & Clouds would have been her *consistent strategy*. Her drive for self-publicity and capacity for self-reinvention may well have convinced you that, just as she dragged down her celebrity star rating in 1992, so too could she yank it up again in years to come. And perhaps she may have learned some lessons from 1992 and be a trifle more circumspect in her future reinventions. Her chart may have looked like Figure 14.3.

Figure 14.3. Would You Have Backed Madonna Ten Years Later?

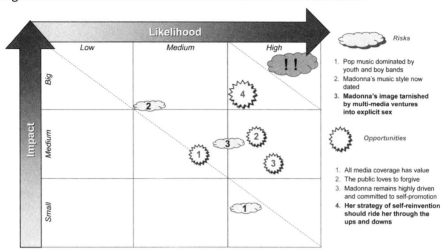

The one thing you know for sure in the world of entertainment is that an entertainer needs to keep her name in the headlines, her face on the front covers of magazines, whether in praise or condemnation. Any news is good news. No news is obscurity. You're aware that in her year of sexual exhibitionism, Madonna had been even more in our faces than before. You may have figured that all she had to do was to continue to reinvent herself, preferably into something entirely different—into an Argentinean folk heroine, perhaps, or an Eastern mystic, or an all American girl, or a devoted mother, or a lady of the manor, whatever—and she could postpone her sell-by date indefinitely. The strategy seemed brilliant. You would surely have backed that strategy and would have been pleased that, 13 years later, in 2006, her *Confessions Tour*, still controversial, with provocative deployment of a crucifix and crown of thorns, became the highest grossing global tour by a female artist ever.

Would You Back Richard Branson's Virgin Galactic?

Here's another example of a consistently successful *Stand-Out!* strategy. Richard Branson is an entrepreneur the like of whom has seldom, if ever, been nurtured in Britain. He has launched successful new ventures in areas of activity as diverse as music and money management, mobile telephony and airlines, all under the brand name of Virgin—the name of his first business after leaving high school in 1970. This was a mail order record business, and he soon followed this with a small record shop on London's Oxford Street. He later opened a recording studio and had a stroke of luck when his first artist produced a first song that sold 5 million copies. Branson didn't look back, and both his recording and retail businesses took off.

In 1984 he made an extraordinary detour, venturing into the airline business. He knew it was risky: "We started the business in 1984 and almost all my colleagues at Virgin said I was completely mad to go into the airline business. The newspapers said calling an airline Virgin was mad." (Source: www.virgin.com) Airlines are indeed notoriously risky enterprises and many investors won't touch them with a bargepole. History is littered with airlines that have gone under. Remember Pan Am? Eastern? Laker Airways, the original no frills, cut-price, trans-Atlantic carrier? Yet all these companies were run and backed by people who knew about airlines, not by music entrepreneurs!

Would you have backed Branson in his Virgin Atlantic venture? You can imagine the Suns & Clouds chart. A fearsome agglomeration of thunderous dark clouds blowing ominously toward the top right-hand corner. With one sun shining defiantly in their midst.

This sun would have been a phenomenal brand name, associated not just with quality, value-for-money service provision and a perception of the little man fighting against the global Goliaths. But one also suggestive of excitement and glamour. This was raised to a new level following the airline launch. Branson embarked on a series of world speed record attempts to keep the brand in the headlines, usually involving Branson himself. In 1986 his boat, *Virgin Atlantic Challenger II,* broke the record for crossing the Atlantic Ocean. A year later he did the same in the hot air balloon, *Virgin Atlantic Flyer.* He later achieved the same feat flying across the Pacific Ocean, before making several attempts to circumnavigate the globe in a hot air balloon. Foiled by weather, these attempts proved unsuccessful, though not so in terms of publicity.

Aided no doubt by this high-profile marketing strategy, Branson's airline has been an astonishing success. It has held its own both with its rival British Airways and with American transatlantic carriers. It has survived two severe downturns in the air industry without government subsidization or resort to Chapter 11.

Branson has now moved on to the new travel frontier: space tourism. His new venture, *Virgin Galactic,* plans to launch six paying passengers at a time (plus two crew) into space from a spaceport in New Mexico. They will be flown to a suborbital altitude of around 60 miles, where they will be allowed to unstrap and experience weightlessness for about six minutes. Would you back him?

You may ask why this question is relevant to this book? Virgin Galactic is a business venture and this is a book about backing you as an individual. The answer is that a business, certainly a new venture, is often little more than the aggregate talents and experience of the entrepreneurs behind it. In this case, you'd be backing Branson.

What would the Suns & Clouds for Virgin Galactic look like? Some would argue that this venture makes even Virgin Atlantic look like a safe bet! At least the backers of a new airline know its cost structure (and sensitivity to fuel prices). They understand the technology and appreciate the risks of technical failure or sabotage.

But for space tourism, technology is unproven and still developing. Investors will be all too aware of the sad demise of space shuttles *Challenger* and *Columbia.* There may also be health risks since space tourists won't have the preflight conditioning and training of astronauts. And the economics are uncertain. How many flights per year per space-craft? How much will people be prepared to pay (once the rich have been there and back)? How many competitors, with how many space-craft?

These risks will shape some formidable clouds in Virgin Galactic's Suns & Clouds. But the one outstanding sun found in the Virgin Atlantic chart will still be shining for Virgin Galactic. The brand name remains stellar. And Branson himself is hot on the marketing trail again with plans for him and his family to be on board for Virgin Galactic's maiden voyage. You can imagine the fanfare and media coverage.

Branson's Stand-Out! strategy, like Madonna's, remains consistent. It hasn't always worked—Virgin Trains hasn't been a runaway success—but more often than not it has. Would you back Virgin Galactic?

Your Suns & Clouds Chart Revisited

After the stellar examples of Madonna and Richard Branson, back, literally, to this planet. Hopefully the strategy you've developed will have made you too more backable.

Take another look at your Suns & Clouds chart of Chapter 8. Have some of the risks diminished in probability or impact as a result of your strategy? Have some of the opportunities shifted to the right?

Has the balance of risk and opportunity improved? May it even have been transformed?

Or has your strategy made your chart riskier, but with potentially higher returns?

Let's hope the answer to at least one of the above questions is a resounding "yes!"—that was the purpose of developing a winning strategy.

Let's recap where you are. In Part I, you concluded that you were backable in your current or pre-MBA business or job. You may not have been wholly satisfied in your work before reading Part I, but afterwards you felt better about it. You proceeded to Part II and followed some techniques on how to make yourself more backable. Hopefully that is what you are now, or are in the process of becoming so.

> *I believe the true road to pre-eminent success in any line is to make yourself master in that line. I have no faith in the policy of scattering one's resources, and in my experience I have rarely if ever met a man who achieved pre-eminence in money making … who was interested in many concerns.* –Andrew Carnegie

If, however, you were not absolutely convinced in Part I of your backability in your current or pre-MBA job or business, and if in Part II those doubts were not lain to rest, then you should move on to Part III. This is primarily aimed at those who found that they were not backable in Part I and are thinking of switching to a new career, one that they feel passionate about.

Could that be of interest to you too?

Is Valerie More Backable?

Valerie is eager to see how her new marketing-led strategy has affected her Suns & Clouds chart for a return to independent economic consulting career after her MBA. She finds it has improved terrifically (see Figure 14.4). The prioritizing and allocating of resources to sales and marketing have improved the balance of risk and opportunity in two main ways:

- The risk of her undisputed weakness in marketing's adverse impact on profit has been substantially mitigated, with cloud 4 moving leftwards on the chart.
- The opportunity of Valerie exploiting her MBA to penetrate the new segment of business strategy will be boosted by the investment in marketing, with sun 5 moving to the right.

The overall balance now looks attractive. Suns 3 and 4 stand out clearly from all risks...with one possible exception—Valerie's attitude.

Figure 14.4. Risks and Opportunities for Valerie's New Strategy in a Return to Economic Consulting Post-MBA

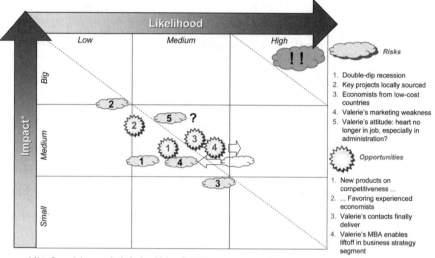

* Note: Over and above *your backer's view* of likely profits in three years' time

Valerie learned from Part I that her heart would no longer be in her independent economic consulting career if most of her projects were in public administration. Likewise, she knows she would continue to relish the job if the projects were in economic competitiveness or, in particular, her target new segment of business strategy.

But might she actually be more passionate about a career in another field altogether? She's 34 years old, so it's better to think about career change now rather than in ten years' time.

There's only one way to find out. Valerie resolves to continue the path set out in this book. Let's see what Part III offers, she thinks, there's nothing to lose.... We'll catch up with her again in Chapter 17.

Is Gary More Backable?

We last came across Gary in Part I, Chapters 8 and 9, where we learned that he was backable in a return to his pre-MBA job as a manager at UtiliCo in North Chicago. Risks were of such low likelihood and/ or impact as to be negligible, other than one: Gary's presentational shortcomings—the only likely constraint on him making it one day to board level.

So Gary pores over Part II of this book. His generic strategy has to be Stand Out!—not in the sense of a Madonna-style performer, but as a manager—very sound, highly competent, the safest pair of hands in the company. He wants to go for the goal, to be the ideal provider (of managerial services) tomorrow. To get there, he recognizes that he also needs to build in some elements of the Sharpen Act! generic strategy.

Gary sums up his strategy in a sentence: To build on his competitive position at UtiliCo through sustained investment of cash, time, and energy in developing managerial competence, namely further varied experience and training post-MBA, especially in presentational skills.

Gary embarks on some research during one of the few and precious breaks from his MBA assignments. He is reticent about contacting his boss at UtiliCo to request formal training. As far as he knows, she remains largely unaware of how diffident he is at presenting. He fears that if he alerts her, she may realize that, yes, Gary isn't really that hot at presenting and perhaps she should use someone else next time. On the other hand, she might be delighted that Gary is seeking to improve his capabilities on behalf of the firm. It's a close call. On balance, Gary doesn't feel like taking the risk.

Gary decides he has to do this further training on his own, in his spare time after the MBA. If necessary, he'll take some time off work. He investigates his strategic alternatives. A few minutes of Googling and he finds a one-week residential course in presentational skills and public speaking for $3,999. The country club setting sounds lovely, but that seems more like the sort of course a company like UtiliCo should pay for! He also finds a two-day, nonresidential course in downtown Chicago for $1,950 and a one-day course for $650. Finally, he finds a seemingly more cost-effective, ten-week, one-evening-per-week course at a local community college for $289—which would be much more what he'll be able to afford after his investment in the MBA.

Gary figures that the one- or two-day courses will probably be a waste of time. He might learn what he was supposed to do, but there would be little chance for him to practice. So he decides to try the local college for a few weeks (alternative A), and if that doesn't help much then he might have to bite the bullet and invest in the country club course (alternative B).

Then Gary's wife calls him on his cell phone. She has just come across an advertisement in *Today's Chicago Woman*, which reads: "Hate, hate, hate public speaking? Call Aileen at 847.876.2455." "Why don't you give her a call?" suggests Gary's wife.

He does. Aileen is delighted, and tells him about this public speaking club she started a couple of years back that meets every two weeks. He is most welcome to come along and check it out. Where is it? Amazingly, it is in the village of Glenview, in Cook County, a mere 10-minute car ride from Gary's home.

From the moment he walks in the door, Gary feels at ease. This is a world apart from the atmosphere at Northwestern, where his fellow MBA students professed mutual support but could not help themselves engaging in covert rivalry! In this public speaking club, Gary feels embraced. He is not alone—all are there to improve their communication skills. All are applauded and encouraged in their efforts. All are evaluated positively and warmly, with helpful recommendations on what to work on next. All are learning and developing in a fun and astonishingly supportive environment.

What is more, and incredible, having invested huge sums on his MBA program, membership in this club would set Gary back all of $16 for the joining fee, then a mere $3 a month in membership dues!

Gary signs up straightaway. He doesn't have to bother with the community college, and certainly not with the country club. Alternatives A or B? In the trash can! He's found the solution. It had been right on his doorstep. And it is all but free!

This is where we'll leave Gary. He was backable before. Now he is highly backable. Suns shine supreme in his Suns & Clouds chart (see Figure 14.5). With an MBA under his belt, a robust strategy of building on his managerial strengths, and his presentational shortcomings on course to being eradicated, he is well on the road to career success.

Figure 14.5. Risks and Opportunities for Gary's New Strategy in a Return to UtiliCo Post-MBA

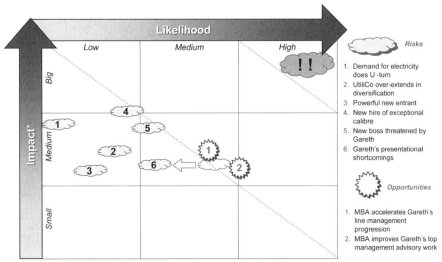

* Note: Over and above Gareth's pay expectations

A Word on Toastmasters International

What was this extraordinary organization that Gary discovered? Does it exist in reality? Indeed it does and it's called Toastmasters International. In Gary's Chicago area alone, including Du Page, Lake, McHenry, and Cook counties, there are more than 60 such clubs. As of November 2010, there are around 12,500 Toastmaster clubs in over 110 countries across the world, with 260,000 members. Three in five members are in the United States, with a further one in ten in Canada. Half of them are female, half male. Seven in ten are aged from 35 to 50, and eight in ten have a college degree. You can find Toastmasters clubs from Alaska to Alabama, Barbados to Brussels, Costa Rica to China. Alumni include management guru, Tom Peters.

I've been a member since 1990, a founder member of London's second oldest club, London Corinthians Toastmasters. Over the years, I've seen scores of people transformed. I've seen petrified speakers learn to control their nerves and ultimately, incredibly, enjoy performing. I've seen dull speakers come alive. I've seen good speakers become captivating.

Presentational and public speaking skills are initially like cycling or typing skills. They're not inherited, they can be learned. They're difficult at first to grasp, easier over time. Once learnt, they become more like the golf swing—best kept tuned up through regular practice. Lack of practice can allow faults to creep in—whether swiping from the top in golf, or hands creeping up to the face in speaking. Toastmasters is the ideal forum for such practice. There are hundreds—thousands— of real-life Garys whose work and social life has been uplifted by Toastmasters clubs across the world.

A chance ad meant that Gary didn't need to evaluate his strategic alternatives. He didn't even need an action plan. It was all too obvious. He just needed to turn up every other Thursday evening and his communications skills would improve, steadily and surely. Irreversibly. He pursued a strategy where the investment costs were not far off zero, the risks negligible, the payback immediate, and the returns astronomical.

For those readers who aren't members of Toastmasters, let me leave you with this thought. You're reading a book on career development, perhaps career change. You're clearly interested in self development. There's no more effective program for self-development worldwide than Toastmasters International. Type the word Toastmasters and the name of your town or county into Google, find the nearest club, and go along as a guest.

You have nothing to lose. You'll come across a bunch of like-minded souls. At worst, you'll have a good evening's entertainment. For free.

At best, it'll transform your life.

Part III
Backing Your Passion

Introduction

> 66 *Ask not what the world needs. Ask what makes you come alive…*
> *then go do it. Because what the world needs are people who have come alive.*
> –Howard Thurman

If you concluded in Part I that you wouldn't back you in your current or pre-MBA job, then Part III helps you to find a post-MBA career that you love *and* where you'll be backable.

It shows you how to back the passion in you.

Part III is also for you if you went to business school straight from your bachelor's and are seeking your first serious job, a job you'll feel passionate about and, crucially, where you'll be backable.

Part III introduces a novel, top-down approach to career change. There are many excellent books that can guide you on finding the right job from the bottom up—identifying your interests, values, transferable skills, and then finding jobs that match them. You can try the classic *What Color is my Parachute?* by Richard N. Bolles, or the clearer, crisper derivative *What Color is my Parachute? For Teens* by Carol Christen and Richard N. Bolles. Or the lucid and methodical *Changing Careers for Dummies* by Carol L. McClelland. Or the energetic *I Don't Know What I Want, but I Know it's Not This* by Julie Jansen. Or if you're thinking of setting up your own business, *Creating You & Co.* by William Bridges. Part III doesn't decry these approaches. On the contrary, they have helped thousands of people make life-enhancing career changes.

This book sets out an alternative. It delivers a *top-down* approach, a *demand-driven* approach, a *passion-driven* approach: starting from where you want to be, where the passion lies, and then assessing just how realistic your chances are of succeeding in that field—and what you can do to shorten the odds.

Part III takes as its building blocks some of the approaches and techniques already laid out in Parts I and II. The market assessment techniques of Chapters 2 and 3, and the competitive position tools of Chapters 4 to 6 will be revisited sketchily in Chapter 16, and in greater depth in Chapter 17. There too you'll find again the Suns & Clouds chart of Chapter 8, as you assess your backability in your short-listed jobs with passion. Chapter 18 returns to the techniques developed in Part II and shows you how to develop a strategy for improving your chances of success in your preferred field.

Part III starts, however, with the discovery of passion. Chapter 15, Where Is the Passion?, asks you to find the field of work where your passion lies. Whose job, or business, do you most covet? If you were in that business, you would be so fired up, so full of passion, that work wouldn't seem like work at all. It doesn't matter at this stage whether you believe you could actually do this job, run this business. The important thing is to imagine what you would love to be doing during the day job. You'll be given some tips on how you can come up with scores of ideas of jobs with passion. Then you'll be shown how to pull out a dozen or so of those jobs with the most passion, ready to be screened in the next chapter.

The purpose of Chapter 16, Screening for Reality, is to screen the long list down to a short list of three or four jobs that not only have passion but also where you could be successful. You'll take a first cut at assessing how attractive the markets are for these jobs and how well placed you would be to get in and succeed in them. You'll be introduced to the *Hwyl* Star chart.

Many of the longer-shot, more aspirational jobs in your long list will be screened out, and it's possible that you won't have enough left to make a short list. That's no problem. This should be seen as an iterative process. You'll return to the full list of the previous chapter and bring forward a new long list of a dozen or so jobs, drawn from the next level down of your passion rating. You'll repeat the screening process, you may even have to do it once again, before finally ending up with your short list of jobs that not only have passion but offer sound prospects of you getting in and succeeding at them.

Chapter 17, Where Best to Back?, will guide you through the work you must now undertake to narrow your field further. You'll need to do further research, especially on the most promising job or business. You'll need to speak to people who do that job, and their "customers". The tools introduced in Part I should now be redeployed in detail. You need to understand where the market is going, how tough is the competition, how well placed you would be, whether you will make your earnings plan, and how risky it would be to back you. You'll be able to firm up the placement of these short-listed jobs on the *Hwyl* Star chart and conclude which you should back, and which should be kept in reserve as a plan B.

Chapter 18, Shortening the Odds, can be crucial. Depending on your time scale, you may be able to improve your prospects of getting into and succeeding in your target job. You need to consider whether some of the tools deployed in Part II can be of help. Do you need to build on your strengths or work on some weaknesses? Which of the Stand Out!, easyU! or Sharpen Act! strategies would shorten the odds of success in your target job? How would that improve its positioning in the *Hwyl* Star chart ? If you were to do the same or similar to prepare for other short-listed jobs, would that change their relative positioning? By the end of this chapter, you will have planned how to go about improving your chances of success in your target job or business.

In Chapter 19, Pursuing the Passion, we'll look at key steps you need to take to start your own business or go for the job with passion identified in Chapter 18. It will not be comprehensive—that's for specialist manuals on the job-hunting process, for example, Daniel Porot's *The PIE Method for*

Career Success: A Unique Way to Find Your Ideal Job. But this book will divulge some tips, such as on interviews, which have been learned by the author along the way, with examples and anecdotes.

Part III will show you how to find your ideal post-MBA job or business and improve your prospects of getting in and succeeding there. It will inspire you to back your passion!

15

Where Is the Passion?

The Bottom-up Approach to Career Change
A Top-down, Demand-driven, Passion-driven Approach
Knowing When You've Found the Passion
Tips on Finding the Passion
Drawing Up Your Long List

> *Life is to be lived. If you have to support yourself, you had bloody well better find some way that is going to be interesting.*
> –Katherine Hepburn

This chapter helps you to find the field of work where your passion lies. Whose job, or business, would you most covet post-MBA? If you were doing that job, you would be so fired up that work wouldn't seem like work at all. The job would consume you with passion. You might even feel the *hwyl*, the Celtic concept of passion, fervor, spirit, which can lift you to extremes of success!

Note: Don't be disheartened by the apparent absence of vowels in *hwyl!* The word actually contains two vowels. There are seven vowels in the Welsh language, the familiar five as in English plus "w" and "y." *Hwyl* is pronounced as "who-yl."

No matter at this stage whether you think you could actually do this job, run this business. The important thing is to imagine what you would love to be doing during the day job. You'll be given some tips in this chapter on how you can come up with scores of jobs with varying degrees of passion. Then you'll be shown how to pull out a dozen or so of those jobs with the *most* passion, ready to be screened in the next chapter.

First, however, let's do a quick review of the traditional, bottom-up, and yes, well-proven approaches to career change.

The Bottom-up Approach to Career Change

There are some excellent books for guiding you through a bottom-up process on career change. Let's take it from the top.

What Color Is Your Parachute? by Richard N. Bolles

Bolles's *Parachute* should be your first stop if you're embarking on a job search. Revised annually since 1970, it's packed with advice, experience, anecdotes, and wisdom.

For a life-changing job search, which is what Part III of this book is about, Bolles suggests you build your own personal flower. This represents pictorially the job of your dreams. There are six petals surrounding the core, each representing an influencing factor, as follows:

- ▷ Where the job should be located.
- ▷ Which field the job should be in (defined by your favorite interests or fields of fascination).
- ▷ What type of organization (taking into account your favorite people environments).
- ▷ What values the organization should have.
- ▷ What working conditions you would expect.
- ▷ What salary and level of responsibility you would expect.

At the core of this flower are your favorite transferable skills. The dream job will not only enable you to apply your favorite skills, but will also satisfy your desires for location, interests, culture, values, working conditions, and service terms. You then attempt a match with reality. You live with your flower, take it around with you, and show it to friends and people whose opinion you respect. Hopefully a picture of the ideal job will begin to emerge. The book then helps you set out to secure it.

Bolles's approach is primarily from the bottom up. You carefully work out what you are good at, what you want, what you believe in, and methodically derive the job that fits you.

Backing You, MBA! takes a different approach, a top-down approach, a passion-driven approach. Here we start by looking at jobs you aspire to do and *then* see whether they fit you.

There are many other good books on career change, on moving to the job of your dreams. They too offer a primarily bottom-up approach. Here are some of the best.

Changing Careers for Dummies by Carol L. McClelland

This book starts on similar territory to *Parachute*. You're encouraged to set the stage for career change by considering your personality or temperament, your values, your health, your hobbies and interests, your desired location and the impact of your family on your work. It then seeks to find out what your ideal work environment would be, in terms of schedule, type of organization, terms of service, and type of colleagues.

The book shows you how to search for your hidden treasure—your passion. It starts by asking you to identify your "skills that make time fly." Here it borrows from Howard Gardner's *Frames of Mind: The Theory of Multiple Intelligences* and asks you to consider which of these innate talents or intelligences are most applicable to you:

> ‣ Do you think in words?
> ‣ Do you think in a logical, organized fashion?
> ‣ Do you connect well with others?
> ‣ Do you have a good eye?
> ‣ Do you have a good sense of your body?
> ‣ Do you appreciate nature and its creatures?

The book asks you to identify your favorite topics, processes, internal drivers, tools, industries, client group, and meaning in work. These are all assembled to record your "hottest interests and passions." Each one becomes a card in a deck of cards and you're asked to deal yourself a succession of hands of four cards each. This technique is used to brainstorm a range of new careers, each grounded in your very own passions.

This is in some ways a similar approach to *Parachute's* flower. But the next part of the book moves on to become a highly informative career guide. Each of the innate intelligences listed above is given its own chapter, and McClelland gives you creative guidance on what career choices may be available to you within each of those intelligences. Under each intelligence, you are given both standard and "out of the box" options on career choice and advice on where to look next. This book is both a stimulating *and* practical contribution to career change.

I Don't Know What I Want, but I Know It's Not This by Julie Jansen

This is a different type of book. It's written in a more chatty style, and it's stacked on each page with examples of people who have tried this, done that. It asks you to consider in Part I what your work situation is, before tailoring Part III of the book to each of five generic work situations, which she describes as:

> Where's the meaning?
> Been there, done that, but still need to earn
> Bored and plateaued
> Yearning to be on your own
> One toe in the retirement pool

For each work situation, Jansen offers a three-step process: complete the self-assessment, explore roadblocks and opportunities, and create an action plan.

Part II of the book covers familiar territory. She asks you to think about where you want to be, by evaluating your values, attitudes and readiness to change in one chapter, and your personality preferences, interests, and skills in another. It's the bottom-up approach again, applied innovatively to the five work situations in Part III of the book.

Creating You & Co by William Bridges

We've come across this distinctive book earlier, in Chapter 13 on *Backing YouCo!* The meat of Bridges's book is a clever variant on the bottom-up approach to career change. He suggests that you should find and then mine your DATA, an acronym that refers to your desires, abilities (talents you were born with), temperament (and vocation), and assets (qualifications and experience). It's a thought-provoking take by a leading academic in organizational and individual transitions. The final part of the book is a useful look at turning your DATA into a business—finding an opportunity, creating a product, and running a micro-business.

Other books you may find useful are:

> *How to Get a Job You'll Love* by John Lees—a leading British careers coach gives his take on values, interests ("your house of knowledge"), skills, personality, and intelligences (again using the Gardner approach). Through a "field generator," Lees guides you on how to identify suitable fields of work.

> ▸ *Do What You Are: Discover the Perfect Career for You Through the Secrets of Personality Type* by Paul Tieger and Barbara Barron-Tieger—these experienced trainers help you identify your personality type and find the job that best suits it. The authors provide career advice and highlight the strengths and pitfalls of each personality type with real-life examples.

> ▸ *The Pathfinder: How to Choose or Change Your Career for a Lifetime of Satisfaction and Success* by Nicholas Lore—the founder of a career counseling network sets out techniques for designing a new career direction to fit your talents, personality, needs, goals and values and "how to deal with the *yeah but* voices in your head that keep you going back to the same ill-fitting job, day after day."

> ▸ *Build You Own Rainbow: A Workbook for Career and Life Management* by Barrie Hopson and Mike Scally—experienced British career counselors lead you through a workbook based on their long running workshops on career and life management. The book is in six sections, addressing these questions: Who am I? Where am I now? How satisfied am I? What changes do I want? How do I make them happen? What if it doesn't work out?

My advice to you is simple, and enjoyable. Take yourself off to a good library, or to one of those super bookshops with sofas and latte, and skim them all. They are all good. Each has its own distinctive take. Any one of them could be of huge help to you. Select the two or three that suit your own preference for approach and style of writing. Then borrow or buy them, get stuck in, learn, and enjoy!

A Top-down, Demand-driven, Passion-driven Approach

This book suggests an alternative to the bottom-up, skills-driven approach. It suggests a top-down, demand-driven, passion-driven approach. Instead of starting bottom-up from what your values, interests, and skills are, it starts top-down with where you'd like to end up.

What job would you love to have? In which job would you be happy?

Which job can you think of where work would no longer be "work"? You would be so fired up that it wouldn't seem like work at all. You would rush to work in the morning and you wouldn't want to leave in the evening.

Who would you most like to be? Whose job, or business, do you most covet? If you were in his or her job, would you consider that you had the dream job?

In which job would you be consumed with the Celtic *hwyl*? You would feel such passion, such fervor, such spirit about the job that you would be uplifted to extremes of success.

That's the top-down approach. It's demand driven, in that it seeks to pinpoint those jobs that attract you to them, that draw you toward them. Rather than supply pushed, where you steer yourself toward a job that suits your values, interests, and skills.

And it's driven by passion. The job will entice you with its promise of passion.

Knowing When You've Found the Passion

You'll know when you've found a job with passion. Just thinking about it is exciting. It'll make your thoughts race. It'll wake you at five o'clock in the morning, and you won't want to go back to sleep.

It'll fill you with drive. To do something about it. To pick up the phone, knock on a door.

Above all, you'll know you've found the passion when you speak about the job. When people talk about something they're passionate about, the voice changes. The pace quickens. The pitch rises. The volume gets turned up a notch or two.

As an extreme example, take a teenage girl in two situations. Imagine her mother or father asking her how school went that day. The answer comes back monosyllabically, monotonously, ponderously. Then the telephone goes and her best buddy's on the line. The voice undergoes a metamorphosis. Suddenly it's animated, rapid, rich in variety of tone, pitch, and volume. Punctuated throughout with laughter. Whatever the two teenagers are talking about, it's surely something that fires them. And it's reflected in the voice.

It's the same in public speaking. I've belonged to a public speaking and communications club for many years (see Chapter 14 on Gary's post-MBA strategy and his discovery of Toastmasters). At every meeting four or five people stand up and deliver a prepared speech for five to seven minutes on a topic of their choosing. All speakers are advised to choose a topic that they are interested in, preferably one they are passionate about. As a result, and this is extraordinary given the range of backgrounds and talents of all these amateur speakers, it's very seldom that we hear a dud speech. Whatever the topic, the speaker's enthusiasm for the topic will be conveyed to the audience through above all her *voice*. No matter how inexperienced the speaker, no matter whether she has learned any of the tricks of vocal variety, the speech will be a winner if the topic brings out the passion in her.

If you want to know whether you truly feel the passion in a particular job, try talking about it to a friend. Talk about its daily routines, the kind of people who work there, their ambitions, their achievements. Talk about the pros and cons. Talk about it in relation to other jobs which inspire you. Talk about it in relation to ordinary jobs, why it inspires you more than your current or pre-MBA job. Ask your friend to observe how you talk about these jobs. When you speak of this passion-filled job, does your voice become faster, more animated, more impassioned?

Or join Toastmasters! Speak about the job to a small audience. Ask your evaluator beforehand if he'll note any difference in your vocal variety on this speech, compared with previous speeches. Will the speech convince him too that the job is fascinating?

The passion will be reflected in the voice. If you speak about a job where the passion lies, your voice will confirm it.

But how to find such a job?

Tips on Finding the Passion

The problem with the top-down approach, I can hear some argue, is in getting started. Suppose you have never heard of or come across the ideal job for you! How can you envision it and then work out whether you're suited for it?

You can't! They're right! This will be the case for some people. In which case, please, please revert to the bottom-up approach. Open *What Color is Your Parachute* and fill in the flower. Geography: North America. Interests: beekeeping and honey. People environment: people who help others. Values: mutual support. Working conditions: outdoors. Salary: at least average earnings. Transferable skills: accounting and (favorite) beekeeping. Then, after the job search, *Eureka!* you find it: a vacancy for a new commune member of the Honey Cooperative in Moose Jaw, Saskatchewan—a job you previously didn't know existed!

These cases I suspect may be uncommon. In the majority of cases, the top-down approach should work too because *you already know of*, or you can get to know of, the kind of work you would like to do. That's not to decry the bottom-up approach, of course. It's proven.

How to find the ideal job for you? How to discover where the passion lies? If you don't already know, and many of you do, here are some tips.

Where is the love? –Black Eyed Peas

Whose jobs do you admire of those you know?

Think of your family. Your friends. Your old school friends. Your former colleagues. Your fellow MBA students. Your kids' friends' parents.

Are any of them in a job or running a business that would inspire you? Have they been in the past? Are they thinking of switching to one?

Take one further degree of separation: What about the family, friends, and colleagues of your family, friends, and colleagues? Do they have jobs that would inspire you?

Take a piece of paper (or open up a Word table on your laptop) and make three columns. In the left-hand column, write down all the names you've just thought of. In the middle column, write down the kind of work these people do, or did. Then in the right-hand column, indicate to what extent the work would inspire you. Try checks ("ticks" in British English). Or a cross for a job that does nothing for you. Give one check for a tolerable job, two for an okay job, and three for a good job. Give an enthusiastic four checks for a great job or business, one where you'll feel the passion.

Then give five checks or more for a job you feel truly, deeply, crazily passionate about. This is a job where the Celtic *hwyl* lies, one that can inspire you to extremes of success!

What jobs do your fellow interest-sharers do?

Do you belong to any clubs, societies, voluntary groups, political groups? Your fellow members in these clubs share at least one thing in common, their interest in the purpose of that particular club/society/group.

All of you in that group like, for example, jazz, or books, or fun running. Or you are all prepared to help out on the charity stall at the summer fete.

Might there be something else you have in common with these people, other than the one common interest through which you know each other? Might you have work interests in common? Are any of them in a job that would inspire you?

And what of their friends and family?

Take out your sheet of paper and add to it some jobs of your fellow interest-sharers.

Do you know a dozen people who found the passion?

Who do you know who has changed careers successfully in their lives? Not many? I bet that's not so. I'm sure you could list a dozen or so with ease. Have any of these career switches been of interest to you? Inspired you?

I can think off the top of my head of a dozen people I know who've made successful career changes. Here they are (names changed, of course):

- ▸ Eleanor, an accountant, who couldn't abide the tedium and switched to her passions of life coaching, color therapy, and percussion workshops.

- ▸ Rhys, a bus driver, who found the London traffic too stressful and passengers too awful, went to evening classes in gardening and then set up on his own as a gardener.

- ▸ Calum, a corporate financier who tired of the greed culture and moved into his passion of garden design.

- ▸ Julia, a solicitor, who found the work unfulfilling and became a music teacher.

- ▸ Carmel, a private equity director and mother of three, who retrained as a mathematics teacher.

- ▸ Paul, an actor and singer in London West End musicals, who set up as a children's party entertainer, later extending the brand into related entertainment services.

- ▸ Lisa, an architect, who found herself redundant during a construction recession and retrained as an osteopath.

- ▸ Kay, a former university lecturer, who after some years as a full-time mom retrained as a stress management counselor.

- ▸ Anthony, Graham, Marcus, and Martin, all former consulting colleagues, who moved into areas of inspirational self-employment, respectively starting a horse-riding school, livestock farming, managing a hotel at an Alpine ski resort, and classical singing.

Now that I've started, I can readily think of a further dozen. Can you rattle off a dozen people you know who've made interesting career changes? Have any of these changes been inspirational for you? Would you have liked to have done the same?

Ask your friends, family, fellow club/society members to list a dozen examples likewise. You could soon have well over a hundred exemplars! Any inspiration there?

Again, take out your sheet of paper and add to it the jobs of people you've known, or people your friends and family have known, who've found passion through their work.

Who do you know *of* whose work inspires you?

So far you've looked to people you know for inspiration. Now take a look at people you don't know, but you know *of*. Think of people you've read about in books who have inspired you. Think of people you've looked at and read about in newspapers, in the supplements, in magazines.

Think of people you've seen on TV. In documentaries, in reality shows, in sports, on the news. People who've inspired you in some way.

Think too of fictitious people. People in novels, in movies, in the theater, in dramas or soaps on TV. People whose imaginary lives have come alive for you through fiction or drama.

Yet again, out with the paper and add in the names of those you know of who've found passion in their jobs and the extent to which (the checks) you would share that passion.

Where do MBAs tend to end up?

Does your business school have charts on what jobs its MBA alumni have moved on to? Almost certainly such charts exist and play a major role in the school's marketing.

Management consulting and investment banking may well feature prominently on the list, especially at the more prestigious schools. But there will be surely be a broad spread of industry sectors alumni have moved on to.

There are numerous national and international surveys undertaken of MBA graduate job destinations. One of the largest is by QS in its Top-MBA.com International Recruiter Survey, which shows that the largest sector of MBA recruiters is, unsurprisingly, financial services, followed by consulting/professional services.

But these two sectors together only make up around 40% of MBA recruitment. Other high MBA recruiting sectors are manufacturing/engineering, electronics, pharmaceuticals/healthcare and energy.

Also interesting are the annual surveys by Universum in the U.S. and Europe of employer attractiveness. In the 2010 U.S. survey, management consulting (McKinsey, BCG, Bain, Deloitte) and investment banking (Goldman Sachs, J P Morgan, Blackstone, Morgan Stanley, Credit Suisse) featured prominently in the top twenty, but other employers perceived as attractive were more diverse—Google, Apple, Disney, Nike, Johnson & Johnson, Amazon, Microsoft, General Electric, Proctor & Gamble, IDEO, and Coca Cola.

Results were similar in the European 2010 survey, but with more consultants and fewer investment banks in the top twenty and European firms such as LVMH, L'Oreal, Nestle, BMW, Unilever, Porsche, and IKEA making a strong showing.

Any inspiration there? If so, jot down some more jobs and/or employers on your piece of paper, and rate them with the appropriate ration of checks.

Even celebrities can change careers

I'm not sure how useful you'll find this section because celebs exist in a bubble of their own, cocooned from the real world by their property, wealth, fame, paparazzi, and bodyguards. But celebrities do sometimes change careers, moving into fields beyond those in which they gained their fame.

Think of Hollywood actors who have moved successfully into politics, such as President Ronald Reagan, Governor Arnold Schwarzenegger, and Mayor Clint Eastwood (all initially standing in California!), or Glenda Jackson, Member of Parliament. Or those who've been active in political pressure groups, such as Brigitte Bardot, Jane Fonda, and Vanessa Redgrave. Or sportspeople who have moved into broadcasting, like John McEnroe, or into acting, like Vinnie Jones. Or actresses who have moved into pop singing, like Kylie Minogue and Jennifer Lopez.

Think too of celebs who have moved into the world of business, such as Paul Newman and his natural food products, Linda McCartney and her vegetarian cuisine, Elle Macpherson and her lingerie line. Or think of dozens of celebs and their fragrance launches, from Britney and Paris to KISS and Donald Trump!

For most celebs, it's their very celebrity that gives them the launch pad for their career change. But in thinking of the career switches of celebrities you've followed, perhaps some of those on the B or C Lists, you may find some inspiration.

Broaden your reading for inspiration

If you're still short of inspiration, then you may need to read around a bit more. You could try making a conscious effort to dedicate your leisure reading time to discovery of fields of work. There's an abundance of material available to help.

In the British *Sunday Times* magazine, there's an amazing one-page feature at the back that has run for years called *A Life in the Day Of,* and every week features one person whose life is typically ordinary but extraordinary. The subjects chosen can range from a movie star to a chambermaid, a political campaigner to a factory worker, a top lawyer to an asylum seeker. All they have in common is their individuality. Read them and similar features in other magazines and discover who inspires you, why and what job they do.

There are also books you can read for inspiration. You could start with *What Should I Do with My Life?* by Po Bronson, a collection of stories of ordinary people who "had unearthed their true calling, or at least those who were willing to try." From the investment banker who became a catfish farmer to the chemical engineer who became a lawyer in his sixties, these are stories of "individual dilemmas and dramatic gambles," not always successful. The tales of the author's subjects are interesting, and at times, inspirational.

Or you could try one of Barbara Sher's books. She's a therapist, motivational speaker, career counselor, and prolific author. You could browse through a range of her books in a bookstore and see which one inspires you. Or read the reviews on Amazon.com. Her bestselling books include *I Could Do Anything If I Only Knew What It Was: How to Discover What You Really Want and How to Get It.*

Then there's the mega-selling phenomenon of the *Chicken Soup for the Soul* series, Jack Canfield and Mark Victor Hansen's moving compilation of extraordinary stories about ordinary people. One story might strike a light for you.

There's also a wealth of examples in the career change books referred to earlier in this chapter, especially in Julie Jansen's *I Don't Know What I Want, but I Know It's Not This.*

Again, pull out your list and add more names, jobs, and checks.

Consult a list

We're starting to scrape the barrel a bit here. If you haven't found inspiration from any of the above sources, it's unlikely that a dry, factual, unemotional list of (thousands of) occupations is going to inspire. But you never know.

There are lots of sources. No need to invest serious cash, when the Internet is around. The best place to start if you live in the United States is the Bureau of Labor Statistics website (www.bls.gov). Once in you can click through to the Occupational Outlook Handbook, which is updated every other year. It's a mine of information. You can search for any occupation that you're interested in, or browse from a menu of occupations, drilling down to the ones of interest. For each occupation, there's information on the nature of the work, working conditions, training and qualifications, employment, job outlook, earnings, related occupations, and sources of further information.

There are also regular reports and tables produced by the Bureau, which you can download. One fascinating table, which you could well find useful, is of the "Fastest Growing Occupations covered in the Occupational

Outlook Handbook" and can be found on bls.gov/news.release/ooh.t01. htm. In the 2006-2007 handbook, the fastest growing occupations likely over the period 2004-2014 include home health aides, network systems and data communications analysts, medical assistants, computer software engineers, dental assistants, preschool teachers, post-secondary teachers, and computer systems analysts. The table gives the number of jobs likely to be created, the percentage increase in employment for each occupation and the level of training required. One of these in-demand jobs may have your name on it!

Similar sites are available on the Internet in most countries. In Britain, you can find whatever labor statistics you need from the website of the Office for National Statistics, statistics.gov.uk. A very useful website for graduates is prospects.ac.uk, which provides a treasure trove of information on every graduate job conceivable. Under each job you get information on the job description and typical activities, salary and conditions, entry requirements, training, career development, typical employers, sources for vacancies, case studies of real people working in the field, and contacts/resources for further information.

Have you found any occupations of interest that you had not uncovered earlier? If so, add them, along with the appropriate checks, to your list.

Take a career test

I'm a bit reluctant to recommend this last route. It really belongs to a bottom-up approach, and I've already referred you to a bunch of good books that will guide you through that process.

Nevertheless, there are some well established career tests around, many of which can be accessed on the Internet. Some may charge a few bucks, others are free. Your best bet is to latch on to jobhuntersbible.com, the website of Dick Bolles, author of *What Color Is Your Parachute*. Then click through to Tests and Advice, and then Career Tests. You should now be on jobhuntersbible.com/library/counseling/ctests.php and Bolles will walk you through the merits of the various tests on offer, including the

Princeton Review Career Quiz, the *Self-Directed Search* by John Holland, the *Career Key* and the *Career Interests Game*, developed originally by Bolles from Holland's work (as the *Party Exercise*), but adapted by the University of Missouri and available on their website career.missouri.edu. It's a fun game and well worth playing.

Any more jobs and checks to add to your list?

How Martha Stewart Found the Hwyl

Many celebrities find fame only after switching from a previous career. Sean Connery was a body-builder, Catherine Zeta-Jones a dancer, and Kelly Clarkson worked as a telemarketer and cocktail waitress in a small town in Texas before having a shot at *American Idol*.

Then there's the phenomenon that is Martha Stewart. A part-time model during her university days at Barnard, studying history and architectural history, Martha Kostyra became a successful stockbroker. She quit in her early thirties to become a full-time mother while undertaking a major restoration of an early 19th century farmhouse. It was from its basement that she started a catering business with a friend from college. Within a couple of years, she had produced a cookbook, *Entertaining*.

The rest is history. The book became a best seller and over the next few years she produced more books, including *Weddings*, wrote articles, made TV appearances and launched her own housewares line at K-Mart. In 1990 she became editor of the magazine *Martha Stewart Living*, which would peak in 2002 with a circulation of 2 million. In 1993 she appeared in a TV show named after her, initially a half-hour a week, then an hour a week, then daily.

In 1997 Martha Stewart secured funding to purchase all the print, TV and merchandising activities associated with her name and consolidated everything into a company, *Martha Stewart Living Omnimedia*. The company was floated on the New York Stock Exchange a couple of years later, making her a billionaire on paper.

Millions were lopped off the company value when she was accused, then convicted, of insider trading, on a deal where she had saved a mere $45,000. But the conviction and her subsequent serving of a short prison sentence did not halt the Martha Stewart express. More lines at K-Mart, more books, more TV programs, the brand has extended even further into the building of Martha Stewart houses.

All this from a former model-cum-stockbroker. She discovered the Celtic *hwyl* in her basement kitchen. She went on to radiate that passion to the U.S. public in print and on TV. She became a brand and the brand went stratospheric.

What passion could you uncover in your own kitchen? Your study? Your backyard?

How Ralph Smedley Found the Hwyl

Not all who find passion in work go on to become billionaires like Martha Stewart! Nor would many of us choose to. Fulfillment can come in forms other than material. For many it comes from helping others. Or in creating structures to be able to help others.

Ralph C. Smedley is an example of this. After graduating from Illinois Wesleyan University in 1903, he took a job as director of education at the local branch of the Young Men's Christian Association. There he soon realized that older boys would benefit from some training in communications skills, so he started a public speaking club.

He called it the Toastmasters' Club, because the activities resembled a banquet with toasts and after-dinner speeches. The boys enjoyed taking turns to make speeches and evaluating them, as well as presiding at the weekly meetings.

Smedley's Bloomington club blossomed, but soon he was promoted to general secretary of the YMCA and transferred to Freeport, Illinois. After his departure, the club folded. Over the following years,

Smedley set up other Toastmasters clubs wherever he was transferred. In Freeport, he invited businessmen and other professionals to join the meetings, but to no long-term avail. The club thrived while Smedley was there but disappeared once its founder moved on. Subsequent clubs in Rock Island, Illinois, and San Jose, California, suffered the same fate.

Smedley must have despaired of ever seeing his creation blossom into a self-sustaining organization. "I observed a tendency among my fellow secretaries at the YMCA to regard The Toastmasters Club as a sort of peculiarity—an idiosyncrasy of mine," he later said. "Perhaps it was not altogether orthodox as a 'Y' activity."

Finally, Smedley arrived in Santa Ana. Yet again he started up a Toastmasters club, but in Southern California's optimistic climate the concept at last caught on. Men (yes, it was all male in those days, but certainly not now) from neighboring communities sought out the group and liked what they saw. Smedley helped them organize their own Toastmasters clubs and these clubs united in a federation.

Smedley had found his *hwyl*. As he turned 50, he resigned from the YMCA to concentrate on developing Toastmasters. He opened a tiny office in a downtown Santa Ana bank with a desk, typewriter, telephone, and second-hand answering machine. He hired a secretary to handle the correspondence, while he wrote materials for the club's use. The organization grew.

Smedley remained involved with Toastmasters until shortly before his death in 1965 at the age of 87. By then, Toastmasters International had grown to a membership of 80,000. It had moved into its own large office building in Santa Ana, and Smedley himself took part in the dedication ceremonies. It must have an emotional occasion, a tribute to one man's vision and drive.

The organization now has over a quarter of a million members, in over 100 countries. The Santa Ana Toastmasters Club, since renamed as the Smedley Number One Club, still reserves a chair for him at every meeting. It is placed alongside the lectern and carries his photograph and the original club charter.

Ralph Smedley backed his passion and lived it, to a grand old age.

(Note: I am grateful to *Toastmasters International* for permission to reproduce part of its biography of Ralph C. Smedley.)

Drawing up Your Long List

If you've been reading about Martha Stewart or Ralph Smedley, it's time to return to the mundane. No offense, but let's face it. Very few of us will turn out to be like them, let alone a Bill Gates or Nelson Mandela. But we do owe it to ourselves to make the most of our time here, preferably benefiting many, not just ourselves. And the first step in this process is to find the passion.

The time has come to review your list. Take out your sheet of paper and see what you've come up with. Hopefully you have by now jotted down plenty of names, jobs, and checks. All those with checks will inspire you to a certain extent. You've looked at people you know, people you've read about, and people you've seen on TV, and thought about those whose jobs could inspire you. You may also have looked at lists or taken a career test. You may have gained inspiration from thinking about successful people who found the passion with a career change.

You may have before you a list of three, four, or more dozen jobs that could inspire you to varying degrees. Now the list needs to be made more manageable.

You need to rearrange the full list (easier if you've typed it out on your laptop) by grouping the jobs by the number of checks received. At the very top group together all those jobs that gained five or more checks. Then those with four, three, and so on. Last, and least, should be those with crosses.

Now you weed out those with the fewest checks. Obviously, you'll start with all the crosses. Then you'll move on to the single checks. Carry on this process, cross-checking your check rating and making any required amendments as you go along. Stop when you arrive at the top dozen or so jobs left. Hopefully each will have received at least three checks, preferably four or five.

No more than a dozen jobs are needed at this stage. You can always return to the list if you have to. A dozen is a reasonably sized list to be taking into the next chapter on screening. This is your *long list* of jobs with passion.

To reiterate: at this stage, it doesn't matter whether you could do these jobs well, or if indeed you could even qualify to do them. The important thing is to derive a manageable long list of jobs that inspire you, ranked *purely* by their passion content.

> " *If you do work that you love, and the work fulfills you, the rest will come…. You know you are on the road to success if you would do your job, and not be paid for it.* –Oprah Winfrey

Where Is Jennifer's Passion?

We met Jennifer in the introduction to this book, but didn't need to look at her in Parts I and II because she is at business school expressly to change career. She has no interest in developing further in her pre-MBA career. She has been with one of the Big Four accounting firms for six years, the last three specializing in financial due diligence. She's at business school because she wants to move on to something more exciting and more remunerative—something, she thinks, like management consulting, private equity, or investment banking.

But which? Or is there another option yet more attractive? It's time to investigate….

Figure 15.1. Jennifer's Full List of Jobs with Passion

Who	Job	Passion
Jennifer, now	Accountant, Transaction Services Group, a Big 4 house	✓✓✓
Her father	Chief Operations Officer, engineering company	✓✓
Her mother	Public relations (formerly)	✓✓✓
Her grandfather	US Army Major	x
Her other grandfather	Banker, branch manager	✓
Her grandmother	Public service administrator	✓✓
Her brother	Doctor	x
Her uncle	Manager, consumer goods company	✓✓✓
Her aunt	Deputy head-teacher, high school	✓✓
Her uncle's ex-wife	Manager, drains claims management outsourcing company	✓
Her brother's friend	Hedge fund director	✓✓✓
Her brother's friend's brother	Private equity investment director	✓✓✓✓✓
Her father's friend	MD South America, global services company	✓✓✓
Her mother's friend's cousin	TV presenter	✓✓✓✓
Her high school buddy A	Marketing consultant	✓✓✓
Her high school buddy B's friend	Model	✓✓
Her high school teacher's wife	Policewoman	✓
Her college buddy A	Executive search executive	✓
Her college buddy B's cousin	E-commerce entrepreneur	✓✓✓
Her MBA friend A	Strategy consultant	✓✓✓✓✓
Her MBA friend B's father	Stockbroking – equities research	✓✓✓✓
Her MBA friend C's sister	Investment banking – mergers and acquisitions	✓✓✓✓
Her neighbor 's ex-partner	Finance director, medium-sized company	✓✓✓✓
Her former colleague A's father	Journalist/Author	✓✓✓✓✓
Her former colleague B's sister	Asset management executive	✓✓✓✓
Her friend's sister	Wall Street bond trader	✓✓✓
Her hockey buddy A	Corporate finance adviser	✓✓✓✓
Her hockey buddy B's mother	Advertising manager	✓
Her boyfriend	Advertising creative manager	✓✓✓✓
Her ex	Musician	✓✓
Her clients A-Z	Private equity executives	✓✓✓✓✓
Steve Jobs	Technology entrepreneur	✓✓✓✓
Katherine Zeta-Jones	Movie actress	✓✓✓✓✓
Barack Obama	President	✓✓✓

Jennifer heads straight for Chapter 15, digests it thoroughly, switches on her laptop, and opens a PowerPoint file for her long list of jobs with passion (see Figure 15.1 for a shortened version). She goes through each job of virtually everyone she knows, irrespective of whether she would want to do it. She thinks of her family, her friends in high school, in college, and in her hockey club; she considers her fellow students at business school, her neighbors, her former colleagues, and all her other friends and acquaintances, present and past. She thinks consciously of *their* friends, families, and colleagues. She thinks of people she knows *of*, from her favorite movie star to the President.

Then she rates them by the passion factor. As instructed, she pays no attention to whether or not she could actually do the job, but by how much she would actually love doing the job. Her ex-boyfriend, for instance, is a musician, a classical double bassist. She would love to be a musician, tough as it is to make ends meet, but, though she has a pleasant alto voice, she struggles to read music. Nevertheless, she includes the job.

Figure 15.2. Jennifer's Long List of Jobs with Passion

Job	Passion
Private equity executive	✓✓✓✓
Strategy consultant	✓✓✓✓✓
Journalist/Author	✓✓✓✓✓
Movie actress	✓✓✓✓✓
TV presenter	✓✓✓
Stockbroking – equities research	✓✓✓
Investment banking – corporate finance/M&A	✓✓✓
Finance director, medium-sized company	✓✓✓
Asset management executive	✓✓✓
Advertising creative manager	✓✓✓
Musician	✓✓✓
Entrepreneur	✓✓✓

It is when she starts to group together the jobs that rate four or five checks (Figure 15.2) that she sees the point of the exercise. Jobs like private equity executive and strategy consultant appear in good company, alongside journalist and movie actor. In all these jobs, Jennifer can tangibly feel the passion. And not far behind are jobs as diverse as equities research analyst and musician.

Just looking at the list gives her a buzz. Private equity, her main aspiration before arriving at Harvard, is in good company....

A Planet of Hwyl

This student at London Business School was taking a walk in Regent's Park, opposite the school, when he came across a Northern Irish girl sitting on a park bench. They fell in love, got married, and set off on honeymoon with "a beat-up old car, a few dollars in the pocket and a sense of adventure" to cross Europe and Asia overland, all the way to Australia. They made it there, "flat broke but happy," having shared an experience "too amazing to keep to themselves." The book that took shape on their kitchen table, *Across Asia on the Cheap*, was published in 1973 and immediately struck a chord with backpackers traveling between Europe and Australasia. It was soon followed by a second, *South-East Asia on a Shoestring*. This author fondly recalls digesting every word of these early travel bibles on his Asian meanders of the early 1980s. Tony and Maureen Wheeler had found their *hwyl* and backed it, finally selling three quarters of Lonely Planet Publications to BBC Worldwide in 2007. The business fetched a sum a planet apart from the homely hostels, savory noodle stalls, and bouncing buses recommended by their books over the years!

16

Screening for Reality

Screening for Backability
>> How Attractive Are the Markets?
>> How Well Placed Are You?
>> How Backable Are You?
Creating Your Short List with the *Hwyl* Star Chart
Iteration

In the last chapter, you derived a long list of a dozen or so jobs or businesses you would very much like or even love to do post-MBA. Some you may stand little chance of getting into, let alone succeeding there once in. Shame, but that's life. Others you may do well in. The purpose of this chapter will be to derive a short list of three or four jobs, ones you're passionate about *and* where you'll be backable.

You'll do very little extra research in this chapter. That's for the next chapter. Here you'll take a first cut at assessing how attractive the markets are for each of these jobs and how well placed you would be to get in and succeed at them. You'll effectively be doing a quick and dirty assessment of how backable you'd be in each job. You'll be introduced to the *Hwyl* Star chart, an adaptation of one that my small business clients have found useful over the years, to help derive your short list of achievable jobs with passion.

Many of the more aspirational jobs in your long list will be screened out, sadly, but at least they'll have come and gone without you wasting any serious time on researching them, let alone pursuing them. It's possible that so many jobs will be filtered out that you won't have enough left to make a short list.

That's no problem. You should see this as an iterative process. You'll return to the full list of the previous chapter and bring forward a new long list of a dozen or so jobs, drawn from the next level down of passion rating—for example three checks, rather than four. You'll repeat the screening process, you may even have to do it once again, before finally ending up with your short list of achievable jobs with passion.

In the next chapter, you'll do some serious research on these shortlisted jobs. But first let's get on with the screening.

Screening for Backability

The first thing to realize is that the screening process has to be objective and dispassionate. The aim is not to provide you with a clearer ranking of which job you'd most like to do. It's to find out in which job you could be *backable*. Out of all those long-listed jobs with passion, where would a backer consider you worth a punt?

This aim has implications for the criteria we'll use in ranking the jobs. Typically, when people are thinking of a career change, they'll list criteria such as pay, working conditions, values, culture, location, type of colleague, status, and so forth. Then they'll use these criteria to rank possible careers for relative attractiveness.

This is all highly valid. But it's not for here. It's for the next chapter, *after* we've screened the long list for backability.

There is little point in spending loads of time doing further research on a career where it's highly unlikely that you'll be backable.

These jobs first need to be screened for hard-nosed, economic, competitive factors. Is the market for these jobs growing? Are there more job-seekers than jobs available? With your skills and experience, would you stand a reasonable chance of getting in and succeeding?

Let's aim to deliver a realistic short list. The long list is the dream list. What gets through the screen and into the next chapter needs to be a short list of achievable, backable jobs with passion.

> 66
> *Follow your own particular dreams. We are handed a life by peers, parents and society; you can do that or follow your own dreams. Life is short; be a dreamer but be a practical person."* –Hugh Hefner

How attractive are the markets?

The first thing we need to consider, from the perspective of a prospective backer, as in Part I, is how attractive are the markets for these jobs.

In Chapter 2 we looked at how to assess market demand prospects, risks, and opportunities. Then in Chapter 3 we looked at the supply side and assessed prospects for competition, and whether there would be balance in labor supply and demand for these jobs over the next few years.

At this stage there's no need for you to do any research on assessing these job markets. Only if the job gets through the screening process is it worthwhile doing serious research.

Gut feel is what's needed. You need to rank your long list by what you feel. You already have a vague notion of market demand and competition for these jobs, because you know something about them. These are jobs to which you aspire, where you believe the passion lies. Let your gut feel provide these preliminary estimates.

You need to rank each of the long-listed jobs or businesses by four criteria:

1. *Number of people engaged in this job or business*—are there many people working in this field, compared to the numbers engaged in other fields?

2. *Growth in jobs or businesses*—is this a field where there will be growing demand for people over the next few years? Or is demand more likely to stay flat, or decline?

3. *Competition for jobs or among businesses*—how ferocious is the competition to get these jobs? To what extent does the supply of people wanting to do these jobs exceed vacancies available? If this is a business, how intense is the competition between businesses? To what extent is it intensifying?

4. *Job market risk*—how risky is this job or business, compared to others?

The ranking can be done in words, checks, or numbers, whatever your preference. Mine is for numbers, and Figure 16.1 shows an example.

Figure 16.1. **Rough Market Attractiveness of Long-Listed Jobs: An Example**

Long-List of Jobs and Businesses	Number of Jobs	Growth in Jobs	Compet-ition for Jobs	Job Market Risk	Market Attract-iveness
A	5	4	3	2	**3.5**
B	4	4	4	3	**3.8**
C	4	3	3	2	**3.0**
D	2	1	2	3	**2.0**
E	3	3	2	4	**3.0**
F	5	2	4	3	**3.5**
G	3	1	4	3	**2.8**
H	4	2	4	3	**3.3**

Key to Rating: 1 = Unattractive, 3 = Reasonably Attractive, 5 = Highly Attractive
(For competition for jobs, remember that the more intense the competition, the **less** attractive the market. Likewise for job market risk: the riskier the market, the **less** attractive. Conversely, and more intuitively, the greater the number of jobs the more attractive; likewise for growth in jobs.)

The chart shows someone's long list of eight jobs or businesses. B seems to be in the most attractive job market. Demand for jobs is sizeable, growing, competition for jobs is not as bad as for most jobs and it doesn't seem too risky once in. Jobs A and F follow, A being a bit more risky than B, and F with slower growth in jobs. D's market seems the least attractive—it's small, declining, and highly competitive.

Suppose job D is this person's most preferred job or business of all? The one with passion in spades? Shame, because even if in the next section she emerges reasonably well placed to get in and succeed in that job, it would be inadvisable to try. The market will be against her. She'll be pushing uphill. She won't be backable.

How well placed are you?

The second stage of the screening process is to assess how well placed you would be to get in and then succeed at this job or business.

As we saw above for assessing market attractiveness, gut feel is again all that's needed at this stage. There's no point in investing hours of time in figuring out customer needs (Chapter 4), Key Kapabilities (Chapter 5), and competitive position (Chapter 6) for each of these dozen jobs if they're unlikely to pass through the screening process. That level of detail is for the next chapter.

We use a shortcut instead. For each job or business, think of two criteria only:

> *Your relevant capabilities*—How you would rate against the capabilities required for the job or business?

> *Your experience*—How you would rate against the experience needed to do the job or run the business?

The first criterion relates to how well you think you would do the job, or run the business, if you got into it. How relevant are your skills, your innate talents, to the skills needed to perform the job successfully? How suitable are your qualifications? If they are currently deficient, how readily could you raise them to the required level?

The second criterion is important in those jobs or businesses where experience is a serious barrier to entry. There may be a whole range of jobs you know you could do well, but your lack of relevant experience would make you difficult to back. Not necessarily because you couldn't do the job. More because prospective employers, or indeed your customers, would be looking for someone more experienced than you to be offering and delivering such a service.

Some words of warning on the experience rating:

▷ When screening a long list, you may think that you have no experience at all of doing a particular job. Don't be dismayed. Think about what elements of your experience to date may at least be *indirectly* or tangentially relevant to that job.

▷ Remember that we're looking primarily for relative comparisons, not absolute levels. We're looking for jobs where some aspects of your past experience may be more relevant than for others.

▷ If you're young (under 30—lucky you), the experience criterion may be less relevant than for those of us who are not so young, especially if over 50. Youngsters applying for jobs are typically assessed less rigorously on experience than on capability. And on *potential* capability. You may choose to drop the experience criterion altogether and just use your capability rating on its own.

Let's return to the example of the woman with a long list of eight jobs or businesses. Figure 16.2 shows her rough competitive position against each of those careers.

From this crude screening process, it would seem that she'd be best placed to succeed in job C, followed by jobs G and H. In C, she believes she would have reasonable capabilities to do the job and some of her past experience would count strongly. As for her dream job D, she doesn't seem well placed to succeed. She thinks she could do it reasonably well, but she can think of no aspect of her experience that would count for much in the interview process.

Figure 16.2. **Rough Competitive Position Against Long-listed Jobs: An Example**

Long-List of Jobs and Businesses	Your Relevant Capabilities	Your Relevant Experience	Your Competitive Position
A	2	1	1.5
B	2	2	2.0
C	3	4	3.5
D	3	1	2.0
E	1	2	1.5
F	1	3	2.0
G	4	2	3.0
H	3	3	3.0

Key to Rating: 1 = Weak, 2 = Below par, 3 = Favorable, 4 = Strong, 5 = Very strong

How backable are you?

Now you need to combine the rough assessment of market attractiveness with the similarly rough assessment of your competitive position. This will give us an idea of how well placed you would be in job markets of varying levels of attractiveness. You need to draw up a screening chart.

Figure 16.3 shows an example. You can either rustle up your own version on PowerPoint or turn to the proforma in Appendix 1, Figure A.14, and you can use or photocopy that.

Plot all your long-listed jobs on the chart. The stronger your competitive position, the further to the right you'll place your job. The more attractive the market, the higher up it should go.

The more backable the job the closer it will be placed around or even above the main diagonal leading from top left to bottom right.

If the job ends up in the bottom left corner, forget it. It's an unattractive market where you'll be poorly placed. It's not for you.

If the job shows up anywhere near the dotted line diagonal in the top right-hand corner, that's terrific news. It's in an attractive market where you'll be well placed (subject to further research in the next chapter). Whether or not it's the "perfect job" will depend on how many checks you gave it in the passion ranking of the last chapter—we'll return to this in the next section.

Let's take a closer look at Figure 16.3, which again uses the example of the woman with the long list of eight jobs.

Figure 16.3. **Initial Screening of the Long List: An Example**

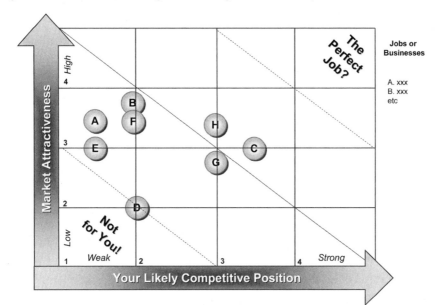

As we suspected, job D is a nonstarter. Her competitive position is weak, *and* the job's in an unattractive market. Jobs A and E are not much better. Jobs B, F and G offer some promise, but it is C and H that seem most promising. They lie to the right of the diagonal.

For C, she is well placed in a job with reasonable market prospects. For H she is reasonably placed in a job with good market prospects.

C and H are where she would be most likely to find a backer. These are likely to be the backable jobs that pass through her screening process and into her short list for further research.

Creating Your Short List with the *Hwyl* Star Chart

There is, however, one final, crucial component that has been left out of the screening process until now. That is the passion factor. Jobs that proceed to the short list need to have not only good market prospects *and* be ones where you'd be reasonably placed to succeed, but they *also* need to be jobs that inspire you. If the jobs poised for short listing were ranked less favorably in the passion listings of the previous chapter, then it's possible the wrong jobs will pass through to the short list.

This is where we add the final touch to the screening chart. We replace the penciled circles with stars and make them proportional in size to the extent of passion the jobs generate. By definition, all the jobs on the long list are jobs with passion, but some more so than others. Give those jobs with three passion checks a small star, those with four a bigger one, and those with five or more the biggest. These are jobs with the Celtic *hwyl*, the passion, fervor, and spirit which can fire you to extremes of success!

Now you'll see at a glance which jobs should be short listed. They will be the largest stars around and about the main diagonal, or preferably to the right.

Let's return one final time to the example of the woman with eight jobs on her long list (see Figure 16.4).

Job H is the runaway winner for the short list. Not only would she be reasonably placed to succeed at this job, and it's a job with attractive market prospects, but it's one of the two jobs that she feels most passionate about. The other job to which she gave five checks, by the way, is D, and that has already been ruled out as a no-hoper.

But the chart also shows that there are two other jobs that merit short listing. We've already mentioned job C, where she would be well placed in a reasonable market. But job G too is promising. She would be reasonably placed for a job with reasonable market prospects *and* it's a job to which she gave four checks in the passion listing.

Figure 16.4. The *Hwyl* Star Chart: An Example

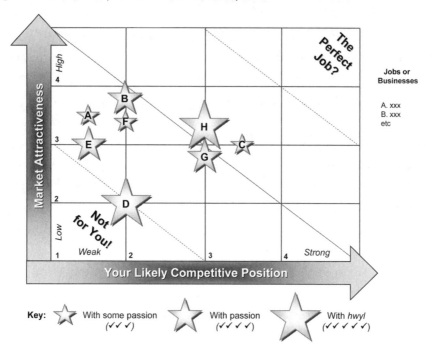

In this example, then, it would be jobs H, G, and C in the long list that would pass through the screening process into the short list of jobs with passion.

Iteration

This screening process will not always work quite as smoothly as for with the woman exemplar chosen. This is because your long list of jobs with passion has taken no account whatsoever of your capability to do them. Many of those jobs at the top of your long list are just wishful thinking, and that's fine. But when you get down to the rough assessment of your competitive position against these fanciful jobs, you may find you don't get anywhere near the diagonal.

This is tough, but hardly surprising. We'd all love to be movie stars, but realistically we're not all going to make it from here!

Don't be deterred. Try another iteration. Go back to your long list and import the next dozen or so jobs. Pass them through the screening process. They should get you closer to the diagonal. Still short of the two or three jobs needed for a short list? Try one more iteration and pull another dozen jobs across. Hopefully by now you'll have found two or three that are sufficiently promising to merit the short list.

You've screened your long list down to a short list of jobs that not only have passion, but where you also may be backable. This needs further investigation in the next chapter.

Jennifer's Screening

Jennifer has drawn up a long list of a dozen jobs, each of which she has rated at least four passion checks. These are jobs she feels passionate about, but how attractive are their markets and how well placed is she to do them? She sets out to learn more.

Of her four most highly rated jobs, each with five passion checks, she senses that private equity and strategy consulting are still licking their wounds after the 2008–10 credit crunch, movie acting remains ultra competitive and only journalism/writing seems to have reasonable market prospects (see Figure 16.5).

Of the jobs with four passion checks, the most attractive market prospects seem to be in finance for medium-sized enterprises, asset management, equities research, and starting her own business.

These are all rough assessments, of course, reflecting her gut feel as to the state and prospects of these markets. She understands that those that pass through the screen will have to be more fully researched in due course.

Figure 16.5. **Rough Market Attractiveness of Jennifer's Long-listed Jobs**

Long List of Jobs and Businesses	Number of Jobs	Growth in Jobs	Competition for Jobs	Job Market Risk	Market Attractiveness
Private equity executive	2.0	1.5	1.5	1.5	**1.6**
Strategy consultant	2.5	2.0	2.0	2.0	**2.1**
Journalist/Author	2.0	2.5	2.5	3.0	**2.5**
Movie actress	2.0	1.5	1.0	1.5	**1.5**
TV presenter	2.0	2.5	1.5	2.5	**2.1**
Stockbroking – equities research	2.0	2.0	2.5	3.0	**2.4**
Investment banking – M&A	2.0	1.5	2.0	2.0	**1.9**
Finance director, SME	2.5	2.5	3.0	3.5	**2.9**
Asset management executive	2.0	2.0	3.0	3.0	**2.5**
Advertising creative manager	2.0	2.0	2.5	3.0	**2.4**
Musician	2.0	2.0	2.0	2.0	**2.0**
Entrepreneur	3.5	3.0	2.5	1.0	**2.5**

Key to Rating: 1 = Unattractive, 3 = Reasonably Attractive, 5 = Highly Attractive
[For Competition for Jobs, remember that the more intense the competition, the **less** attractive the market.
Likewise for Job Market Risk: the riskier the market, the **less** attractive. Conversely, and more intuitively, the
greater the Number of Jobs the more attractive. Likewise for Growth in Jobs]

As to her prospective competitive position (Figure 16.6), Jennifer figures she will be best placed in finance directing, followed by private equity, where she can put her three years' experience of financial due diligence to direct effect, and in strategy consulting. Equities research, asset management, and corporate finance follow not far behind.

At the other extreme, she suspects that a sub-editorial contribution to her high school magazine will not serve as a leg up in a journalistic career. Nor perhaps her supporting roles on stage at college, fun but hardly Oscar-worthy, for a career in movie acting. She will be least competitive, however, in a musical career—sure, she can sing a bit and strum a guitar, but when it comes to true potential, she has to be honest about her limitations.

Figure 16.6. Jennifer's Rough Competitive Position in Her Long-listed Jobs

Long List of Jobs and Businesses	Her Relevant Capabilities	Her Relevant Experience	Her Competitive Position
Private equity executive	3.5	3.0	**3.3**
Strategy consultant	3.0	2.5	**2.8**
Journalist/Author	2.5	1.0	**1.8**
Movie actress	2.5	1.5	**2.0**
TV presenter	3.0	1.5	**2.3**
Stockbroking – equities research	2.5	2.5	**2.5**
Investment banking – M&A	2.5	2.5	**2.5**
Finance director, SME	3.5	4.0	**3.8**
Asset management executive	2.5	2.5	**2.5**
Advertising creative manager	2.0	1.5	**1.8**
Musician	1.0	1.0	**1.0**
Entrepreneur	2.0	2.5	**2.3**

Key to Rating: 1 = Weak, 2 = Below par, 3 = Favorable, 4 = Strong, 5 = Very strong

Jennifer eagerly draws up the initial screening chart (Figure 16.7) and is surprised to find such an outright winner, finance directing at a medium-sized company (circle H). On further reflection, she realizes she is indeed rather well placed to move into a comparatively attractive job market.

Figure 16.7. Initial Screening of Jennifer's Long List

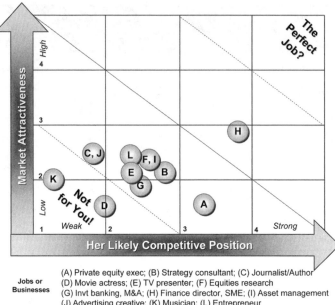

Jobs or Businesses

(A) Private equity exec; (B) Strategy consultant; (C) Journalist/Author
(D) Movie actress; (E) TV presenter; (F) Equities research
(G) Invt banking, M&A; (H) Finance director, SME; (I) Asset management
(J) Advertising creative; (K) Musician; (L) Entrepreneur

Other jobs lie far behind, the closest to the main diagonal being private equity, strategy consulting, equities research, asset management, and starting her own business (A, B, F, I, L).

One thing is for sure, though. Movie acting (D) and music (K) are not for Jennifer!

Now Jennifer adds the final ingredient, the extra dimension—the passion (see Figure 16.8). Finance directing (H) remains the winner, of course, but it is only a four-check job. Private equity (A) and strategy consulting (B), with their five checks, now stand out from the likes of equities research (F) and asset management (I) and might even be mounting a challenge to finance directing.

Figure 16.8. Jennifer's *Hwyl* Star Chart

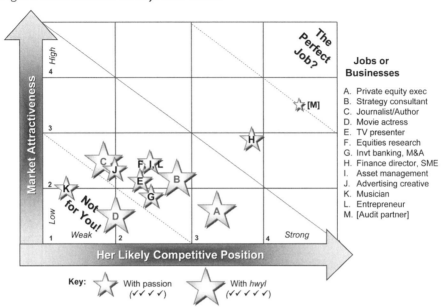

Three jobs, then, clearly pass through Jennifer's screen—finance directing, private equity, and strategy consulting. Time for further research, she thinks—and, in the meantime, if some movie director or newspaper editor happens to chance upon her in the Harvard library one sunny afternoon, she can always revisit the currently abject positioning of those jobs on her *Hwyl* Star chart!

When She Wished Upon a Star

It is intriguing to imagine what the *Hwyl* Star chart of this Long Islander looked like as she graduated with a Harvard MBA. At Princeton she had wanted initially to be a doctor, but switched to economics and ended up marrying a doctor instead. So maybe two of her five-checked stars would have been doctor and top manager of a large corporation. Setting out for the latter, she became a brand manager at Proctor & Gamble, and a consultant with Bain & Company in San Francisco, before taking her first senior corporate post at Walt Disney—where she worked for 10 years. She then hopped from one to another senior corporate management position before landing the role of CEO at a dot-com, which had just 30 employees but big plans. She headed eBay for 10 years, steering it into a global giant. She left to venture into politics, and entered the history books by spending a record sum (over $150 million) on her ultimately unsuccessful candidacy for Governor of California in 2010. To have that much political ambition, conviction, and passion, we must have omitted a very large star from Meg Whitman's *Hwyl* Star chart. But is it placed near the center or to the left? Time will tell....

17

Where Best to Back?

In the last chapter, you short listed the most promising two or three jobs or businesses with passion. But your screening process was done on the back of minimal research. It was largely gut feel, and that will be remedied in this chapter. You will do some serious research and your hypotheses of the last chapter will be put to the test. The outcome should be the discovery of the job or business that not only fires your passion but is one where you are backable.

This chapter will guide you through the further research needed. You'll need to read all you can about the short-listed jobs, and speak to people who do them. And to their "customers." You'll confirm that these jobs will inspire you. And that they fulfill the other aspects of job satisfaction that matter to you. You'll dust off the tools introduced in Part I and set them to work on the short-listed jobs. You'll need to *really* understand where the market is going, how tough the competition is, how well placed you would be, and how risky it would be to back you in your target job.

In summary, you'll need to find out just how rosy these short-listed jobs or businesses really are. Are they really for you? You'll firm up the placement of these jobs on the *Hwyl* Star chart and conclude which job you should back yourself in—and which should be kept in reserve as a plan B.

In the next chapter, you'll see what you can do to improve your chances of getting in and succeeding in the target job or business. You may need to build on your strengths, or work on some weaknesses. You may use some of the tools introduced in Part II of this book. You'll see how you can improve the placement of that target job on your *Hwyl* Star chart.

But first you need to firm up on which of the short-listed jobs you're going to research first. There are three main areas for further research before you can draw firm conclusions:

- ▸ How satisfying are these short-listed jobs?
- ▸ How attractive are their markets?
- ▸ How well placed would you be in these jobs?

Let's take them one at a time.

Job Satisfaction

Let's recap. The two or three jobs or businesses that have made it into your short list are those that inspire you, fill you with passion. Hopefully they will be among those which you rated with five, or at least four, checks in Chapter 15.

But how much do you *really* know about them? To what extent has your understanding of them been colored by what you have read in newspapers or magazines, what you have seen on the TV, what your friends or family have said about them?

Do you really understand what these jobs are like? How well paid are they? Do you have to excel to make good money? What are the working conditions like? Will your desk be near a window? Will you have to work long hours? Where will you work? Will you have to spend long periods away from your family? What day-to-day work will you actually do? Will you find that fulfilling? What values are your colleagues likely to have? Will they be compatible with yours? What status will this job have in the community? Is that important to you?

You won't yet have answers to most of these questions. Nor should you be expected to. You're contemplating career change, after all, and it's unlikely at this stage that you'll know everything about the career you are thinking of changing to.

But you need to know. And now's the time to find out.

> *If you do achieve what you want with your life, what about you would you like to have remembered, after you are gone from this earth?*
> –Richard N. Bolles

First you need to establish what job satisfaction means to you. Loads of money? Perhaps, but at what cost? Would you accept bucketfuls of bucks if it meant you were expected to work in unhealthy or unsafe conditions? What if you had to compromise, even abandon your ethics? What if it meant being entirely self-centered, with no regard for others less fortunate? What if the *de facto* mechanism for personal advancement was the metaphorical rapier thrust in the back of a colleague? What if you had to bury your true self, contain your sense of humor? What if you had to be cavalier with the law?

I remember discussing with a consulting colleague a few years ago the merits of seeking a job in private equity. To do well, to get to the top in buying and selling companies, I opined, you need not only to be business savvy and financially astute, but you also had to have a genuine hunger to make money, an all embracing ambition to become rich, really rich. "I've never had that hunger," I said, "that's why I'll probably stay in consulting. What about you?" There was a pause. He looked at me with a wild-eyed determination bordering on the desperate, before answering, with no trace of irony: "I'm flipping starving!" If he gets in, he'll do well. Good luck to him.

For most human beings, however, there are many diverse aspects of job satisfaction to take into account, not just piling up the gold. Job satisfaction criteria can be grouped under six heads:

- ▷ *Pay*—Is this job (or business) likely to meet or exceed your desired level of remuneration? And pension? If pay is to be performance-related, whether through a bonus scheme, profit share, or equity participation, what are the risks of pay falling below your expectations?

- ▷ *Working conditions*—Will this job meet your expectations of type of work, hours of work, independence, work/life balance, location, frequency of overnight travel, and other working conditions?

- ▷ *Fulfillment*—Will this type of work enable you to fulfill your manual, intellectual, and creative talents?

- ▷ *Values*—Will the culture of the organization, the nature of the work, the character of your colleagues be compatible with your values?

- ▷ *Status*—Will this job confer the requisite status and importance, whether to your own self-esteem or to the community?

- ▷ *Passion*—Will this job inspire you, consume you with passion, fervor, spirit? Joy? Fun?

So far, you've ranked prospective jobs or businesses using only the last criterion, passion. It's the best place to start, but it's now time to see whether your short-listed jobs measure up to your other job satisfaction criteria.

You must first decide which of the job satisfaction criteria matter most to you. Clearly, pay was what mattered beyond all else for my former colleague referred to above. How does it rank for you?

Go through each of the six job satisfaction criteria and assign each the appropriate level of importance—whether low, medium, high, or somewhere in between. Open up a spreadsheet on your laptop and allocate in the first instance a 20% weighting for a high rating and 10% for a low one. The weightings won't add up to 100% on the first run, but you can nudge each weighting up or down as appropriate until they do. Don't get pseudo-scientific about this—a rating of 13.5% would be spurious accuracy, to the nearest 5% should be fine.

Now rate each of your short-listed jobs against each of the six job satisfaction criteria, with a score of 5 being highly satisfactory and 1 un-satisfactory. Let your spreadsheet work its magic to produce a weighted average job satisfaction score for each job.

Is the job with the highest score the same as the one with the highest passion rating? Hopefully it is, but if it isn't not to worry. Remember that all two or three short-listed jobs are worthy of further research—it's just a question of which you'll research first.

The soundest advice would be to start with the job that emerged best from the screen of Chapter 16. If that's just a four passion check job, so be it—that may well be the one for you.

Advice from the heart, rather than the head, would be to start with the short-listed job with either the highest passion rating or the overall highest job satisfaction rating.

It's really up to you. Whether you proceed with head or heart, proceed you should. Select one of those short-listed jobs as your target job.

Let's return to the example of the woman we followed in the last chapter who screened her long list of eight jobs into a short list of three (see Figure 17.1).

Figure 17.1. Satisfaction Rating of Short-Listed Jobs: An Example

Job Satisfaction Criteria	Importance	Weighting	Job H	Job G	Job C
Pay	High	20%	3	4	5
Working conditions	Very High	25%	5	4	2
Fulfilment	Med	15%	5	4	4
Values	Low/Med	10%	5	5	3
Status	Low/Med	10%	5	5	4
Passion	High	20%	5	4	3
Overall		100%	4.6	4.2	3.4

Key to Rating: 1 = Unsatisfactory, 2 = Not so satisfactory, 3 = Satisfactory,
4 = Very satisfactory, 5 = Most satisfactory

Her main priority in seeking to switch careers is to gain more flexibility around working hours, to enable her to shape her working day around school drop-off and pick-up times. So she gives this job satisfaction criterion a higher importance than pay, or even passion. She finds that job H ranks highly against all her criteria, bar one: it doesn't pay very well. But it is one of the few jobs she has given a five-check passion rating to and working hours are highly flexible.

Job G pays better, and still offers some flexibility in working hours, while job C pays really well but would demand her presence on occasions irrespective of whether her children needed picking up or were unwell. She also thinks that job C would be less fulfilling, less in tune with her values (given her would-be colleagues' fixation on the bottom line) and would lend her less status in the community than either of the other two.

Overall, job H seems like a clear winner, subject to further research. Pay wouldn't be so good, but she figures she'd be able to cut her cloth accordingly and that would be a small sacrifice to enable her to do a job she'd love. Job H will be her target job for research.

> " *Whoever renders service to many puts himself in line for greatness—*
> *great wealth, great return, great satisfaction, great reputation, and great joy.*
> –Jim Rohn

Reusing Part I Tools for the Target Job

It's now time for some serious research on your target job or business.

You need to assess how backable you would be in this target job. Imagine taking your proposition to a professional investor. Would he back you? Would you back you?

Perhaps, but only if your job analysis is backed up by research. You'll need to answer detailed, difficult questions. When you assessed your backability in your current or pre-MBA job, in Part I of this book, questions were relatively easy to answer. That was your job—you work in this field, you know or can readily find out what's going on.

But now you'll have to answer tough questions about a field you know little about. And if you can't answer them, you won't be backable. Why should you be, if you're not serious enough about this career switch to even research it properly?

In short, you need to repeat, more or less, Part I of this book! But not for your current or pre-MBA job or business. For your short-listed target job.

My recommendation is that you proceed to do full Part I research on the target job. And at the same time do some limited, desk-based research on a backup job, the runner-up in the screening process. This should give you work enough to be getting on with as you dig up data, talk to people, draw up charts, build the storyline.

If further research suggests that the target job may not be the best bet then at least you have a backup. You can upgrade research on the backup job to full Part I analysis, while starting desk-based research on the third placed job. And so on, always keeping a backup if prospects for your target job grind to a halt.

In the example in Figures 17.1, the woman would be well advised to undertake serious research on job H, while at the same time doing some desk-based research on job G.

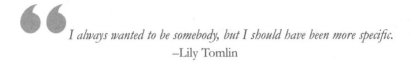

I always wanted to be somebody, but I should have been more specific.
–Lily Tomlin

How attractive is the market—really?

The first main area of further research needed is market attractiveness. You need to firm up on the rough assessment you made for Chapter 16's screening process. You know how to do it. You've already done it once, in Chapters 2 and 3, for your current or pre-MBA job or business. You just need to do it again, for the target job!

To establish how attractive the markets really are for your target job, you need to assess for each major business segment:

> ▷   Market demand prospects, risks, and opportunities.

> ▷   The nature of competition, its intensity, and how this is likely to change.

You'll start by assessing market demand prospects. Just as you did in Chapter 2 of this book, you need to:

> ▷   *Assess past growth trends*—check how market demand has grown in the past.

> ▷   *Assess past drivers of growth*—identify what has been driving that growth in the past.

> ▷   *Assess changes in growth drivers*—identify whether there will be any change in influence of these and other drivers in the future.

> ▷   *Forecast future growth*—forecast market demand growth, based on the influence of future drivers.

> ▷   *Assess market demand risks and opportunities.*

I won't go into further detail on how to do the above here. It's all there in Chapter 2. Suffice to say that this will be trickier to research than when you did it for your current or pre-MBA job or business. Some tips on how to go about finding the necessary information are set out later in this chapter.

Then you need to assess trends in competition in your target job or business. Again, just as you did in Chapter 3 of this book, you need to:

- Establish who your new competitors will be in each major segment.
- Assess whether competition is tough and/or getting tougher, using Professor Porter's Five Forces;

  » Internal rivalry
  » Threat of new entrants
  » Ease of substitution
  » Customer bargaining power
  » Supplier bargaining power

- Assess the market demand-supply balance and the implications for future prices or earnings.
- Assess competition and pricing risks and opportunities.

The above listing of a few bullets masks a lot of hard work, in both research and analysis. But it'll be worth it, and it has to be done if you are to convince yourself that you should switch to the target job.

How do your researched findings compare with the rough assessment you made of the market attractiveness of this target job or business in Chapter 16? More or less attractive? Why?

How well placed are you—really?

Next you need to firm up on how well placed you would be in this target job or business, confirming the rough assessment you undertook during Chapter 16's screening process.

Again, you know how to do it. You did it in Chapters 4, 5 and 6 for your current or pre-MBA job or business.

You need to work your way carefully through the three-stage process undertaken in Part I, establishing:

> ▸ "Customer" needs for people in your target job (Chapter 4)
> ▸ What needs to be done to succeed in that job (Chapter 5)? What are the Key Kapabilities (K2s) needed?
> ▸ How you would measure up against those K2s (Chapter 6)? What would your competitive position be?

First, you need to assess what the needs of your customers are going to be in your target job. Just as you did in Chapter 4 for your current job, you'll try to establish customer needs relating to the E2-R2-P2 of your target services, namely effectiveness, efficiency, relationship, range, premises, and price.

You'll find out what level of importance customers attach to each of their needs, how this differs by business segment, and whether this will change over time.

Undertaking this part of the research won't be as easy as when you did it for your current job. Then, you only had to talk to your own customers, or if you were an employee, to your colleagues and bosses. Here, you need to talk to your target job's "customers," the users of the services you aspire to provide. I'll set out some tips later in the chapter on how to go about this.

Second, you need to work out what the Key Kapabilities for your target job or business are. Just as you did in Chapter 5 for your current or pre-MBA job, you need to translate customer needs into what providers of that service must do to meet those needs and succeed in that job. You need to apply weights reflecting the importance of each of the K2s, taking into account not just skills, qualifications, and experience, but also such factors as market share and management. And how crucial a K2 is attitude in your target job?

Now you're in a position where you can assess how well placed you'd be in your target job or business, just as you did in Chapter 6 for your current or pre-MBA job. How would you rate against each of the K2s, in particular in relation to your peers currently performing that target job? How would your overall competitive position compare with theirs?

You must be careful here. Most people doing your target job or engaged in your target business already have much more experience than you. Their competitive position is likely to be much stronger.

Don't be dismayed. While working out your initial competitive position, think about what your rating could be *in three years' time*, and what you could work on to improve it. At the very least, the gulf in experience between you and those presently doing the job will have narrowed considerably.

And remember there's one Key Kapability where you're going to be at least on a par with those already in the field. And hopefully you may surpass many of them. That is *attitude*. The whole reason you are targeting this job is because of the passion. Some of those currently in this field may have grown jaded over the years, others may never have thought of it as their ideal job.

Not so for you. From day one your enthusiasm will be radiant and your energy levels volcanic. At least on this K2, you'll be top of the tree.

These are only first cuts at your competitive position. Where you're particularly unsure how you'd rate yourself, stick in a question mark. You'll revisit your rating once you've done your further research, in particular talking to some practitioners in the field, as well as their customers.

You've now worked out how well placed you'd be in your target job or business upon entry, and if things go according to plan, in three years' time. How does that compare with the crude assessment you made for this job during the screening process of Chapter 16? Better placed or worse? Why? What risks?

How Do You Find Out?

How can you find out about job market attractiveness and your prospective competitive position in a field you know little about? It's not as difficult as you may think. But it does involve picking up the telephone.

As set out in Chapter 6, there are two main sources of information available for researching job markets and your potential positioning:

> The Internet and other sources of third-party market research

> Structured interviewing

The Internet is a boon for doing desk-based market research—please take another look here at Chapter 2 and the section *Weave Your Web of Information.*

Then there's structured interviewing, first encountered in Chapter 6. But things were easier then. For employees, information on customer needs and the extent to which you perform and meet those needs, in relation to your colleagues, could be readily gleaned just from talking to your boss. For the self-employed, you could derive such information through a structured interview program with your customers.

But these were users of your services. They were your colleagues (if you were an employee) or your very own customers (if you were self-employed). Who then are the customers of those currently doing your target job or business? And how do you get to talk to them? For that matter, who are the providers of your target job? It's not you any more. This is not your current job, it's a target job. How do you get to talk to these current practitioners?

You need to talk to both sets of people—providers and customers of your target job.

You need to talk to the providers to get a firmer idea of how satisfying the job would be. You need to accumulate further information on the nature of the work, the hours, the travel, the culture, and so forth. You need to wheedle out their views on what it takes to be successful in their field.

You should talk to their customers to find out their needs and what providers need to have and do in order to meet them.

Again, as in Chapter 6, the answer is through structured interviewing. But this time with two additional complications:

> ▸ You need to interview both customers *and* providers.

> ▸ You may well not know any customers *or* providers!

It's not as daunting as it may seem. Think of market researchers or salespeople cold calling. They are trying to find out information from you or sell you something that is typically of little interest, relevance or usefulness to you. Imagine how difficult that job is. They deserve a break, which is why I try to be polite as I thank them, through gritted teeth, for their call and replace the receiver gently!

It is nowhere near as hard for you. You'll have a storyline with which *people can empathize*. You're interested in this field of work and would like to find out more about it. You're not threatening. You'll encounter a range of people, from those who have no time or inclination to talk to you, though even they will typically be polite and well wishing, to those who'll be delighted to chat and inform and encourage you. The biggest challenge is actually summoning the guts to pick up a phone in the first place and call a company cold.

Here in summary is how to conduct a structured interviewing program for your target job or business, which is an approach similar to that of Chapter 6:

> ▸ Select a representative range of provider and customer interviewees, preferably with some sort of a referee to break the ice.

> ▸ Prepare your storyline.

> ▸ Draw up a concise questionnaire for providers, and a separate one for customers.

> ▸ Interview them, through email, telephone, or, best of all, face-to-face.

> ▸ Thank them and give them some feedback.

This approach is set out in some detail in Appendix C.

Further research through structured interviewing is the key to confirming your assessment of these aspects of your target job or business:

> ‣ How attractive is the market really for this job?
>
> ‣ How well placed would you be really for this job?
>
> ‣ How satisfied would you be in this job?

These are of course the three components needed for your *Hwyl* Star chart. It's time to reexamine it.

Your *Hwyl* Star Chart revisited

You've done your research. You now have a much firmer idea on how attractive the market is for your target job or business. Likewise you're clearer on how well placed you'd be in that job and how satisfying it would be.

Has your research confirmed that this is a job that would meet all, or most, of your satisfaction criteria? That it remains a job not just with passion, but with pay, working conditions, fulfillment, values and status that would, on balance, rank it above other short-listed jobs or businesses?

And where does your target job now sit on your *Hwyl* Star chart? Has it shifted significantly from your earlier drafting in Chapter 16?

Has it shifted, disappointingly, to the left, or downwards? Worse, has it headed toward the bottom left-hand corner? Is it now looking less promising than other short-listed jobs or businesses?

Is it indeed time to draw a line through this target job? Rather than embarking on a job hunt in this field, with all that entails—job searches, application letters, chase-up calls, interviews and all else—should you cut your losses now? And move on to researching your backup job?

Or has your research left your target job more or less where it was on the *Hwyl* Star chart? That should be encouraging. Even better, has the research improved the job's positioning, shifting it a tad upwards, or to the right, or even toward the top right-hand corner?

Has the research improved your chances of being backable in your target job or business?

Meeting Your Earnings Aspirations

As we saw in Part I of this book, there are four pieces of the Risk Jigsaw: market demand risk, competition risk, your competitive position risk, and your plan risk. The research you've done in this chapter has helped you address the first three jigsaw pieces for your target job or business. What about the fourth? Are your earnings aspirations likely to be met?

What are your planned earnings in your target job in three years' time? If you'll be an employee, what's your planned pay? If you're aiming to be self-employed, what are your planned revenues and profits?

Are these plans consistent with what your research suggests will happen in the market? Are they consistent with your likely lowly competitive position when you start the job? Do they realistically reflect the likely improvement in your competitive position over the first three years of you doing the job, or running the business?

What are the risks of you not making that plan?

Perhaps you may benefit from a quick look back at Chapter 7 of this book, where the examples given highlight the need for *consistency* in the assumptions in your plan.

Are You Backable in Your Target Job?

We're there! You now have all you need to draw up a Suns & Clouds chart for you switching career to your target job or business.

Have a quick skim through Chapter 8 to remind you how to do it, then give it a go! How does it look? Hopefully there will be a reasonable balance between risks and opportunities.

Don't be disheartened if the overall picture looks rather cloudy! What did you expect? You're shifting career. You'll be new to this job. It's bound to be risky!

But what is this life if you take no risks? Nothing ventured…

Are you sure, however, that there are no showstopper risks? If there is, even just the one, back out now. Don't waste any further time or effort switching to this job.

Are there any risks sitting uncomfortably close to the showstopper area? If so, is there anything you can do to mitigate those risks?

Would you back you in your target job or business?

Let's hope so. But before you start sending out those application letters, shouldn't you be thinking about how you can improve your chances of getting in? And once in, how you can improve your chances of succeeding there?

That's for the next chapter.

Is Jennifer Backable in a Career Switch to Private Equity?

Three jobs have passed through Jennifer's screen: finance directing, private equity, and strategy consulting. First things first, Jennifer checks to see whether their job satisfaction rankings will emerge similarly to their passion rankings of Chapter 15.

She finds that all three rate highly in job satisfaction, but, to her surprise, strategy consulting ranks just ahead of private equity. Yet she'd quit her job in transaction services to do an MBA with the primary aim of switching to private equity! What's going on?!

Sure, private equity wins hands down on pay (see Figure 17.2), and she has always known that working hours will be arduous—though no less so than in her pre-MBA job and in strategy consulting. And in terms of status and passion, private equity is right up there along with consulting.

Where she's now hesitating is in terms of fulfillment and values. Jennifer suspects that she may gain more professional fulfillment in devising ways for a client to grow a business than in concocting a clever financial structure to optimize equity returns. And her main values of collaboration and mutual support seem to favor more the culture of consulting than private equity.

Figure 17.2. Jennifer's Satisfaction Rating of Short-listed Jobs

Job Satisfaction Criteria	Importance to Jennifer	Jennifer's Weighting	Private Equity	Strategy Consulting	Finance Director
Pay	Very High	25%	5	4	3.5
Working Conditions	High	20%	3	3	5
Fulfilment	Med	15%	4	5	4
Values	Low/Med	10%	3	5	5
Status	Low/Med	10%	5	5	4
Passion	High	20%	5	5	4
Overall		100%	4.3	4.4	4.2

Key to Rating: 1 = Unsatisfactory, 2 = Not so satisfactory, 3 = Satisfactory, 4 = Very satisfactory, 5 = Most satisfactory

Meanwhile, the job that came through Jennifer's screening process as a clear winner, finance director of a medium-sized company, has also emerged well from the job satisfaction ranking, even though marginally below the other two jobs.

But these are rough, preliminary findings and merit further research. Jennifer decides to put heart before head, passion and job satisfaction before backability, and proceed for the time being with private equity as her target job, with strategy consulting as a back-up.

Research in private equity presents no problem for Jennifer. She has been doing transaction advisory work for many private equity executives over the last three years. When she leaves a voicemail for those she deems most likeable and communicative, they get back to her quickly—if only because they think she may have a lead for them!

Within a couple of weeks, Jennifer has done structured interviews with nine of them, including two face to face, along with three telephone interviews with managers at investee companies. She has also trawled the business school library and conducted Internet research on market trends. She fills in the charts of Appendix A on market demand for private equity (Chapter 2), competition in the private equity industry (3), customer (corporate) and stakeholder (asset manager) needs (4), K2s of private equity practitioners (5), her likely competitive position upon entry and in three years' time (6), and her business plan (7). Finally Jennifer gets to the Suns & Clouds chart (Chapter 8) and examines it carefully (Figure 17.3).

Figure 17.3. Jennifer's Risks and Opportunities in Switching to Private Equity

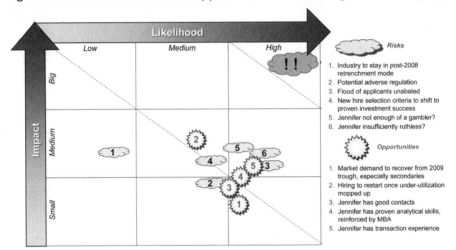

The chart looks inclement—too many clouds in the wrong places. While there can be little doubt that Jennifer is intellectually and analytically well suited for the job—viz. sun 4, and she has exceptional transactional experience for a new applicant (sun 5), it's not clear that her contact list (sun 3) will be of much help since her private equity contacts know her as an advisor and supplier as opposed to a peer, and it might be hard to change their mindset.

More worryingly, Jennifer's interviews have confirmed what she had suspected but pushed to the back of her mind. Private equity directors are seeking to engage not just brilliant analytical minds, but investors, even gamblers (see risk 4). One or two anecdotes have proved illuminating: One contact had been asked at his interview whether he preferred betting on the horses, on roulette, or on futures. When he answered none of them, his interviewer seemed deflated, but perked up when the contact said he preferred investing in equities! Jennifer prefers to place her savings in tax-efficient unit trusts—not an answer that would impress, she suspects (cloud 5).

Finally, Jennifer has picked up further feedback about the type of individual who thrives in the private equity industry, especially from two interviewees who have quit. Success, it seems, depends on an element of ruthlessness in the individual, understandably when applied to those on the opposite side of the negotiating table, but less so when displayed in dealings with employees and investee company managers, and especially come bonus time, with fellow colleagues. Jennifer suspects she may lack, and has little desire to cultivate, the hard edge to succeed in the business (cloud 6).

It is with a sense of dread that Jennifer completes the Part I analysis by drawing up the storyline (as in Chapter 9) to answer the question: Would you back you in a shift to a career in private equity? Here it is:

In a still tight private equity market, Jennifer may not have the full set of capabilities and experience needed to get in and prosper:

- *Market demand prospects:* Private equity is recovering slowly from the credit crunch of 2008–10, but recruitment will remain at a low ebb for some time.
- *Competition:* Competition for the few posts available remains ferocious and may become more so as recruiters place more emphasis on investment track record.
- *Jennifer's competitive position:* Jennifer has transactional experience and proven analytical capabilities, but her personality seems more attuned to a role as an adviser.

- *Jennifer's plan:* Jennifer's earnings expectations will certainly be met if she succeeds as a private equity executive, but the risk of an early exit would linger.
- *Risks and opportunities:* Risks of tough competition and Jennifer's lack of capitalistic oomph and steel overshadow the opportunities of her transactional past, analytical skills, and contacts.

That's it, then. Jennifer has learned that she's not backable in a switch to private equity. Tough, but that's life.

And no harm done. She has only invested a couple of days of her life researching the possibility. It has been a learning experience. But it's time to draw a line in the sand.

Of course she's tempted to have a go at it anyway and send out a bio to her many private equity contacts. But that would be foolish. She should now look at private equity as she did movie acting and music in the last chapter—as history.

Time to move on to her back-up job and raise it to target status. She has already been through the business school library and careers office files on strategy consulting. Now she upgrades this job to the structured interviewing phase. A couple of weeks later she has drawn up her Suns & Clouds (see Figure 17.4).

This chart looks altogether more clement. Jennifer's main opportunities shine through clearly. Her many contacts in strategy consulting, alongside whom she has worked on many deals, are advisers, just like she is. Her proven analytical skills, reinforced by the MBA, will be valued even more highly in a consultancy. And her transactional experience will give her an edge over some of her prospective colleagues.

Figure 17.4. Jennifer's Risks and Opportunities in Switching to Strategy Consulting

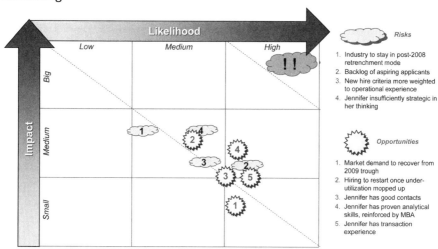

On the other hand, there are some concerns. A couple of interviewees have told her that firms tend to be recruiting those with more hands-on, corporate operational experience these days—though the balance may shift back to strategists in future months. Most worryingly, Jennifer's track record in financial due diligence may give hirers the impression that she is a historical thinker. Strategists need to think in the future. But here Jennifer can come up with a number of examples where she has worked alongside top-tier strategy consultants in firming up base case cash flow forecasts.

Jennifer does a Chapter 9-style storyline and concludes that she is backable in a switch to strategy consulting. It's no slam dunk, but nothing worth achieving ever is.

She decides to give it a shot. And if she finds it difficult to get into one of her target strategy consulting houses, she'll brush off the cobwebs on her next back-up job, finance directing for medium-sized companies.

First Jennifer needs to do more groundwork and prepare an entry strategy for strategy consulting. That's for the next chapter....

Is Valerie Backable in a Career Switch to Strategy Consulting?

We last saw Valerie in Chapter 14 after she had followed the approach of Part II and developed a robust strategy to return to her former job as an independent economic consultant after her MBA.

But there was a nagging doubt in her mind. Would she be more inspired shifting to a new job altogether? And, if so, would she be backable?

Nothing to lose, she figures, so she tackles the approach of Part III, with these results:

- She finds that strategy consulting tops her long list of jobs with passion, alongside charity management (preferably working in economic development), medicine (preferably with the Red Cross or Médecins Sans Frontiers), and Member of Parliament—each of which receives five passion checks (Chapter 15).
- Her pre-MBA job of economic consulting gets four and a half checks —it would have had five, even six, if only there were more work around in economic competitiveness or, even better, business strategy.
- It's neck and neck between charity management and strategy consulting in the screening process, with both similarly well placed on the *Hwyl* Star chart (Chapter 16); she opts for strategy consulting as her target job, with charity management as the back-up.
- She undertakes a similar market research and structured interview program as Jennifer's and speaks with many involved in strategy consulting (Chapter 17).
- She draws up her Suns & Clouds for a shift to strategy consulting (see Figure 17.5).

Figure 17.5. Valerie's Risks and Opportunities in Switching to Strategy Consulting

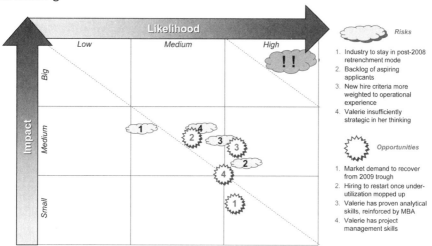

Jennifer is dismayed. The chart doesn't yield an outright no, but it is hardly a ringing endorsement. On balance, clouds 2, 3, and 4 seem to outweigh sun 3.

Market-wide risks (1 and 2) and opportunities (1 and 2) remain unchanged from those of Jennifer's Suns & Clouds (Figure 17.4). Likewise sun 3, Valerie's proven analytical capability (as for Jennifer), reinforced by an MBA, is the outstanding opportunity.

But in Valerie's case, risk 3 becomes more prominent. The more mature the applicant to strategy consulting, as in most other jobs, the more directly relevant the experience has to be. This is less important for the younger Jennifer. For Valerie to slot into a strategy consulting firm, her experience would need to be not too dissimilar to that of a current employee of around her age, mid-30s, someone at senior manager knocking on partner level.

Valerie's experience is in working with government departments in less developed countries, not with private sector companies in the developed world. She wouldn't be able to take on a managerial role on a typical strategy consulting assignment without further in-house training and ongoing supervision. She becomes a risky hire, a reasonable prospect in a tight job market, an unlikely prospect when the supply of applicants greatly exceeds demand.

Valerie is not evidently backable in a shift to strategy consulting. She may decide to give it a try and float her bio around a few firms to see what happens. Better would be to move on to further research on the back-up job, charity management.

But Valerie has seen enough of Part III. She is now certain what she wants to do. She will return to economic consulting with the marketing-led strategy she developed in Part II.

She is going to return to her passion, focus, and work hard. She will sparkle, specialize, and sweat. And she will succeed!

Is Hari Backable in His New Venture?

In Chapter 13 we saw Hari and his new wife Concha resolve to start their own business in designer quality cases for laptops. They know what they are passionate about, so they skip Chapters 15 and 16, and dive straight into the research of Chapter 17.

They are initially stumped over "How Attractive Is the Market Really for the Target Job or Business?" Because theirs is a new venture, a fresh start, they wonder how they can realistically assess market demand.

It's the standard question in a startup. By definition, there are no customers, so where does one go to find out?

The answer is to talk to potential customers. In a B2B startup, you should talk to prospective clients. In a B2C startup like Hari's, you often have to do some pilot consumer test marketing.

So Hari and Concha rustle up a couple of buddies, drive North along the bay to the financial district of San Francisco, and stand on California Street at lunchtime armed with a clipboard and some sketches, accosting any elegantly dressed office workers that pass by. Their findings are encouraging. Within a certain price range, almost two fifths of respondents say they might be interested in buying such a laptop case if it existed!

Meanwhile, Hari makes some enquiries through the Thai wife of a friend and finds that the unit cost of production, assuming an initial batch of 1,000, could lie well within the upper limit needed for viability.

Things are looking promising, but there seem to be all sorts of risks. So Hari draws up his Suns & Clouds chart to put them in perspective (see Figure 17.6).

Figure 17.6. Hari's Risks and Opportunities in Launching UCo

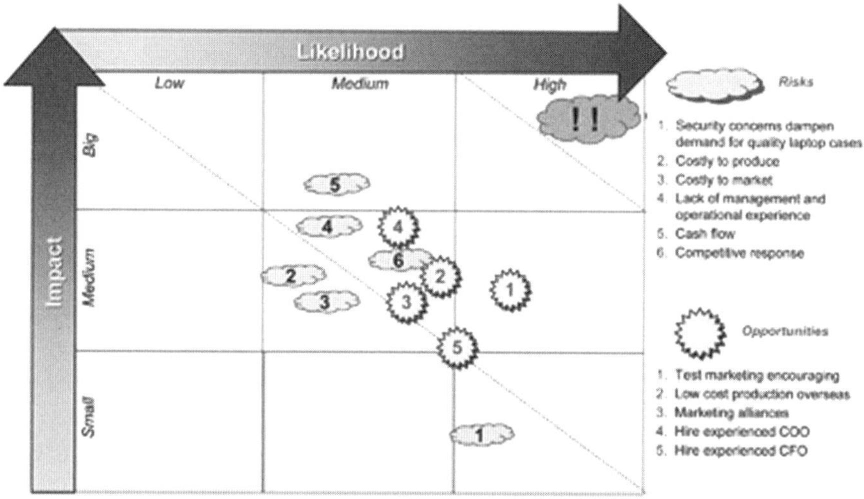

Hari finds that most risks appear largely containable. For nearly every risk there is a mitigating factor. The risk that the case will be too costly to manufacture (number 2) is offset by the opportunity of low-cost production overseas, perhaps in Thailand (2). The risk that it will be costly to market (3) can be minimized through a strategic marketing alliance with companies which offer similar products (3). And the risk of his inexperience in running a company (4) can be mitigated through the engagement of a chief operating officer (4) who has experience in small business startups.

The overall balance of risk and opportunity looks promising. The main risks of competitive response (6) and cash flow difficulties (5) in the first couple of years, hopefully mitigated by the appointment of a competent chief financial officer and a supportive venture capital backer, should be eclipsed by the shining sun (1) of the test marketing results. Indeed, a few people Hari spoke to said they would be prepared to pay top dollar for such a product, even above the stated guide price range!

Hari thinks his YouCo looks backable. But what can he do now to make him *more* backable before he takes it to a venture capitalist? That's for Chapter 18.

18

Shortening the Odds

Reusing Part II Tools for the Target Job
  » The K2 Gap
  » Your Entry Strategy
Becoming More Backable in Your Target Job

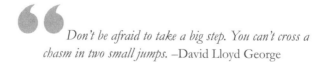 *Don't be afraid to take a big step. You can't cross a chasm in two small jumps.* –David Lloyd George

In the last chapter, you found a job or business where the passion lies and, with an MBA in your pocket, you may well be backable.

Let's pause there for a moment. That's already some achievement! You've found a job of your dreams where you'll be backable. Or not far off. Isn't that amazing? You're on the verge of setting off on a course that could change your life.

But before you do, there's one further step. From all the research you conducted in the last chapter on your target job, did you find anything that you could or should be doing *now*, *before* you set off in pursuit of this new job or business?

Before you embark on this journey, are you well prepared? If you were planning to go on a long, long hike, wouldn't you put in a good few week-ends of practice covering plenty of miles with a hefty load on your back? Wouldn't you ensure you assembled the right provisions and equipment? The right map? Compass? Tent pegs? Stove? Waterproof clothing? Pre-served foods? Water? Plasters for the inevitable blisters?

How should you prepare before you embark on this journey of career change? What will equip you to give you the best chance of reaching your destination?

This is where the tools deployed in Part II of this book can help. How can you build on your strengths, or work on your weaknesses, before you set off, or while you are pursuing your target job?

Which of the *Stand Out!*, *easyU!* or *Sharpen Act!* strategies (Chapter 12) would shorten the odds of success in your preferred field? How would they impact on positioning in the *Hwyl* Star chart? If you were to do the same or similar to prepare for other short-listed jobs, would that change their relative positioning? By the end of this chapter, you'll have planned how to go about improving your chances of success in your job shift.

You'll have ensured that you're as well provisioned as possible before you set off on the journey of the next chapter, Now Pursue the Passion!

Reusing Part II Tools For the Target Job

The K2 gap

First you need to envision what the ideal provider of services in your tar-get job or business will look like in three years' time. To an extent you've already done this. In the last chapter, you assessed customer needs and the Key Kapabilities needed to do the job well.

Here you can push that analysis a bit further. You could try thinking a little more "out of the box" about how things may evolve in the markets and companies you will be serving in this new job. You could try building scenarios ("What if such and such happens?") about what may happen in the future. You could then work out what capabilities the ideal provider of services would need under each scenario, and which of those capabilities would be common to all or most of the scenarios.

If you think this approach could be useful, take a look at Chapter 10, where it's all set out, step by step. But there is, of course, one main difference. You'll be doing it not for your current or pre-MBA job, but your target job with passion.

The next step is to identify the gap between your likely competitive position in your target job and that of the ideal provider. The gap will be wide at present, but it should narrow over time, if only by virtue of your growing experience as time goes by. But that may not be sufficient.

To what extent does the gap differ in the various business segments in your target job? You may choose to draw up a Strategic Bubble Bath, with your likely competitive position along the x-axis and the market attractiveness of each business segment along the y-axis—as we did in Chapter 11 for your current or pre-MBA job.

Think about where you could be in three years' time in your target job. Be realistic. You won't make it to the ideal provider within three years. But how close can you get? How close did you assume you'd get when you assessed your competitive position in the last chapter? Should you now stretch your sights and make your plans more ambitious? Should you "go for the goal"?

In the light of your reset sights, what then is the shortfall between your expected capabilities after three years and the capabilities to which you aspire—the K2 gap?

The drawing up of the K2 gap is set out in detail in Chapter 11. Now you'll be doing it for your target job.

Your entry strategy

Okay, you've established the K2 gap for your target job or business. How are you going to bridge it?

You'll need to select an entry strategy. In Chapter 12, you were introduced to the three main generic strategies, which we called Stand Out!, easyU! and Sharpen Act! You were shown how to develop strategic alternatives around that generic strategy, investing in areas such as marketing and training for an employee, possibly self-financed. For the self-employed, further areas of investment could be in premises, equipment, staff, or partnership. You were shown how to evaluate these alternatives and how to build a realistic action plan.

Again, I won't repeat here what's already written in Chapter 12 except for this: You'll have a much better chance of getting in and succeeding in your target job if you have a sound entry strategy, if you know where you want to be in three years' time, and a plan on how you're going to get there.

And this: A Stand-Out! or easyU! strategy will get you into your target job more readily than a Sharpen Act! strategy. If there is something distinctive and differentiating about you, or if you are offering a quality service at a competitive price, you'll be raising your head above the parapet.

The Sharpen Act! strategy, where you work on some evident weaknesses, is really more applicable to progressing in your current or pre-MBA job. If one of your known areas of weakness is an important Key Kapability in your target job, you should think again. Should you really be aiming for a job which doesn't play to your strengths? Having said that, if the target job is the one of your dreams, and you could raise your capabilities in that area to at least parity over time, then why not have a go?

Having selected your generic entry strategy, what are your alternatives for realizing it? If you're to be an employee, what investment should you make in marketing or training? If self-employed, what investment do you need not just in those two areas, but also in equipment, premises, staff, and partnering? Take another look at Chapter 12 for further discussion on this.

Decide on the most effective strategic alternative and draw up an action plan (see the example in Chapter 12 again).

Becoming More Backable In Your Target Job

You've envisioned the ideal provider of your target job or business, reset your sights, identified the gaps, selected a generic entry strategy, firmed up the optimal strategic alternative, and drawn up an action plan. You'll be in better shape to embark on your job hunt.

How will that impact on the competitive position chart you drew up in Chapter 17? Has your likely position in year three been strengthened appreciably?

Has your Suns & Clouds chart of Chapter 17 become sunnier? Has the balance of risk and opportunity shifted in your favor?

Have you shortened the odds of getting in and succeeding in your target job or business?

Have you become more backable in your career switch?

Shortening Jennifer's Odds in Strategy Consulting

Jennifer has decided to aim for a career in strategy consulting after her MBA. Now she needs to improve her chances of getting in there. And succeeding once in.

She turns to Part II and kicks off with some brainstorming. Jennifer is not the sporty type and relaxation for her comes with pampering. She heads off to the spa, emerges scrubbed, roasted, and tenderized, cooks herself some vegetarian pasta, cracks open a bottle of 2001 vintage Californian red, and ponders the future of strategy consulting.

She comes up with three scenarios, which she names:

- *Purse Zipped!*—public sector consulting opportunities are far fewer in the recessionary era of austerity.
- *Baby Come Back!*—deal flow returns, following a two-year trough, as private equity opens its coffers.
- *Dirty Knees!*—hiring continues to favor those with corporate operational experience.

Implications for the ideal provider of strategy consulting services she sees thus:

- *Purse Zipped!*—a track record of public sector work will not be an advantage.
- *Baby Come Back!*—expertise in strategic due diligence and financial analysis will become revalued.
- *Dirty Knees!*—those with corporate operational experience will be at an advantage.

Jennifer doesn't see much commonality of K2s here, but the findings are nevertheless useful. Scenario 2 is to her benefit, 1 and 3 are not. She needs to exploit Scenario 2.

Figure 18.1. Jennifer's Strategic Bubble Bath and Sights Setting

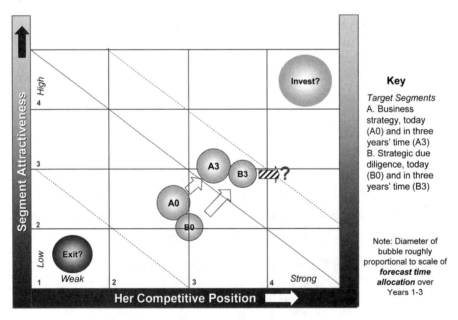

Jennifer sets herself high sights. She aspires to be Ms. Ideal Provider Tomorrow. That means raising her competitive position from where it is now, and where it might otherwise be in three years' time, to new levels. The markets should become more attractive with economic recovery, and Jennifer's position should improve over time, but how can she go beyond that (see her Strategic Bubble Bath in Figure 18.1)?

Her MBA will help, but she needs to specialize further. She must be an exceptional candidate, with a distinctive Stand Out! strategy. In a sentence: To build on her competitive position in strategy consulting through sustained investment of cash, time, and energy in one area of specialization, namely strategic finance.

She identifies three strategic alternatives:

- Take the key strategy electives, like mergers, acquisitions, and alliances, global strategy, strategies for growth, and so on, but attend or shadow key finance electives, like advanced corporate finance, options and futures, or structured finance, and join relevant clubs, e.g., the private equity club.
- Undertake a project for, or do a summer internship with, an investment bank, private equity house, or finance-orientated strategy group.
- Embark on a corporate finance evening program once she graduates, or perhaps one year later.

Jennifer is a driven and hard-working student, but even she wonders whether A is achievable. She's no Hermione Granger, armed with a Time Turner! B seems achievable, with no extra investment of time or money, unlike C—the merits of which Jennifer can see, but she may have had enough of the lecture hall by then!

She opts for alternative B, for sure, plus as much of A as a muggle can realistically achieve. She will also think again on C if her strategy consulting employer doesn't give her enough further training.

Now Jennifer re-examines her Suns & Clouds (see Figure 18.2). Her strategy should make risk 4 less likely to occur, pushing cloud 4 to the left. This single shift improves the overall balance of risk and opportunity appreciably.

Figure 18.2. Risks and Opportunities with Jennifer's Entry Strategy in Switching to Strategy Consulting

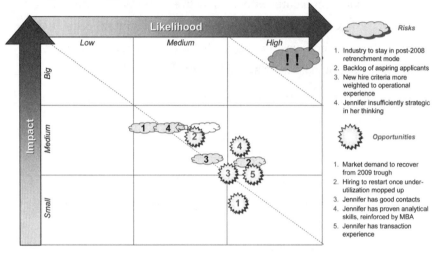

Jennifer's entry strategy has made her more backable. She has shortened the odds of a successful career shift to strategy consulting.

Shortening Hari's Odds in YouCo

Hari and Concha do some brainstorming, lying lazily in bed one rainy Sunday morning, armed with coffee, croissants and, as a treat, an assortment of their favorite tropical fruits—mango, mangosteen, and pomelo. They consider a range of scenarios, ranging from the grim—product malfunction—to the cheery—celebrity endorsement. But the one they keep coming back to is competitive response.

Once they have a product in the market, selling well, others will follow. Barriers to entry are low, and even lower for the main potential competitors—handbag producers. There is a danger that the laptop producers themselves might choose to sell more downmarket versions of their case, whether leather or faux leather.

One Key Success Factor (for a business, as opposed to a Key Kapability for an individual) needed to withstand this risk will have to be strength of brand. Hari and Concha will have to come up with not just a stellar name, but a thorough plan on how they will build this brand, at what cost, and by when.

Armed with a robust brand development plan, umbilically linked to his business plan, Hari will be able to approach a venture capitalist. He'll be more backable.

19
Pursuing the Passion

Twelve Tips on Winning Your Target Job
- » Find Your Ideal Employer
- » Land the Interview
- » Perform at the Interview
- » Follow Up the Interview

Launching Your Own Business
Backing the *Hwyl*!

> 66
> *The greatest glory in living lies not in never falling, but in rising every time we fall.* –Nelson Mandela (from Confucius)

In Chapter 18, you developed an entry strategy for your post-MBA target job or business.

Now it's time to go out and get that job. Or start that business.

It's time to pursue the passion!

This chapter considers what you need to do to land that dream job, or start that dream business. It's not comprehensive—that's for specialist books on the process of job-hunting. This chapter merely pulls out a dozen choice tips on how to back the passion, many of which have been learned by the author the hard way, along a meandering career path.

Here they are.

Twelve Tips on Winning Your Target Job

Find your ideal employer

Okay. You've found your dream job. You've prepared and provisioned yourself for it. You finish your MBA, take a few months off backpacking round South America, then start the job-hunting process in earnest. Smart? No!

Tip #1—It's best not to "quit your job" until you have the next one lined up!

You're a special case. You've already quit your job, probably, to do an MBA—at least a one year investment, probably two. Good for you.

Happily, employers will regard your doing your MBA as doing a job. Employers like their applicants to be in full time work when they apply. They like to think their prospective employees are highly marketable, worth courting, worth pinching. They themselves are rushed of their feet. They feel uncomfortable with applicants who have too much time on their hands.

And from your perspective, applying while doing the MBA, like being in a full time job, will sharpen you up. When you're working, your responses are smarter, your energy levels higher, your time tighter, and this will come through in the interview.

Take a few months off, or worse a gap year, and you will have lost that sharpness when you go knocking on doors. It's brutal, but true. In the old days, old timers used to say that it didn't matter what you did in your 20s, as long as you knuckle down in your 30s.

No more. People who take time off are regarded by investment banking or management consulting employers as not serious about their careers, almost as drifters. Forget about the mind-broadening benefits of traveling the world, as I did for twelve years. In today's ultra-competitive world, such indulgence equates with unemployability.

Land the job first, while still at business school. *Then* ask them if you can defer the start date by a few months…

Okay. You sit yourself down in the Careers Center at business school and trawl through the correspondence files. You scan through job postings, checking out the online sites, as well as the traditional sites in newspapers, magazines, journals. You write to two dozen headhunters who seem to be active in your chosen field. Smart? Yes and no!

Tip #2—Don't wait for the employer to come to you. Go to the employer!

By the time you get to see a job posting, even a letter direct to your Careers Center, it may be too late. The employer may already have someone in mind, advertising the post just to check the right boxes on equality of opportunity. And your response to the ad will be one of many, possibly one of hundreds. It'll be difficult to stand out from the crowd.

Likewise with writing to headhunters. They may agree to meet you, but "Don't call us, we'll call you when something comes up" is their typical response. Don't hold your breath. The odds of that one headhunter receiving the mandate for the job you want are low. The odds of her then calling you, having since met scores of other hopefuls, are likewise low. Multiply those probabilities together and your chances of being asked to an interview on a specific job vacancy are very low. Some get lucky, of course, but the odds aren't great.

The best strategy by far is to pick out the companies you want to work for and approach them directly. After all, you know quite a bit about them by now. You've conducted your research in Chapter 17, you've even spoken to practitioners. You may even have spoken to people who work in the very companies you wish to apply to.

They may well have no vacancy. But one may become available soon. And they could consider an additional place just for you. Why? Because they'll receive an approach, whether by letter or telephone, preferably both, from you, that will be passionate. You'll inject that passion into all your communication with the company.

They'd be fools not to take you on board. Think what they'd miss if you went to a competitor!

Land the interview

Okay. You find a dozen companies who employ people in your target field. You get the addresses, draw up a pro forma cover letter, and insert the addresses into each cover letter, maybe with some mail merge software. Smart? No!

Tip #3—Wherever possible, start the cover letter with a referral.

Most unsolicited letters enquiring about a job opportunity end up if not in the trash can then in a huge folder, to be dealt with via the standard, pro forma rejection letter. You know the one: "Very interested to receive your letter…most impressed with your qualifications and experience…however (and here it comes!)…no appropriate opportunities available at the moment…will keep you on our books…we wish you all the very best for the future…"

Your chances of receiving one of these will be reduced if you can sneak some sort of a referral into the opening paragraph. For example, *Dear Mr. Ford, Diana Lopez from your performance improvement practice kindly suggested that I write to you…* should be more effective than simply writing *Dear Mr. Ford, I am writing to enquire whether you have any vacancies in your performance improvement practice…*

Even this rather tenuous referral shows that you have taken the trouble to find out about the company and call, speak to, possibly even meet a member of staff. It's a signal of interest, enthusiasm, and initiative that could place you in a different category from other applicants.

Best of all, of course, is a genuine referral from someone you know, or someone who knows someone you know, and who actually recommends you for this job. Assuming the referee is a person of stature and known to the recipient of the letter that can be sufficient to get you through the door.

The referral is one reason why your cover letters shouldn't be standardized. But even in the absence of a referral, your cover letter should be customized. The cover letter, along with the enclosed résumé, is your key to getting in the door of a company. And the more you can show in that letter that you are worth opening the door to, the better your chances.

Tip #4—Customize the cover letter for *that* job in *that* company.

The cover letter is an opportunity to show that you have a sound understanding of the company and why it would be to their benefit to hire someone like you. The first paragraph is introductory, preferably with a referral. In the space of three further paragraphs—the cover letter should be just one page, with plenty of white space and not too much type—you need to communicate the following:

- Paragraph 2: Your understanding of the company, its needs, and how the company would benefit from recruiting the ideal employee for this job.
- Paragraph 3: Your background, leading up to why you are applying for this job.
- Paragraph 4: Why you are exceptionally well placed to meet the company's needs (highlighting your strengths against Key Kapabilities) and why you would do so with enthusiasm and passion.

This means that each letter must be special to the company to which you are writing. Much more work for you, of course, but we're talking here about switching to a job you're passionate about! Surely that's worth a couple of extra hours on the Internet, backed up preferably by a couple of calls?

Okay. You update your résumé, photocopy it a dozen times, and enclose it in each of the dozen, individually crafted cover letters. Smart? No!

Tip #5—Tailor your résumé for *that* job in *that* company

Remember, the résumé, along with the cover letter, is your key to getting in the door of a target company. Is there any one element of your experience or qualifications that could be more relevant to that company? If so, could this be highlighted in some way in your résumé?

For example, suppose you are applying for a job in strategy consulting. You write to one company that specializes in the fast moving consumer goods sector. So you highlight in your résumé any client interaction or projects you've worked on over the years with relevance not just to strategy, but also to consumer goods companies or related sectors such as food, drink, retail, logistics, and consumer services like travel or insurance.

Likewise, you should highlight how areas of responsibility in your past jobs are of direct relevance to specific responsibilities likely to be demanded in the job for which you are applying.

The more tailored your résumé, the more customized your cover letter, the better your chances of getting through the door.

Okay. You've sent off your customized letters and tailored résumés. All you have to do is sit and wait for the mail or for a phone call. Smart? No!

Tip #6—Chase!

If you hear from the company within two to three weeks, fine. If not, call them. Chase them. Remember, this is a job with passion you're after. Maybe the delay is because they're moving your application around between departments. Fine. Maybe it's because they've made their decision, one way or another, but they've been too busy to get round to notifying you. Maybe it's because the letter got lost in the post, lost in the company, buried in one executive's in-basket. Not so fine.

You need to know. Chase!

Perform at the interview

Okay. You've landed an interview or two or more! The more the merrier, in fact, because it's good to get interview practice, even for jobs you're not hugely keen on or where they probably won't be keen on you. Practice makes perfect.

All you have to do now is roll up for the interview, be yourself, and the job's yours! Smart? No!

Tip #7—Dress to impress!

Here's a rule of thumb: Be as well dressed as the best-dressed person in the room.

Companies tend to recruit in their own likeness. Period. That means looking how they look, not how you want to look. If you're a casual sort of guy and will only feel comfortable working in the kind of organization that is relaxed about dress, fine. But don't take the risk of showing up sloppy at the interview, thinking it's a laid-back organization. The organization may be, but what if your interviewer isn't? Suppose she comes into the room looking drop-dead smart. No matter what the organization, sloppy dress will come over as disrespectful. You may not be taken seriously.

Even if you know it to be an open-shirt type of organization, play it safe. Wear a tie.

I remember going for an interview in London in the early-1980s. I'd been working overseas for many years and went to the interview wearing a two-tone brown suit, the jacket in light herringbone pattern, which I'd bought years earlier in Carnaby Street—then at the heart of London's Swinging Sixties. It had been fashionable at the time but had become dreadfully dated—and wholly inappropriate for a firm where the dress code was dark suit and tie! I didn't get the job.

Okay. You put on a smart suit, walk through the door and tell the interviewer all about your past career and hopes for the future. Smart? Yes, and no!

Tip #8—Talk about why the company needs you!

Sure, you need to convey where you've been and where you hope to go. But what really impresses the interviewer is when you know about the company and what you could do for them. You should bubble with information and views on where the company is heading and how you can help them get there.

In today's world, it's so easy to get up to speed on most companies, their markets, their competitors. There's tons of information sitting there on the web, begging to be read. It's just a matter of taking the time to dig around and locate it.

Imagine this: The interviewer tells you that you'll be expected to spend a day or so a month going to regional team meetings, whether in the Miami, New Orleans, or Atlanta offices. And you say, "Great! I didn't know the company had more than one office in the southeast." What's the interviewer to think? That's publicly available information, accessed with just a couple of clicks on the website. "This guy didn't bother to find out much about us," she'll think. "He's not keen."

Whatever information there is on the company available in the public space, you should know about it before you walk into the interview room. And you should let the interviewer know that you know it.

Okay. You're dressed up and clued up on the company, all you have to do now is relax and chat about yourself and how you can fit in with the company. Smart? No!

Tip # 9—Sit alert!

Interviews should not be relaxing. Relaxing is dangerous. The more you relax, the less impressive you come over.

Of course, you shouldn't be tense either. If you're anxious, nervous, and jumpy, that's hardly going to impress the interviewer either.

You need to be alert, on the button. That's what does the trick. And the best place to start is how you sit. Not reclining in the chair. Not leaning on the table. But in the classic TV interview pose. Upright, but leaning slightly forward. At around 75 degrees. You will appear at your most alert. It also enables you to perform orally at your best while seated.

I remember another of my laid-back interviews in the mid-1980s, where I got on so well with the guy that we talked for a half-hour about my travels round the world. He'd visited on holiday some of the countries I'd lived in and was genuinely interested in finding out more. We shared stories and anecdotes, thoroughly enjoying each other's company. By the time we finally got round to my work experience, I was so relaxed that I'd slipped right down in my swivel chair. I wasn't far off horizontal! I didn't get the job.

Okay. You're clued up, dressed up, and sitting up, all you need to do now is tell your story. Smart? Yes and no!

Tip #10—Perform!

It's not just what you say, it's how you say it. This one hour interview is a momentous occasion for you. This is for a job with passion. It could be for the job where you feel the ultimate in passion, the Celtic *hwyl*. Imagine you're on stage. The curtain rises, the lights come on, and yes, it's show time! Time to perform!

Your enthusiasm for this job needs to come through not just in your words and ideas, but in you. In how you communicate. In your voice—its pitch, pace, volume. In your facial expressions. In your hand movements (and please, don't allow your hands to go anywhere near your face, especially your mouth—don't block your main instrument of communication!). In how you perform.

Easier said than done, you say. Dead right. But there's a simple solution. Join Toastmasters.

I've already given a plug for Toastmasters International in Chapter 12. But I'd be remiss in not reinforcing it here when discussing personal communication skills.

The skills you learn at Toastmasters will fully equip you for the interview process. You'll learn how to communicate better, not just speaking to a roomful of people, but one-to-one. You'll learn how to use your voice, your face, your hands, your body in improving your communicating skills. You'll learn how to work with words. You'll learn how to persuade, inspire, and entertain.

You'll learn how to perform.

But Toastmasters will help with more than just communication skills. It'll provide you with group support. You're embarking on a life-enhancing career switch. This is self-development at its zenith, and that's what Toastmasters is all about. It's full of like-minded souls.

Use Toastmasters as a forum to try out your ideas. Construct a speech on why you want to change career, then deliver it and receive the feedback of your peers. And another speech on how your target job could transform your life. Try a humorous speech about your horrors of picking up the phone, or being interviewed. Get their feedback. Discuss your life-enhancing career plans in an empathetic milieu. There will be dozens like you, discussing similar themes. You are *so* not alone!

One final word on the interview. Most interviewers these days believe that the way to get the best out of interviewees is to make them feel at ease. This was not always the case. In the 1980s some companies deployed the hostile interview. This is where the interviewee is made to feel uncomfortable to test how he will react in adverse situations. It was a ridiculous concept, now entirely discredited—but see the inset box for a memorable experience!

Follow up the interview

Okay. You've had the interview. It went pretty well. All you have to do is wait to hear from them. Smart? No!

Tip #11—Send a note.

You enjoyed the meeting. Write and let the interviewer know. Tell her that you hope she enjoyed it too and found it useful. Remind her of your contact details. And let her know that if she needs any further information you'd be pleased to let her have it.

Your letter can be by email or snail mail—or both, whatever you feel appropriate to the way that company does business. When in doubt, write a letter.

The interviewer should receive your note preferably within a day or two of the interview. If your interview is in the morning, you should write in the evening, enabling the interviewer to receive the email the following morning. If it's a letter, she'll receive it the morning after that.

Okay. You've had the interview, written a note, now you can lean back in your chair and wait! Smart? No!

> *…I walked in and there was a man with his feet up on the desk, reading a report. He gestured to me to sit down and continued to read, ignoring me completely. Time went by, one minute, two. What was I supposed to do? Should I pull out my newspaper? Powder my nose? Punch his? Finally, after five minutes, he raised his eyes slowly from his report and asked, "Who are you?" I kept my cool and politely told him my name. He pondered on that, for another minute or two, and then sneered: "And why should a company like ours employ someone like you?" This was a tricky one. I was tempted to counter with, "Why should someone like me join a company that employs jerks like you?" But I couldn't. The situation was so Groucho Marx. I just stood up slowly, said, "Thank you very much for telling me so much about your company" and walked out the door. I didn't get the job.* –Vaughan Evans (extract from a speech to London Corinthians Toastmasters, September 2003)

Tip #12—Chase (again!)

Allow the company three to four weeks. If you haven't heard anything by then, send a gentle prompt. Ask them if there's been any further progress, or if they've had any further thoughts. Ask them if there's anything further they'd like to discuss with you, or anyone else they feel you should meet. Chase them—by email or post, depending on how you sent the post-interview note.

Give them a further two weeks to reply to your chaser. If there's still no reply, call them. If you can't get past the PA, leave a message on the interviewer's voicemail. If there's no reply to the message in two days, call again. And so on. Pester them. Show them you're keen. Hound them until you find out, one way or another.

Okay. That's a dozen tips. You should follow them.

Smart? Yes!

Launching Your Own Business

> " *This is the true joy in life, being used for a purpose recognized by yourself as a mighty one. Being a force of nature instead of a feverish, selfish little clod of ailments and grievances complaining that the world will not devote itself to making you happy…. Life is no brief candle to me. It is a sort of splendid torch which I've got hold of for the moment and I want to make it burn as brightly as possible before handing it on to future generations.* –George Bernard Shaw

On the other hand, the target career where your passion lies that emerged from Chapter 17 may be starting your own business. Like our fictional Hari in his new fashion concept (Chapter 13). Like Martha Stewart in switching from stockbroking to catering/writing/presenting (Chapter 15).

The great thing about going solo is that you won't have to do any of the above hustling for interviews and pretending you're someone you're not in the interview. Even better, you won't have to do any crawling to the boss. Ever. You're the boss.

But do think twice. It's not for everybody. It can be hard. You'll find yourself having to do "interviews" again and again, except that they'll be to customers. They're pitches for work.

And although you're the boss, you're also the coffeemaker, the copier, the laptop debugger.

These and more pros and cons are set out in detail in Chapter 13. Have a serious read of that, and of other recommended books, and if it's for you, go for it!

Remember, you'll have one enormous advantage in starting this business. It's one that grew out of the passion listing of Chapter 15, and survived the screening process of Chapter 16 and the research of Chapter 17. It's a career choice that will consume you with passion.

Work will no longer seem like work. You'll want to carry through this "work" into the evenings, and at weekends, because it's a passion.

You'll be Shaw's "force of nature."

Your competitors may not, or may no longer, feel the passion. You'll have an edge.

Backing the *Hwyl*!

Life is in the living of it. –Leo Tolstoy

In Part I of this book, you concluded that you weren't backable in your current or pre-MBA job or business. In this Part III you looked at a broad range of jobs or businesses with passion (Chapter 15). You screened them (Chapter 16), researched those that came through the screen and identified the target job where you're most backable (Chapter 17). You then embarked on an entry strategy to make you more backable (Chapter 18).

You've been reminded of a few practical tips to help you land that job (this chapter).

You're as ready as you'll ever be. Don't procrastinate. Take the plunge. A new work life beckons. One with passion, one maybe with that all consuming Celtic *hwyl*.

You won't work to live. You won't live to work. You'll live.

It's time to back you, back the passion in you, back the *hwyl*!

Good luck. *Pob hwyl*.

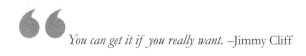

You can get it if you really want. –Jimmy Cliff

Conclusion

In the introduction to this book, we assumed that you are one of the majority of MBA students who entered the program with minds and eyes open about which path to take following graduation. You see one of the main benefits of the program as the chance to learn about, think about, and discuss alternative career options.

You may have been one of those who thought things seemed rosier elsewhere. But you found out from Part I that you are in fact better off carrying on with your current or returning to your pre-MBA job or business. That's where you'll be most backable.

You then applied in Part II some techniques on how to make yourself yet more backable in your current job. And hopefully more satisfied, more fulfilled.

On the other hand, you may have learned from Part I that you weren't backable in your current job. This may have been due to issues affecting your addressed market as a whole, or affecting just you or your company. It may be because you no longer enjoy the job. And this shows through in your attitude.

Or you may have come to business school direct from your bachelors.

So you followed the techniques of Part III and found a job or business where not only your passion lies but also where you'll be backable. You drew up an entry strategy to make yourself yet more backable. You're ready to set off on a new career, a new life.

Whether you've chosen to move forward in your current or pre-MBA job, or move across to one with greater passion, perhaps where the *hwyl* lies, I hope you're now more backable.

And I hope you'll carry on *Backing You, MBA!*

Appendix A
Your Charts

Here's a set of blank charts for you to fill out as you work your way through this book. They are grouped as follows:

- ▷ Figures A.1 to A.8 relate to Part I and should help you in deciding *Would You Back You?*
- ▷ Figures A.9 and A.10 relate to Part II and you *Becoming More Backable*
- ▷ Figures A.11 to A.16 relate to Part III; they are to help you in *Backing Your Passion*

Each chart gives some basic instructions (in italics, with arrows indicating where to fill in what), but they are not and cannot be expected to be self-explanatory. They should be completed in conjunction with the explanations found in the relevant chapter.

The first few charts relate to market prospects or your competitive position in one of your main business segments. If you are active in more than one, you may need to photocopy the relevant charts and complete one set for each of your main segments. Alternatively, pick up a pencil, ruler and a blank piece of paper and quickly sketch a copy of the chart. None are complex, so shouldn't take more than a minute or two to sketch.

I hope you enjoy filling them in as much as I've done—whether for Valerie or the Beatles, Jennifer or Oprah, or, frequently over the years, for me.

Part I: WOULD YOU BACK YOU?

Figure A.1 **Market Demand Prospects in** ....

Enter one of your main business segments

Enter drivers

Demand Drivers	Impact on Demand Growth			Comments
	Recent Past	Now	Next Few Years	
Overall Impact				
Market Growth Rate				

Enter pluses or minuses as appropriate— see key

Enter numbers or words

Key to Impact
+++   Very strong positive
++   Strong positive
+   Some positive
O   None
–   Some negative
– –   Strong negative
– – –   Very strong negative

For help with this chart, see Chapter 2

Figure A.2 .... Risks and Opportunities

in ....

Enter one of your main business segments

Enter whether these are risks and opportunities concerning Market Demand (Chapter 2), Competition (Chapter 3), Your Position (Chapter 3), or Your Plan (Chapter 7)

Risks	Likeli-hood	Impact	Comments

Opportunities	Likeli-hood	Impact	Comments

Enter whether low, medium, or high

For help with this chart, see Chapters 2, 3, 6, and 7

Figure A.3 Competition in ....

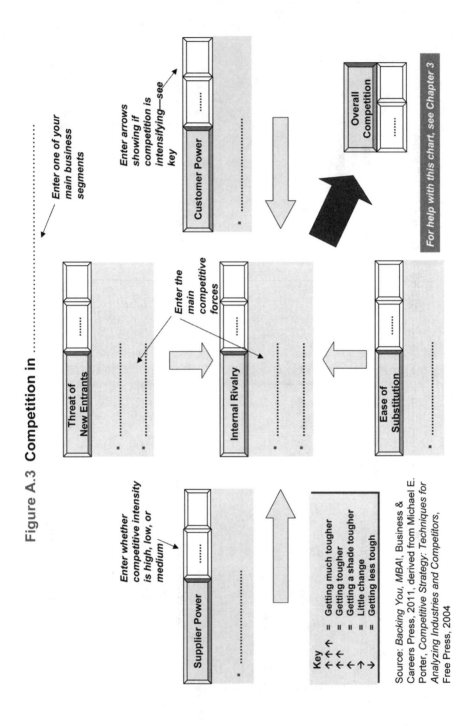

Enter one of your main business segments

Enter arrows showing if competition is intensifying—see key

Customer Power

Overall Competition

For help with this chart, see Chapter 3

Enter the main competitive forces

Threat of New Entrants

Internal Rivalry

Ease of Substitution

Enter whether competitive intensity is high, low, or medium

Supplier Power

Key
↑↑↑ = Getting much tougher
↑↑ = Getting tougher
↑ = Getting a shade tougher
↑ = Little change
↓ = Getting less tough

Source: *Backing You, MBA!*, Business & Careers Press, 2011, derived from Michael E. Porter, *Competitive Strategy: Techniques for Analyzing Industries and Competitors*, Free Press, 2004

Figure A.4 Customer Needs and Associated Key Kapabilities
in ....

Enter one of your main business segments

For help with this chart, see Chapters 4 and 5

Customer Needs		Importance	Change	Associated Key Kapabilities
Effectiveness - Skills	•			• ....
- Knowledge	•			• ....
- Experience	•			• ....
Efficiency	•			• ....
Relationship	•			• ....
Range	•			• ....
Premises	•			• ....
Price	•			• ....

Enter customer needs, under E2-R2-P2 headings

Enter whether the need is of high, low, or medium importance

Enter arrows showing if the need is becoming more important over time

Enter K2 required to meet each customer need

Figure A.5 Your Competitive Position in ....

For help with this chart, see Chapter 6

Enter one of your main business segments

Enter your main competitors

Enter rating for each competitor against each K2 on a scale of 1-5 (see key below)

Key to Rating:
1 = Weak
2 = Below par
3 = Favorable
4 = Strong
5 = Very strong

Weighted average

Key Kapabilities	Weighting (%)	U!	....	....
Relative Market Share				
Cost Factors:				
Management Factors:				
Service Factors:				
Competitive Position	**100%**			

Enter weighting which reflects the relative importance of each K2, taking care to ensure weightings add up to 100%

Enter Key Kapabilities needed to compete in this business segment

Figure A.6 How Achievable Are Your Planned Revenues or Pay?

Your Business Segments	Your Revenues or Pay ($000)	Market Demand Growth (% / year)	Your Competitive Position (0-5)	Your Planned Revenues or Pay ($000)	Your Planned Revenue Growth (%/year)	Your Backer's View: How Achievable?	More Likely Revenues or Pay ($000)
	This Year	Next Few Years	Next Few Years	In Three Years	Next Three Years		In Three Years
1	2	3	4	5	6	7	8
	Source: Chapter 1	Source: Chapter 2	Source: Chapter 6	Source: Chapter 1	Source: Chapter 1	Source: Chapter 7	
A.							
B.							
C.							
Others							
Total							

Enter what your backer would think, not what you think, to be achievable!

For help with this chart, see Chapter 7

Figure A.7 The Risks and Opportunities of Backing You

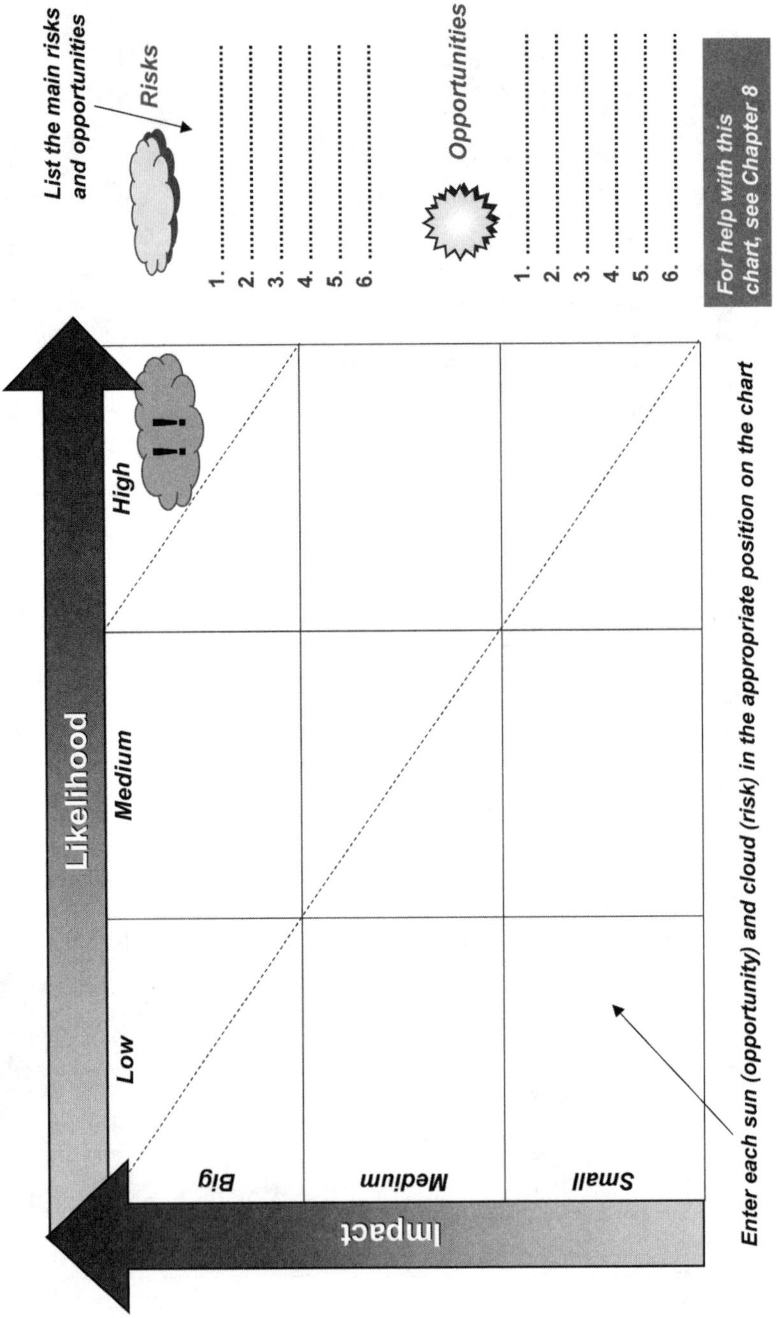

List the main risks and opportunities

Risks

1. ......
2. ......
3. ......
4. ......
5. ......
6. ......

Opportunities

1. ......
2. ......
3. ......
4. ......
5. ......
6. ......

For help with this chart, see Chapter 8

Likelihood

Low Medium High

Impact

Big Medium Small

Enter each sun (opportunity) and cloud (risk) in the appropriate position on the chart

Figure A.8 Would You Back You?: The Storyline!

Enter your overall conclusion,
summarising the headlines below

Market Demand Prospects: .... → *Your conclusions
from Chapter 2*

Competition: .... → *Your conclusions
from Chapter 3*

Your Competitive Position: .... → *Your conclusions
from Chapter 6*

Your Plan: .... → *Your conclusions
from Chapter 7*

Risks and Opportunities: .... → *Your conclusions
from Chapter 8*

For help with this chart, see Chapter 9

Part II: BECOMING MORE BACKABLE

Figure A.9 How Attractive Are Your Business Segments?

Business Segments	Market Size	Market Growth	Competitive Intensity	Market Risk	Enjoyment	Overall Attractiveness
A.						
B.						
C.						
D.						
E (new?)						

Enter rating of attractiveness for each business chunk, using Key or, if you prefer, words or ticks

Average of ratings in previous five columns

Key to Rating: 1 = Unattractive, 3 = Reasonably Attractive, 5 = Highly Attractive
(For competitive intensity, remember that the more intense the competition, the *less* attractive the market. Likewise for market risk: the riskier the market, the **less** attractive.)

For help with this chart, see Chapter 11

Figure A.10 How's Your Strategic Bubble Bath?

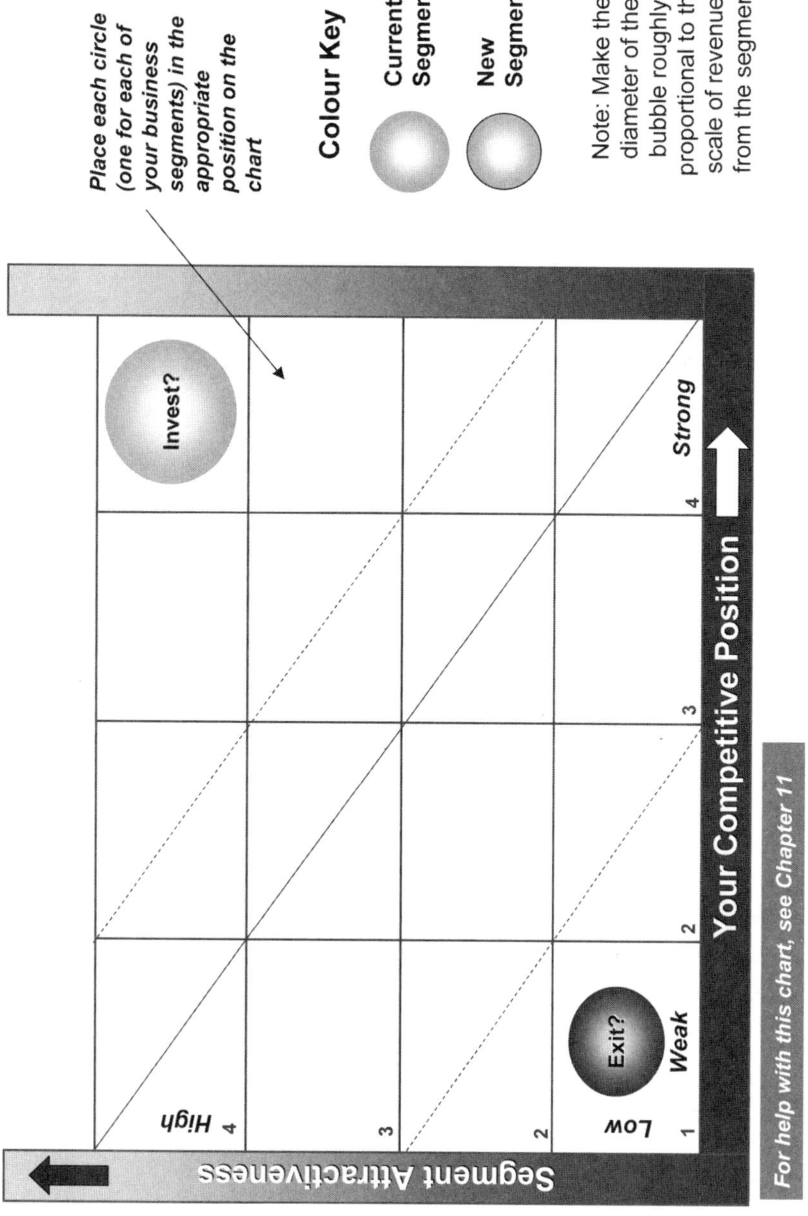

Place each circle (one for each of your business segments) in the appropriate position on the chart

Colour Key

Current Segment

New Segment

Note: Make the diameter of the bubble roughly proportional to the scale of revenues from the segment

Segment Attractiveness

High 4

3

2

Low 1

Weak

Exit?

Invest?

Strong

2   3   4

Your Competitive Position

For help with this chart, see Chapter 11

Part III: BACKING YOUR PASSION

Figure A.11 Your Long List of Jobs with Passion

Job	Passion
	✓✓✓✓✓
	✓✓✓✓✓
	✓✓✓✓✓
	✓✓✓✓✓
	✓✓✓✓✓
	✓✓✓✓✓
	✓✓✓✓
	✓✓✓✓
	✓✓✓✓
	✓✓✓
	✓✓✓

For help with this chart, see Chapter 15

Enter at the top those jobs from your full list with five passion ticks, then those with four ticks and so forth

Figure A.12 How Attractive (Roughly) Are the Markets of Your Long-Listed Jobs?

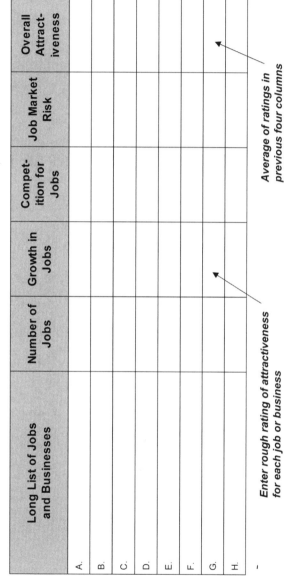

Long List of Jobs and Businesses	Number of Jobs	Growth in Jobs	Compet- ition for Jobs	Job Market Risk	Overall Attract- iveness
A.					
B.					
C.					
D.					
E.					
F.					
G.					
H.					
–					

Enter rough rating of attractiveness for each job or business

Average of ratings in previous four columns

For help with this chart, see Chapter 16

Key to Rating: 1 = Unattractive, 3 = Reasonably Attractive, 5 = Highly Attractive

(For competition for jobs, remember that the more intense the competition, the *less* attractive the market. Likewise for job market risk: the riskier the market, the *less* attractive. Conversely, and more intuitively, the greater the number of jobs the more attractive, likewise for growth in jobs.)

Figure A.13 How Well Placed (Roughly) Would You Be in Your Long-Listed Jobs?

Long List of Jobs and Businesses	Your Relevant Capabilities	Your Relevant Experience	Your Competitive Position
A.			
B.			
C.			
D.			
E.			
F.			
G.			
H.			

Average of ratings in previous two columns

Enter your likely ratings (very roughly at this stage) for each job or business

Key to Rating: 1 = Weak, 2 = Below par, 3 = Favorable, 4 = Strong, 5 = Very strong

For help with this chart, see Chapter 16

Figure A.14 Initial Screening of Your Long-List

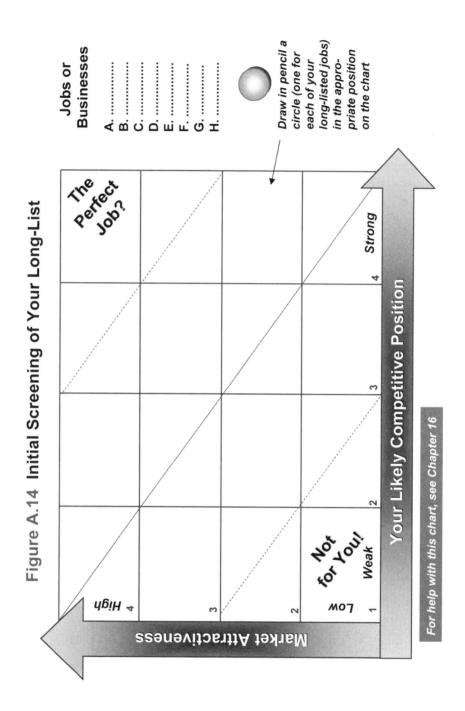

Jobs or Businesses

A. ....
B. ....
C. ....
D. ....
E. ....
F. ....
G. ....
H. ....

Draw in pencil a circle (one for each of your long-listed jobs) in the appropriate position on the chart

The Perfect Job?

Not for You!

Market Attractiveness

High 4

3

2

Low 1

Your Likely Competitive Position

Weak 1   2   3   4   Strong

For help with this chart, see Chapter 16

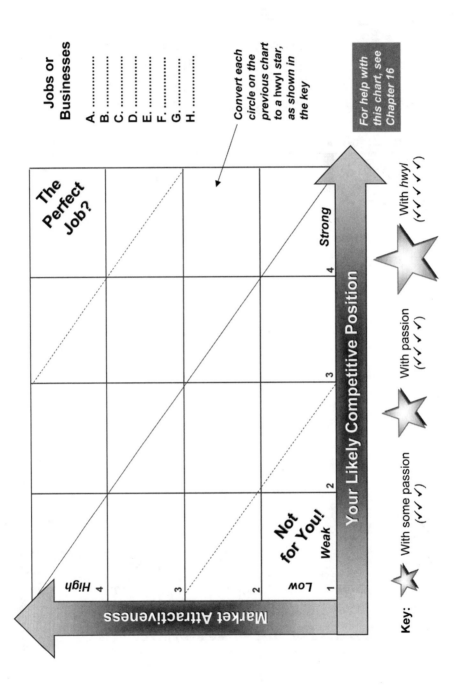

Jobs or Businesses

A. ....
B. ....
C. ....
D. ....
E. ....
F. ....
G. ....
H. ....

Convert each circle on the previous chart to a hwyl star, as shown in the key

For help with this chart, see Chapter 16

Market Attractiveness

High 4
3
2
Low 1

Your Likely Competitive Position

Weak 1 2 3 4 Strong

The Perfect Job?

Not for You!

Key:

With some passion (✓✓)

With passion (✓✓✓)

With hwyl (✓✓✓✓)

Figure A.16 Your Satisfaction Rating of Short-Listed Jobs

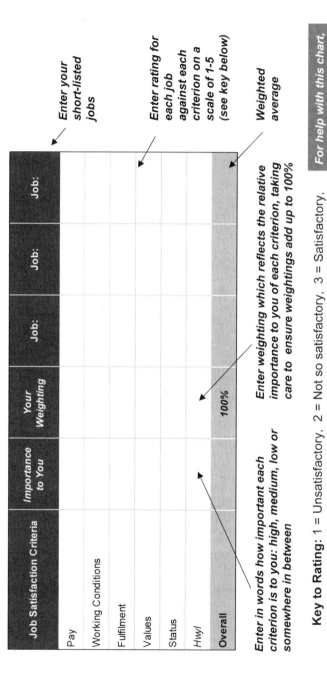

Enter your short-listed jobs

Enter rating for each job against each criterion on a scale of 1-5 (see key below)

Weighted average

Job Satisfaction Criteria	Importance to You	Your Weighting	Job:	Job:	Job:
Pay					
Working Conditions					
Fulfilment					
Values					
Status					
Hwyl					
Overall		100%			

Enter in words how important each criterion is to you: high, medium, low or somewhere in between

Enter weighting which reflects the relative importance to you of each criterion, taking care to ensure weightings add up to 100%

For help with this chart, see Chapter 17

Key to Rating: 1 = Unsatisfactory, 2 = Not so satisfactory, 3 = Satisfactory, 4 = Very satisfactory, 5 = Most satisfactory

Appendix B
Structured Interviewing of Customers

Chapter 6, *How Do You Measure Up?,* advised that a structured interviewing program of customers provides a methodical way for the self-employed to find out their competitive position.

Here's how to do it:

▷   Select a representative range of customer interviewees.

▷   Prepare your storyline.

▷   Prepare a concise questionnaire.

▷   Interview them, through email, telephone, or face-to-face.

▷   Thank them and give them some feedback.

The Interviewees

The interviewees should represent a broad cross-section of your business, including:

▷   Each of your main business segments.

▷   Your top six customers in terms of revenue.

▷   Long-standing customers as well as recent acquisitions.

▷   Customers who also use, or used to use, your competitors, so they can compare your performance from experience rather than conjecture.

> Customers with whom you've had problems.

> Would-be customers, currently using a competitor, but on your target list.

> Former customers who switched to a competitor

That sounds like a lot, but you'll be selective. A dozen should suffice.

The Storyline

Here's your opportunity to put a positive light on your business. Compare these two storylines:

1. "Sorry to waste your time but can I ask for your help in figuring out how well I do my work?"

2. "As you know, my business has been rather busy over the last couple of years. But I thought I should take some time out to ask some of my most important customers how their needs may be changing over time and to what extent I can serve those needs better."

Guess which line will get the better response *and* put your business in a favorable light? The first storyline conveys a negative impression and is all about you and your needs. The second leaves a positive impression and is all about your customer's needs. Stick to the second!

The Questionnaire

The questionnaire needs care. It must be taken as a guideline, not as a box-ticking exercise. It stays with you, and it doesn't get handed to the interviewee. It's a prompter to discussion, no more. It needs to be simple. And concise.

It should be in four parts:

1. The storyline

2. Customer needs—which, how important, now and in the future?

3.   Performance—how you and others rate against those needs

4.   The future—how you can better serve customer needs

The storyline

The storyline should be written out at the top of the questionnaire and memorized. It must be delivered naturally and seemingly spontaneously. Stick in the odd pause, "um," or "er" to make it seem less rehearsed.

Customer needs

These are the main questions to put on your questionnaire:

> What are your main needs in buying this service? What do you expect from your providers?

> How important are these needs? Which are more important than others? How would you rank them?

> Will these needs become more or less important over time?

> Are any other needs likely to become important in the future?

You should allow the customer to draw up her own set of needs, but it's best to prepare your own list to use as prompts, in case your customer dries up, or she misses an obvious one.

Performance

Here are some performance-related questions:

> How do you think I meet those needs? How do I perform?

> How do others perform? Do they better meet those needs?

> Who performs best against those most important needs?

Again you should allow the customer to select who she thinks are her alternative providers of your service, but you should include a prompt list of your main competitors—which you may or may not choose to use. No need to alert her to a troublesome competitor she's not yet aware of!

The future

What should I be doing to better meet your needs?

The Interview

Interviews are best done face-to-face. Then you can see the nuances behind the replies—the shifting glance, the fidgeting, the emphatic hand gestures. But they are the most time consuming, unless you happen to be seeing your customer as part of your service delivery anyway.

If the interviews are done over the phone, they are best scheduled in advance. You can do this by email or with a preliminary phone call. After you've delivered the storyline, then add: "I wonder if you could spare five to ten minutes to discuss this with me. I know you're very busy, but perhaps we could set up a time later in the week for me to give you a call."

The call itself must be carefully managed. Don't launch into the questionnaire without a warmup. Ask her how she's doing, how's work, how's the family, whatever. Then gently shift to the storyline: "Well, as I was saying the other day…"

After you've finished the structured interview, don't forget the cooldown at the closing. Return to one of the topics you discussed at the outset and gently wind up the discussion, not forgetting to thank her sincerely for giving so freely of her valuable time.

The Thanks and Feedback

A few hours, a day, a couple of days, or a week later—whenever you feel it's appropriate—thank your customer again, officially. By letter is best, but that may feel overly formal for you in this electronic world. Email is probably fine, but use your judgment.

The email should be cheerful and full of sincere gratitude. If possible, it should contain a snippet of information that could be of interest or use to your customer. One or two sentences should suffice. It could pick up on one aspect of the discussion and compare what another customer had to say on the same thing. You could give her an indication of the results of your survey: "Interestingly, most customers seemed to think that experience was their most important need" or "Amazingly, most customers seemed to think my punctuality wasn't all that bad!"

That's structured interviewing. Now all you have to do is compile the results, whether on a piece of paper, on an Excel worksheet, or simply in your head, and feed them into your ratings against each K2—for you and for each of your competitors.

The intriguing thing then is to compare these customer-derived ratings with your first draft, do-it-yourself ratings. You may be in for a surprise!

Appendix C
Structured Interviewing for Your Target Job

Chapter 17, *Where Best to Back?,* advised that a structured interviewing program on those who currently do your target job, and their customers, provides a methodical way of finding out what you need to know about the job.

Here's how it's done, with an approach similar to that of Appendix B:

> Select a representative range of provider interviewees, preferably with some sort of a referee to break the ice.

> Likewise for their customers.

> Prepare your storyline.

> Prepare a concise questionnaire for providers and a separate one for customers.

> Interview them, through email, telephone, or face-to-face.

> Thank them and give them some feedback.

The Interviewees

If you have to go in cold in each interview, this program could be a struggle. But you'll still need to do it. Preferable by far is to go into the interview warm, or even hot.

A warm interview in marketing-speak is one where someone you know has recommended that you speak to this person. A hot interview is where you actually know the interviewee.

The first step is to make a list of all those you know who are engaged in your target job or business, or who are their customers. This will be your hot list, but for many people this may only amount to one or two prospective interviewees, perhaps none.

The next and most important step is to draw up a warm list. Speak to people you know who may know people in your target job or business. Speak to your family, your friends, friends of your family, family of your friends, your former class-mates, your kids' friends' parents, your colleagues, past and present, friends of your colleagues, your fellow sport, society or interest group members. Speak, for example, to a friend of the family of a member of your colleague's sports club!

And then, of course, you have your business school resources. Go first to the list of alumni and see who is working in your target job. What year did they graduate, who might they have known? Speak to your lecturers, your course administrators, the librarians, the teams in the careers and alumni offices. Who else do they know working in this field? Speak to your fellow MBA students. What of their friends, family, colleagues?

Defined like this, your "network" of contacts may soon run into the hundreds! Surely out of all these contacts there could be one, two, even more people who are active in your target job or business. Or at least customers. These will form your warm list.

By now, hopefully, you'll have a few names of providers or customers to whom you won't have to go in completely cold. But you'll need about a dozen interviews if you're to satisfy a backer. You'll probably have to do some cold-calling too.

It's easy enough to find out the names of organizations that operate in your target field. Your careers office should have a stack of information and you can update this as appropriate with some research in the school library and on the web.

The difficulty is often in finding out the actual names of people doing your target job in a firm. In the old days, you had little choice but to call the switchboard and bluff your way through to the right person. With the Internet and Google, that can sometimes be easier. Not always, with many companies preferring to disclose as few names as possible. Investment banks and management consulting groups yield little information on individuals on their websites, presumably fearful of predatory headhunters, while private equity firms typically set out their whole team.

If you can, do try to get a name before calling an organization. If you can't, then that's too bad. You'll just have to try the old route and be prepared to duck and dive with the gatekeeper.

In summary, your interview list should be, in order of preference:

> *Hot names*, where you know the person.

> *Warm names*, where someone you know knows the person.

> *Cold names*, where you know of the person.

> *No names*, freezing cold calls, where you don't know whom you should speak to.

If all this fills you with horror, you might try some further guidance. John Crystal in his book *Where do I Go From Here With My Life?* suggests you should go out and talk to anybody about anything before embarking on a job-hunt-related interviewing program. Just getting out there and practicing talking should help build your confidence in talking eventually to people in your target job or business.

Daniel Porot builds on this in *The PIE Method for Career Success: A Unique Way to Find Your Ideal Job.* The I in PIE is for informational interviewing, which is similar to what is here termed structured interviewing. The E in PIE is for employment interviewing, where you are face-to-face with your would-be employer. But the P is for pleasure, and this is similar to what Crystal suggested. Porot suggests you take any subject you like to talk about and practice talking to like-minded people. You can talk about your likes, your interests, your hobbies, your views on hot issues—whatever gives you pleasure to talk about. It'll warm you up for the structured interviewing process to come.

The Storyline

The storyline in a structured interview program is much stronger if you can start with a reference, something like this: "Hi, Emily. My name is Vaughan Evans, and I was recommended to talk to you by Jane Smith, whom I believe you play hockey with."

When she finds out that you don't actually know Jane (!), but that she's a friend of your daughter's former classmate's mother, she may be a trifle disappointed. But you've still managed to break the ice and she may be impressed that you've gone to so much trouble to locate her. Whatever. Your chances of progressing to a five-minute discussion about her job are still higher than if you had gone in cold.

Next you proceed to tell her why you're calling. As in Appendix B, you must take care to present an upbeat message. Compare these two storylines:

1. "Look, Emily, I'm sorry to be a bore, and I'm sure I'll be wasting your time, but could I have a chat with you for an hour or two about your job?"

2. "Anyway, Emily, the reason for my call is that I'm trying to find out a bit more about working in capital markets (for example). I was wondering if you could spare just a few minutes telling me a bit about your job. Your kind of work has long struck me as being really stimulating and rewarding, certainly compared to the work I used to do before my MBA, and I'm seriously thinking of changing career, perhaps to capital markets."

What's the betting that Emily reply to storyline 2 will be: "What sort of work do you do at the moment?" You can then mildly disparage your former job, making Emily feel pleased that she's in an altogether more satisfying occupation. And away you go! What do you think her reply to storyline 1 would be? How about: "Look, I'm a bit busy at the moment/ these days/this month. May I suggest you return to the switchboard and ask for our PR department?"

If you have to go in cold, then storyline 2, without the reference warm-up, is all you're likely to have. It's going to have to be warm, friendly, positive, upbeat, and leave the interviewee feeling good about herself.

The Questionnaire

For Customers

If you're interviewing a customer of your target job or business, you can use a similar questionnaire format to that suggested in Appendix B, with slight amendments and one addition:

> The storyline

> Customer needs, now and in the future

> How current providers rate against those needs

> How future providers can better serve those needs

> Future market demand for such services, compared to the supply of these services

The main amendment concerns the fourth bullet. You'll be asking how future providers, including possibly yourself, can better meet that customer's future needs.

The addition is the fifth bullet. You'll be taking the opportunity to get a customer's views on whether there are too many people already in this field, too few, or round about the right number. And whether market demand for such services is, in the customer's opinion, likely to grow in the future. And if so, how fast? Faster or slower than the likely number of people providing such services? Why? What are the barriers to entry? Are there likely to be too few providers, too many, round about the right number in the future?

Market information you get from customers will greatly help your assessment of the market attractiveness of your target job or business. It will supplement, and hopefully corroborate, the information you'll have found on the Web.

For a further breakdown of the questions you need to ask under each of the headings in your customer survey, take a look back at Appendix B.

For Providers

If you're interviewing a provider, that is, someone who's actually doing your target job or business, your questionnaire should be in four parts:

- ▹ The storyline
- ▹ The nature of the job
- ▹ What you need to be good at it
- ▹ How to get in

The storyline should be typed out at the top of the page but don't read it. Learn it by heart and make sure it comes out naturally and enthusiastically.

You'll have stacks of questions relating to the nature of the job. You've already had a go at rating this job against each of your job satisfaction criteria in the first section of Chapter 17. To recap, these were grouped under pay, working conditions, fulfillment, values, status, and passion. Now's your chance to have your initial views confirmed or challenged.

Make out a list of questions under each of the job satisfaction criteria that you'd like answered. Questions under working conditions, such as hours of work, frequency of overnight travel, or holiday leave, are the easiest to ask of your interviewee. Few people really mind talking about these things. Likewise it's easy enough to ask about what sort of work they tend to do on a day-to-day basis, which will be a guide on how fulfilling this would be for you.

Questions on values are a bit more tricky, but you could try asking oblique questions on their colleagues. Do people in your line of work tend to form close friendships with their colleagues? Do they meet after work? Are they mutually supportive? Or is the workplace highly competitive, even cutthroat, and the last person you'd want to see at a Saturday night party would be a colleague?

You can touch on passion a little—do you really enjoy going to work in the morning?—but this is a highly personal criterion. What's passion-inducing to one person may be anathema to the other. Different strokes for different folks.

Toughest of all are questions relating to pay. It's inadvisable to come right out and ask, "How much do you earn?" People tend to be secretive and often sensitive about their pay. But you could try some devious comparative questions: "Is it true that stockbrokers tend to earn more than asset managers?" or "Has pay in stockbroking been growing reasonably over the last few years, in comparison with, say, for asset management?"

The next set of questions concerns what you need to have or do to be good at that job or business. Have a look through your initial assessment of Key Kapabilities and their importance, as well your first cut competitive position, in the fourth section of Chapter 17. What questions should you ask to get further comfort on how well placed you would be in this job?

You'll probably want to ask about qualifications and training. What's essential? What's good to have, but not absolutely necessary? What sort of skills should one preferably have? What's the minimum experience to get started? Would some of your earlier experience count as genuinely applicable for doing the job? How important is efficiency, as opposed to effectiveness? What sort of relationships does one need to form with customers?

The final set of questions relates to getting in. They may be the most important. What tips does she have on how to get in? What types of organization should you write to? To whom should you address your letters? HR or directly to your boss? Whom to talk to? What to emphasize in your résumé/CV?

There are lots of questions. You won't be able to ask them all. You'll run out of time. For each of the three sets of questions, pick out the three most important. The three you really need answers to before you can realistically evaluate how well placed you would be in this job or business, and how attractive a job it is.

The Interview

The first thing to establish in an interview is how much time you have available to you. Then you can scope your questions accordingly.

If no time limit has been set, despite your prompting, you'll still have to prioritize. Assume that you'll only be able to get five minutes with her over the phone. Assume she'll be too busy to agree to a follow-up discussion, let alone a face-to-face meeting. Of course, you'll try for one or the other, but it's best if you assume you won't get them.

In that case, if you only have a five-minute shot, *what do you really need to know?* What *must* you find out from every one of the interviews to fill in your information gaps? To meet your backer's key concerns?

Under "nature of the job," which of your three most important questions do you most need to know about? If you place greatest importance on working conditions, such as the flexibility of working hours, make sure you get that question in early.

Under "what you need to be good at it," which aspect is most critical to you? Will a diploma do, or do you have to have a degree?

Remember to leave time for a final, most important question on "how to get in." For example, what type of organization has most vacancies for this kind of work?

If you manage to get these questions answered, together with the inevitable follow-up questions, in under five minutes, great. Return to the "nature of the job" and ask the second most important question to you under that heading. And so on. Ask her how much time you have left for further questions. Then ask some more from the other sections and carry on until your time has run out.

If the call ends and not all your most important questions have been answered, that can't be helped. If necessary, make them a higher priority on your list of questions for your *next* call and get them in early.

The objective must be to get at least half a dozen good responses to each of the three most important questions under each of the three headings.

With these answers under your belt, you'll be in possession of valuable information. Information that will help you decide on whether you are backable.

The above has been written assuming that your interview will be over the phone. Most will be. But you should try to get one or two interviews face-to-face. There is no substitute for seeing the visual response to a question, not just the oral. And it's more awkward for an interviewee to shoo you out of the door after just five minutes!

If your interviewee is too busy during working hours, invite him to lunch. Or for a coffee. Or to a drink after work. Or to dinner. Invest in your target job! Surely the potential returns from landing your target job are worth investing in an odd meal or three? And the information you'll draw out of him over a drink or a meal should be more abundant than that gleaned from a five-minute call during working hours.

The Thanks and Feedback

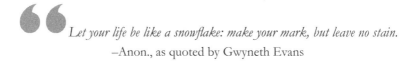

Let your life be like a snowflake: make your mark, but leave no stain.
–Anon., as quoted by Gwyneth Evans

As advised in Appendix B, you must thank all interviewees. Both at the end of the call, and again some time later in writing—by email, snail mail, or both, as appropriate. And if you can throw in some element of feedback, even better—for example, "It was interesting that most respondents, like yourself, seemed to think that strategy consultants put in longer hours than corporate financiers, despite being paid less."

Remember, this is your target job or business. The provider interviewee may be able to help you land a job. Likewise the customer interviewee may one day know of a provider with a job vacancy. Try and stay in touch with them for you never know when they may be able to help you—or you them. Write to them so they will remember your courtesy, enthusiasm, and good cheer.

Appendix D
Recommended Reading

Here are some books on career development that have been recommended in Parts I and II of this book:

Marcus Buckingham & Donald O. Clifton, *Now, Discover Your Strengths*, Free Press, 2001

Paul & Sarah Edwards and Laura Clampitt Douglas, *Getting Business to Come to You*, Tarcher Putnam, 1998

Charles Handy, *The Elephant and the Flea*, Harvard Business School Press, 2003

William Bridges, *Creating You & Co*, Perseus Books, 1997

C. J. Hayden, *Get Clients Now*, Amacom, 1999

Roy Sheppard, *Rapid Referral Results*, Centre Publishing, 2001

Toastmasters International, *Competent Communication, a 10 Project Manual*, 2007

Also referred to are a couple of pioneering books on business strategy, one little nugget on entrepreneurship and one on the quintessence of business planning:

Michael E. Porter, *Competitive Strategy: Techniques for Analyzing Industries and Competitors*, Free Press, 2004 (First Edition 1980)

Robert M. Grant, *Contemporary Strategy Analysis: Concepts, Techniques, Applications*, Blackwell, 2008 (1991)

Ken Blanchard, Don Hutson and Ethan Willis, *The One Minute Entrepreneur*, Headline, 2008

Vaughan Evans, *The FT Essential Guide to Writing a Business Plan: How to Gain Backing to Start Up or Grow Your Business*, Financial Times Prentice Hall, due November 2011

Books recommended for further reading about Part III's career change are as follows:

Richard Nelson Bolles, *What Color Is Your Parachute? 2011: A Practical Manual for Job-Hunters and Career-Changers*, Ten Speed Press, 2010 (1970)

Po Bronson, *What Should I Do with My Life? The True Story of People Who Answered the Ultimate Question*, Ballantine, 2005

Carol Christen and Richard N. Bolles, *What Color Is Your Parachute? For Teens*, Ten Speed Press, 2010 (2006)—also useful for graduates

John Crystal and Richard Nelson Bolles, *Where Do I Go from Here with My Life?*, Ten Speed Press, 1983

Vaughan Evans, *Backing U!: A Business-Oriented Guide to Backing Your Passion and Achieving Career Success*, Business & Careers Press, 2009

Vaughan Evans, *Backing U! LITE: A Quick-Read Guide to Backing Your Passion and Achieving Career Success*, Business & Careers Press, 2009

Jonathan Fields, *Career Renegade: How to Make a Great Living Doing What You Love*, Broadway Books, 2009

Howard Gardner, *Frames of Mind: The Theory of Multiple Intelligences*, Basic Books, 1993

Barrie Hopson and Mike Scally, *Build You Own Rainbow: A Workbook for Career and Life Management*, Management Books 2000, 2004

Julie Jansen, *I Don't Know What I Want, but I Know It's Not This*, Piatkus, 2010 (2003)

John Lees, *How to Get a Job You'll Love, 2009/2010 Edition: A Practical Guide to Unlocking Your Talents and Finding Your Ideal Career*, McGraw-Hill Professional, 2008 (2001)

Nicholas Lore, *The Pathfinder: How to Choose or Change Your Career for a Lifetime of Satisfaction and Success*, Fireside, 1998

Carol L. McClelland, *Changing Careers for Dummies*, For Dummies, 2005 (2001)

Daniel Porot, *The PIE Method for Career Success: A Unique Way to Find Your Ideal Job*, JIST Works, 1995

Don Sutaria, *Career and Life Counselling from the Heart*, iUniverse, 2008

Barbara Sher, *I Could Do Anything if I Only Knew What It Was: How to Discover What You Really Want and How to Get It*, Dell, 1995

Paul Tieger and Barbara Barron-Tieger, *Do What You Are: Discover the Perfect Career for You Through the Secrets of Personality Type*, Little, Brown, 2007 (1995)

Nick Williams, *The Work We Were Born to Do: Find the Work You Love, Love the Work You Do*, Element Books, 2000

And finally, just in case this book has stimulated you into writing a nonfiction book, here are a few books that have inspired and guided me:

Blythe Camenson, *How to Sell, Then Write Your Nonfiction Book*, Contemporary Books, 2002

John Kremer, *1001 Ways to Market Your Books*, Open Horizons, 2008 (1986)

Mark McCutcheon, *DAMN! Why Didn't I Write That: How Ordinary People are Raking in $100,000 or More Writing Nonfiction Books & How You Can Too!*, Quill Driver Books, 2001

Dan Poynter, *Self-Publishing Manual: How to Write, Print and Sell Your Own Book*, Para Publishing, 2007 (1979)

Marilyn Ross and Sue Collier, *The Complete Guide to Self-Publishing: Everything You Need to Know to Write, Publish, Promote and Sell Your Own Book*, Writers Digest, 2010 (2002)

Appendix E
Glossary

Backable – a word coined for purposes of this book, meaning worthy of being backed.

Backing you – investing in / putting money on / supporting / having faith in the future career of you, a potentially backable entity, whether you're self-employed or an employee.

Business segments – product/market segments of your business or job, having distinct services (or products) and customer groups (Chapter 1).

Business plan – where you plan to be in your career in three to five years' time, strategically and financially, and how you're going to get there (Chapter 7).

Competitive intensity – a measure of how tough competition is in the marketplace for your job or business (Chapter 3).

Competitive position – how you stack up compared to your competitors Chapter 6).

Customer needs – what customers need from their service providers (Chapter 4).

Demand drivers – factors which influence market demand (Chapter 2).

easy U! – a generic strategy focusing on being a low cost provider (Chapter 12).

Going for the goal – stretching your sights and aiming for the ideal provider (Chapter 11).

Ideal provider – the provider who rates most highly against each Key Kapability (Chapter 10).

Hwyl – a Celtic concept of the passion, fervor, spirit which can drive you to extremes of success (Part III).

K2s – see Key Kapabilities.

Key Kapabilities – what service providers need to have or do to succeed in their job or business (Chapter 5).

Market demand – the aggregate will of consumers in your marketplace to purchase the services provided or products produced (Chapter 2).

Must-have K2s – those essential K2s in a marketplace without which a service provider cannot begin to compete (Chapter 6).

Risk and opportunity – it is the balance of risks and opportunities, assessed by likelihood of occurrence and impact should they occur, which will determine whether you are backable in your career plans (Chapter 8).

Service provider – a self-employed businessperson engaged in providing a service for customers, or likewise an employee for his/her managers or "customers" (Chapter 1).

Sharpen Act! – a generic strategy focused on improving competitiveness, including working on weaknesses (Chapter 12).

Stand Out! – a generic strategy focused on differentiating through your strengths (Chapter 12).

Strategy – how you deploy your scarce resources to gain a sustainable advantage over the competition (Chapter 12).

YouCo – your own business, whether a self-employed sole trader or with employees engaged (Chapter 13).

Index